MW01608688

THE
SALVATION ARMY
AND
THE PUBLIC

THE
SALVATION ARMY
AND
THE PUBLIC

Historical and Descriptive Essays

R.G. Moyles

AGM Publications
2000

©2000, AGM Publications

Canadian Cataloguing in Publication Data

Moyles, R.G. (Robert Gordon), 1939—
    The Salvation Army and the public: historical
and descriptive essays

Includes bibliographical references.
ISBN 0-9686898-0-9

    1. Salvation Army--Public opinion--History. 2.
Salvation Army--History. I. Title

BX9715.M69 2000   287.9'6'09   C00-900351-7

AGM Publications
Box 82058
Edmonton, AB T6J 7E6

PRINTED IN CANADA
Select Graphix & Printing Ltd.
Edmonton, Alberta

TABLE OF CONTENTS

Introduction

The Salvation Army. These words today conjure up a variety of images. Brass bands on snowy street corners. Doughnut girls in war-service canteens. Uniformed ladies visiting senior citizens' homes. Christmas kettles in shopping malls. Downtown hostels and rehabilitation centres. Thrift stores. Hospitals. Children's villages. Barracks and citadels. . . . Each image will differ with personal experience, but hardly any of the experiences, whether real or vicarious, will have produced a negative response. For The Salvation Army is now, and has been for many decades, one of the world's most trusted and respected socio-religious organizations.

It was not always so. In the early years of its history, roughly 1865 to 1890, the novelty of Salvationist methodology shocked, even horrified, the British public. It was not so much that William and Catherine Booth had commenced a "soup to salvation" mission in East London, as the fact that they had departed so audaciously from accepted religious practices. An *army* of religionists? Bands, drums, flags, and tambourines? Marches through the streets? Songs that sounded like music-hall ditties? All-night prayer and praise meetings? Female preachers, still in their teens? *Orders and Regulations*? Gutter and Garrett Brigades? Safety-match factories? A poor man's insurance society? Salvationists were nothing if not brash; they were noisy, insistent, and ready to perform cartwheels for the Lord. Eyebrows were raised, public denunciations (by prominent people) were written, sermons were preached against them, rotten eggs (and worse) were thrown at them, and Skeleton Armies smashed the Salvationists' brass instruments and sometimes their heads as well.

But what William and Catherine Booth knew was this: public opposition denoted a recognition far beyond what mere acquiesence could —if some men cared enough to fight against a new idea or institution, many more would care enough to support it. "Persecution," William wrote to his officers, "ensures publicity. Persecution has done more to make a Corps known in a Town or

District in one day than would have been done in twelve months without it."[1] And so it proved. For every negative criticism, there was a positive contradiction. Newspapers and journals which might otherwise have ignored the Army, took up its cause when others denounced it; they reported on its doings and illustrated (often quite graphically) its meetings and social outreach. And thus, from about 1878 to 1900, The Salvation Army was one of the most publicized features of British religious life. The Army, capitalizing on that unprecedented publicity, attracted thousands to its meetings, launched one of England's most ambitious social-reclamation schemes, and thereafter endeared itself to a public previously suspicious or downright antagonistic.

The essays which follow attempt to describe and assess the public's obsession with The Salvation Army in its early years —to define the public's perception of Salvationism, its opposition to it, and its possible influence on the Army's progress; and to then show how, after the turn of century, that perception changed to the point where the Army became a revered institution. To accomplish this, each essay will deal with a specific historical event or a single aspect of Salvation Army endeavour. It will then examine how the public, through its newspapers and journals, reacted to that event, dealt with its social implications and, perhaps, even influenced its outcome.

The introductory essay offers a general overview of the kinds of public reactions to early Salvationism and the various ways in which these were communicated. Subsequent essays deal with such issues as the physical opposition encountered by early Salvationists at Worthing and Eastbourne and the parliamentary action which ensued; the public interest in and debate about Booth's social ventures as exemplified in the 'Maiden Tribute' affair and the 'Darkest England Scheme'; the issue of autocracy (often called 'Boothism') as it affected the Army's work in Canada and the United States; and how the British public reacted when one of 'their own,' Catherine Booth, the founders' eldest daughter, was jailed and expelled from the Canton of Geneva.

The final three essays reveal just how successfully the Army survived the 'sticks and stones' of public opposition —how it became an admired and much-eulogized British institution. We shall see how the Army became a public icon, immortalized in literature by some of the world's great writers such as George Bernard Shaw and Vachell Lindsay. So much so, that, when William Booth died in 1912, the world put on one of its greatest displays of sympathy and adulation; the dead General, once reviled, was now hailed as "The Greatest Apostle of the Age." And, even when The Salvation Army underwent its severest test of public loyalty, during what is known as 'The Bramwell Booth Affair' of 1929, the public reaffirmed its faith in the Army's worldwide mission.

Taken altogether, the public commentary is both voluminous and fascinating. From amusing dismissals to vilification; in articles, plays, short stories and poems; in court sentencings and national edicts we see just how The Salvation Army emerged from an era of public denunciation to become the much-loved organization that it is today.

It only remains to state that these essays are not primarily concerned with the accuracy of the events described, or with the truth of the commentaries on them. Their purpose is to assess *perceptions* of The Salvation Army as promulgated by the press and believed by the public. That is, whether The Salvation Army could justifiably be called 'rowdy' or 'corybantic' (as T.H. Huxley labelled it) is not being addressed; that the public *believed* Salvationists to be 'rowdy' is. In some instances it will be manifestly clear that journalists were wrong-headed in their views; that they misrepresented the Army's mission; or simply had no firsthand acquaintance with Salvationism. And yet the public believed them, wrong or right, much as they did when the same journalists wrote about wars, politics and society. Public opinon was a fact of life. And The Salvation Army, though sometimes hurt by it, very often benefitted from that fact.

It is my privilege to acknowledge the assistance and expertise of several people and institutions who have helped make the writing of this book an enjoyable task. Most of my research was carried out in the Collindale Newspaper Library of the British Library in London, England, and the staff there is always gracious and kind. It was on sabbatical leaves granted by the University of Alberta that much of the research was undertaken: my thanks to that great University. To Dr. Rowland McMaster and Professor Nurman Murdoch, who read the manuscript and made many valuable suggestions, a sincere thank-you. And to Ada, my wife, who proofread the whole and kept me sane throughout, my love.

Essay One

The Salvation Army 'Unveiled': Early Journalistic Scrutiny

In 1865, when William and Catherine Booth established The East London Christian Mission, the British public, as represented by the Fourth Estate, barely noticed. And although the Mission flourished, and soon expanded to cities as far away as Cardiff, only occasionally did any secular London newspaper or magazine comment on its presence. Indeed, for the first decade of its existence, the Booth enterprise was considered by most people merely a passing fad —one of the many such religious eccentricities of English life. England was, as the adage went, the "mother-country of religiosities." They came, and they disappeared, as did a new toilet-fashion from Paris or a new opera song from Venice or Milan. The Christian Mission was therefore largely dismissed as just another sectarian flash-in-the-pan, unworthy of much concern or interest.

In 1878, however, the British public was jarred into awareness. The Christian Mission changed dramatically —it became *The Salvation Army*. As W.T. Stead later remarked: "From the moment that the Army received its title its destiny was fixed. The whole organization was dominated by its name."[1] Unorthodox religious worship was now augmented by pseudo-military display: 'officers' and 'soldiers' marched through the streets with bands and flags and tambourines. They sang 'war songs,' adhered to 'Orders and Regulations,' saluted commanding officers, and generally formed themselves into military units called Corps. Using female preachers to flamboyant advantage, the Army invaded pub territories, and engaged in a scheme of social-reclamation that upset traditional notions of poor relief.

By such innovative daring, The Salvation Army not only attracted a committed following of thousands but began to impose itself so insistently on the public imagination that indifference was impossible. In fact, almost from the moment its new title was chosen, this 'new-fangled religion' became one of the most popular objects of journalistic scrutiny in Great Britain. It was lampooned, cartooned, debated, described, dissected, denounced and sometimes praised in almost every newspaper and periodical in the country.

From the prestigious London *Times* to the lowly *Morning Advertiser*; from *The Graphic* to *St. Stephen's*; from the *Pall Mall Gazette* to *Blackwood's Magazine* —journalists vied with each other to 'unveil' the secrets of this new religion. Between 1880 and 1895, in British popular magazines alone, there were more than one hundred and fifty articles and commentaries on Salvation Army activity and methodology. If one adds to this a massive amount of newspaper commentary, one hardly exaggerates in suggesting that The Salvation Army's 'war' occasioned almost as much journalistic colour —as much debate and controversy— as had the Crimean War some thirty years before.

The commentary itself took a wide variety of forms, catering to a similar variety in tastes and reading habits. At a populist level, there were the many artistic representations of Salvationism, nearly all by well-known illustrators, carried by such famous weeklies as *The Graphic, Illustrated London News, Harper's Weekly*, or *Frank Leslie's Illustrated Weekly* —illustrations depicting everything from the inside of "A Salvation Army Women's Shelter" to "The Wedding of Commissioner Railton at Exeter Hall." Some of them —*St. Stephen's Review* and *Punch*, for example— catered to a public taste for the sensational by offering descriptions, satiric cartoons and verse parodies of what they called "Salvation antics":

Salvation stock is 'humming',
Every day,

Utopia nearer is coming—
So they say:
Now when Booth has banked his cash,
And has cooked the Devil's hash,
He'll wave his blood-red sash,
And away!![2]

So captivated were they by Salvationist mannerisms, and so conspicuous were these, that the best cartoonists considered it apropos to ridicule leading citizens —Oscar Wilde, William Gladstone— by dressing them as Salvationists and making lame jokes at the Army's expense. For example, according to *Punch* William Booth's reply to the Archbishop of Canterbury, on being invited to join the Church, was this: "Have heard of a Stall in a cathedral, but have never seen a Booth in a church."

At a more intellectual level, the public could assess a continuing debate about Army methods and beliefs in any of several leading journals. At one extreme there were those periodicals (in the minority) which unabashedly welcomed the Army's soup-to-salvation mission, the most notable among them being the London *Review of Reviews* whose editor/owner, W.T. Stead, was as much an iconoclast as William Booth himself. At the other were magazines like *The Saturday Review* and the *Monthly Review*, mostly with fixed allegiances, which fought vigorously to prevent Booth's "dancing dervishes" from gaining a foothold in British society. And, in between, were the more neutral, liberal magazines which preferred to debate the relative merits of Army methodology (most often praising its social outreach but deploring its religious fanaticism). In the pages of the *Fortnightly Review, Contemporary Review, Eclectic Review, National Review*, and others, the debate was carried on with great gusto, often by such well-known people as Cardinal Manning and Archdeacon Farrar, offering the curious public opinions on everything from female officership to 'hallelujah' praise meetings.

And finally, if the public was not already tired of reading about The Salvation Army, or had a personal (almost prurient) interest in its affairs, there were, in its first two decades, dozens of small books and pamphlets devoted to analysing or exposing Army practices. Most of these, with such as titles as *Pope Booth* and *The Salvation Army as a Money-Making Concern*, were decidedly antagonistic. One, especially, created quite a stir in 1885 when the Reverend Samuel Charlesworth, in a book titled *Sensational Religion*, told of how the Booth's had enticed his daughter, Maud (later to become Mrs. Ballington Booth), away from his affection and into Salvation Army service. Such stories excited public indignation and spurred public curiosity.

As did several books by defectors and dissidents. These came from the pens of men (curiously, no women) who had joined the Army, little knowing what they were getting into nor what demands would be placed on them. As a result, disappointment, ending in defections and resignations, was a common feature of early salvationism.[3] And those who chose to 'expose' Army practices —in such books and articles as J.J.R. Redstone's *An Ex-Captain's Experience of the Salvation Army* (1888), J.T. Cudmore's *The Doctrines of the Salvation Army and the Bible Compared* (1889), Arthur Sumner's *The New Papacy* (1889), Wyndham Heathcote's *My Salvation Experience* (1892), Peter Philpott's *New Light* (1892), and John Hollins's "The Salvation Army: A Note of Warning" (1898)— catered to a public eager to know the truth about the Army's 'secret' manual (its *Orders and Regulations*), its Jesuitical practices, its family feuds, and so forth. They provided that public with plenty of sensational reading; and opponents with plenty of misinformation with which to buttress their virulent attacks.

That some of the views expressed in that voluminous commentary were idiosyncratic, written as a result of personal affront or pique; that some of it contained opinions unsupported by a firsthand acquaintance with Salvationism; and that much of it catered to a public seeking anything sensational, we may take for granted. Yet it is possible, by eliminating extremes, to discern common concerns, criticisms and kudos which fairly represent what the general public thought of The Salvation Army. We can see just what the British (and later, the American) public found either distasteful or fascinating in Salvation Army worship and style —what attracted and repelled them. And it is not far-fetched to suggest that the picture of the Army presented by early commentators —when the criticism was valid— may have helped the Booths shape the progress of their organization. For public attention lent a notoriety to Army activities without which the organization would never have made the phenomenal progress that it did.

In subsequent essays we shall encounter the views of newspaper journalists and editors as they informed the reading public and often persuaded it to take sides on such issues as Booth's 'Darkest England Scheme' and the Army's involvement in 'The Maiden Tribute Affair.' In the essay which follows immediately I will concentrate on commentaries about the Army published in major British and American journals such as *Contemporary Review*, *Harper's Magazine*, and *National Review* and on early *exposés* of the Army in books by former officers. The question being asked is: what dominant impressions of the Army would the public have gained from such commentaries? Or, what, if we were to believe such commentaries, was The Salvation Army like in its early days?

"Grotesque" — "Rowdy" — "Irreverent" — "A Parody of Religion." These were the chief recurring descriptions of early Salvation Army warfare. And understandably so. For the Army was, above all, obtrusive. Its physical presence and external trappings were what people first identified; it was visible and it was loud. The Army practised an overt kind of religion —for the most part carried out in the open-air, with the shrill music of brass bands and blatant placards and circus tricks to attract audiences. It was intended as a way of bearding evil in its den.

In its places of worship —called 'barracks'— Army services were generally boisterous, informal, and unscripted; they were marked by joyous singing (religious words set to popular tunes), 'volleys' of praise, short exhortations ("nobody ever speaks long"), and loud testimonies which involved the whole congregation ("all them as is saved must have a cut in"); and it could be highly charismatic, with much waving of hands and handkerchiefs, body swaying, dancing in the aisles, and emotional conversions. It was extroverted and unabashed. And, when described in the Army's weekly magazine, *The*

War Cry (to which the public had full access), it may have seemed more vaudevillian than religious. Here is Elijah Cadman's account of one such meeting:

> The meeting began, the Holy Ghost came to our help at the beginning, and at three o'clock the waves of glory broke over us. When I gave the invitation to those who were seeking to be holy on earth, 700 men and women came down, the men on one side, the women on the other, and the Holy Ghost broke upon them, and fell upon us all in such a manner, it seemed to nearly carry me out of my clothes. I had hard work to stop on earth. Some jumped, and jumped, till they jumped into the third heaven. When they got the blessing, they swam about the floor in glory. One was a Quaker, who had never quaked till that night. . . . 'Pull Soldiers, pull, pull the glory down' was sung by Major Dowdle, and set the whole platform in motion, some pulling vigorously at imaginary ropes.

It is not surprising, then, that most of the commentaries dwelt on these externals —on the so-called 'antics' of Salvationism. Nor that most of them deplored such unconventional worship. "In all that we read of the apostles of our Lord," wrote an anonymous 'Investigator' in 1882, "one finds nothing akin to the proceedings of these Salvationists. They did not dress themselves in mock military accoutrements, nor claim high-sounding titles, nor proclaim their own successes, nor herald themselves with drums and trumpets in noisy processions, nor did they swim about the floors in glory." Religion, this writer contended, was (though joyful) quite a "serious thing" and was quite incompatible with "irreverence and grotesque performances."[4]

"That Christianity could ever have been made 'rowdy'," wrote the well-known Irish social activist, Frances Power Cobbe, "would have seemed an impossible feat, but the Salvation Army has accomplished it; and the very grave question presses, whether by this deplorable dereliction it is not doing a mischief for which the immediate and ostentatious 'conversion' of hundreds of drunkards and sinners would fail to compensate. I suppose no one will dispute that this rowdyism really prevails in the processions, hymns, services, and publications of the Salvation Army."[5]

Not many would, it seems. Indeed, as this anonymous poem published in *Punch* magazine in 1890 attests, most commentators were just as anxious as Cobbe to expose this 'grotesque' behaviour:

Some talk of Wagner chorus, of war's wild rataplan,
Or of the well-thumped tom-tom of happy Hindostan;
But sweetest of all shindy to which man's ear may list,
Is the tow-row, tow-row, tow-row of the loud Salvationist!

They muster in their thousands on market-place, or green,
With blatant brazen brayings, and thump of tambourine.
Are you at prayer, asleep or sick? What odds? You're forced to list
To the tow-row, tow-row, tow-row of the loud Salvationist!

They throng with thunderous tramplings the city thoroughfare.
In rural nooks their shoutings are on the summer air;
Though sea-side peace be pleasant, its spell may not resist
The tow-row, tow-row, tow-row of the loud Salvationist!

The Corybantic clangor was cheerful, in its way,
But Hallelujah Lasses the cymbals can outbray.
O raucous throat, O leathern lung, O big belabouring fist!
O tow-row, tow-row, tow-row of the loud Salvationist!

"A nuisance! Nay, my children!" ('Tis Grandam Justice speaks.)
"Town butterflies may think so, and so may country 'beaks.'
The Oracle in Ermine declares you shan't resist
The tow-row, tow-row, tow-row of the loud Salvationist!

"Traffic may be obstructed, and tympanums be rent,
The noise may torture sufferers with sickness well-nigh spent;
But these be merely trifles. Your anguish may assist
The tow-row, tow-row, tow-row of the loud Salvationist!

"Our self-appointed saviours must work their noble will.
These shouters have small faith in the voice that's small and still.
Blown brass and beaten parchment taken heaven by storm. Then list
To the tow-row, tow-row, tow-row of the loud Salvationist!

The priests of Baal were noisy, but not so loud as Booth.
Charivari and clamour are vehicles of Truth.
At least that seems the notion of which these seers insist,
With the tow-row, tow-row, tow-row of the loud Salvationist!

That sick child in her chamber may press an aching head,
The mother, bowed and broken, bend deafened o'er her bed.
Regrettable, but needful, since freedom must exist
For the tow-row, tow-row, tow-row of the loud Salvationist!

So Justice, in zeal's bonnet, so Jurymen in haste!
What *are* the claims of comfort, health, common-sense or taste,
Compared with those of brainless Noise, our new evangelist,
And the tow-row, tow-row, tow-row of the loud Salvationists![6]

Just as disturbing as the physical demonstrations, though perhaps not so manifest, was the language used by Salvationists to both promulgate the message and promote the war. Some of the bill-board announcements and the headlines in *The War Cry* read as follows: "Join the Fight Against Old Nick," "A Baptism of Fire," "A Hallelujah Gallop," "Great Charge on the Devil," "A Salvation Charge," "Licking the Devil," "Souls to Mend," "Fire and Brimstone," "Great Exhibition of Hallelujah Lasses," and "Pulling the Glory down." The familiarity with which Salvationists addressed, implored and generally talked about The Almighty ran along these lines: "I say, Lord, make us all like you" and "we are boiling over with Holy Ghost power"; and the parodic songs, bellowed with such gusto, included "For He's a wonderful Saviour, which nobody can deny." Their prayer sessions were called 'knee-drills'; they gave 'blood-and-fire' salutes, held 'Holy Ghost meetings,' 'exhibitions of trophies,' 'holiness conventions' and many 'councils of war', and engaged in 'pool plungings,' the occasional 'hallelujah go' and frequent 'glory dances.' It was enough to make a staunch Anglican —or even a Methodist— cringe, as Frances Cobbe was not loath to point out:

> To such of us as can recall the profoundly solemn spirit which characterized the old Evangelical type of piety, there is something more

William Booth caricatured as a kind of 'dancing dervish'
in *St. Stephen's Review*, Feb. 20, 1882.

Harry Furniss's cartoon which
accompanied *Punch's* poem "The
Lay of the Loud Salvationist"
(Jl 12, 1890).

"FINDING SALVATION."

Punch's depiction of two leading British politicians who supported The Salvation Army. April 21, 1894.

"GENERAL" BOOTH.

His Own Trumpeter.

An 1883 *Punch* cartoon showing William Booth 'blowing' his own trumpet.

than painful, even abhorrent, in the irreverence which now confronts us. The awe-inspiring psalm of our youth is changed to a music-hall melody whistled about the streets; and the sublime image of Religion is dressed up as a merry-andrew. Muscular Christianity did much, not always wisely, but on the whole well, to break up the gloom which had settled on Evangelical piety of the Cowper stamp, and to stop the tendency to twaddle and cant which its baser imitators exhibited. . . . . But far beyond all these, at the furthest swing of the pendulum, we now behold parading our streets the Salvation Army, amongst whom scarcely a vestige of religious awe, or even of decorum in touching things reverenced by their neighbours, can be traced. The French divine who some years ago disgusted the English readers of his book on Prayer by insisting that God was *débonnaire*, has been left far behind, and the stillness of Heaven itself is broken to our ears by vile talk of 'rows,' 'Hallelujah gallops,' and 'jolly' prophets ascending in 'fiery vans.' Nothing is left for awe or solemnity above or below."[7]

Among those who deplored such 'irreverence,' it was generally conceded that "no amount of good effected by the Salvationists [could] justify the use of profane and even blasphemous language," especially when united to a style of worship "more suited to the pantomime of a theatre than the solemn worship of Almighty God."[8] In Cardinal Manning's opinion, one of the biggest mistakes made by Salvationists was "to think that to speak of God and of Divine things in low language" would make the truth more accessible to the poor and uneducated. "Low words," he maintained, "generate low thoughts: words without reverence destroy the veneration of the human mind. When man ceases to venerate he ceases to worship. . . When levity or coarseness is permitted in preaching, or prayer, or hymns, we fear that it will deaden the reverence of some and provoke the blasphemy of others."[9]

The whole argument was summed up, from a Catholic point of view, by A.F. Marshall in *The Catholic Review* in 1890: "[W]e would suggest to the Salvation Army that the Christian religion is a deep (divine) philosophy, not a childish emotional tickling of the sentiment; and that in the Army there is nothing to fall back upon but natural feelings —the most delusive and the most purely human of tribunals.

Backbone —there can be none in such a religion. The intellect is completely swamped in sensibility. The Army must be able to realize this every day, by their observation that their preachers are obliged to humor expectant audiences with graphic and piquant stories and similitudes; appealing always to the warmly-kindled imagination, not to the still, anxious depths of the conscience."[10] The Army's habit of "profaning holy things" was a symptom of "spiritual disease" and would, in spite of its seeming attractiveness, eventually bring about its demise.

Unless, of course, the Booth's reliance on female preachers would do that sooner. For, one of the notable (and most conspicuous) features of The Salvation Army was its 'female ministry' —Booth's officer contingent being, at any given time, composed of slightly more or less than fifty percent women. The Booths prided themselves on this fact, Catherine Booth herself having written two book-length defences of 'female ministry' in her Army.[11] Nor was she merely paying lip-service to the cause. Having taken a leading role in the development of the Army's theology and teaching, she had a just claim to being called the co-founder of the Army. Her daughters, as well, just as capable as their mother, assumed prominent positions and propelled the Army across the English Channel and then across the ocean. Some of the Army's finest evangelists were women; and most of Booth's 'toughest' invasions had been carried out by young, single females.

For many commentators, especially females such as Mary A. Lewis, Mrs. Charles Garnett, Agnes Maule Machar and even Frances Power Cobbe, the Army's position regarding women posed no problem, was even applauded. For some men (generally churchmen), however, flouting the well-known Biblical injunction was cause for much concern. The Reverend Andrew Wilson disliked the Army's policy —and the whole Army— so much that he devoted a whole book called *The Salvation Army: Its Government, Principles, and Practices* (1884) to an in-depth denunciation of its 'principles and practices.' In it, in addition to savagely denouncing everything from 'blasphemous language' to 'all-night prayer meetings,' Wilson singled out the Army's female ministry for special mention:

In the Army, so far as its officers and exercises are concerned, there is neither male nor female, all are one and the same. It is nothing to them that God has enjoined, by His inspired apostle, 'Let women learn in silence. For Adam was first formed, then Eve, and Adam was not deceived, but the woman being deceived was in the transgression' (1 Tim. ii, 11). Also, in his first epistle to the Corinthians, fourteenth chapter, 'Let your women keep silence in the churches; for it is not permitted unto them to speak, but they are commanded to be under obedience, as also saith the law. And if they will learn anything, let them ask their husbands at home, for it is a shame for women to speak in the church.' The reasons given for these strong injunctions are as cogent today as when they were first penned. Yet in the Army women are made lieutenants and captains, to preside over and command the Army's corps. This practice is not only inconsistent with the position in which it has pleased God to place women, but, also, with that modesy which is such an ornament to her sex.[12]

C. Raleigh Chichester, a spokesperson for the Roman Catholic Church, had a different, more amusing, slant on the issue:

Let us now, without controversial reference to St. Paul, reason on this ministration of the Gospel by women. Men and women mutually attract each other, but, as it seems to me, in a very diferent way. Woman sees in man an object on which, and through which, to exercise that lovingness, that desire to help, which is of her nature. She is attracted not so much by what is intrinsic in him as by what is extrinsic. To him, on the contrary, she is attractive for herself. Hence, for the most part, the man pursues and the woman is pursued, not indeed that the pursuit need be of fatiguing length.

If this theory is correct, it will be seen at once that the presence in the Catholic churches of a celibate clergy presents the minimum, as the presence of women on the platforms of the Salvation Army presents the maximum, of disturbing force.... Hence, when a man sees on the platform a young and pretty woman, between whose mind and his no difference exists, or can be created, on the subject in which they are both interested, he cannot fail to contemplate her beauty. Let him close his eyes, her attractiveness will sink into him through the portals of those ears by which they say men, like rabbits, should always be held. It is impossible but that the fact that she is a woman should force itself on his attention in some way or other, leading him away from what she is saying, to what she is.[13]

If very few commentators thought it strange that a military-styled organization should indulge in 'rowdy' worship or use women as 'invasion' commanders; if they did not express surprise that a group of people in uniforms and subject to military rules and regulations, should indulge in what they called 'religious frenzy,' the reason seems clear. Most of them believed that the Army's military style was, as far its converts were concerned, largely a mannerism —it was, especially for the soldiers, mostly an adopted style. As a novelty, they admitted, militarism attached to religion was a great attraction. The titles of captain, lieutenant, colonel and commissioner; the uniform and insignia; the flags and marches— they all exerted, as one writer put it, a "great charm on the holders and coveters of the same. Yesterday a drunkard and today a Salvation Army Captain is an immense transition —laugh at it as you may." They therefore saw the military style as mainly a "means to an end" —in itself of little importance. It would be silly, suggested the Dean of Canterbury, Archdeacon Farrar, to think that flags, and drums, and trumpets, and tambourines (all military paraphernalia), had much to do with essential Christianity, nor did the Army suggest that they did. They were no more than "the crosses, and banners, and processions, and acolytes in surplices and scarlet cassocks, and thuribles, and broidered stoles of our ritualistic churches. The drums and trumpets are not even remotely associated, as are the gorgeous adjuncts of modern Anglicanism, with the insinuation of any doctrine. They have no purpose in the world but the very innocent one of attracting the people to gatherings where they may hear something which benefits their souls."[14]

But there was one feature of Salvation Army militarism which gave rise to considerable debate and criticism: in age of growing democracy, William Booth's assumption, in title and fact, of 'supreme commander' gave rise to heated controversy. Words like 'autocracy,' 'nepotism,' and 'Jesuitism,' frequently found their way into the commentaries, and the Army's *Orders and Regulations* were closely scrutinized by Booth's detractors, especially by disaffected ex-officers.

That Booth exercised "absolute power" over his troops —calling it a "settled, absolute, regular system of using men to accomplish a common settled purpose"— and expected nothing less than 'blind obedience' to his commands, was not in itself considered such a bad thing. Certainly, it had achieved a success beyond reason, and could not be faulted in theory. What rankled most observers was the loss of individual freedom which such a system imposed. In the Army, they pointed out, there were rules and regulations for every human action (there being twelve different sets published during Booth's generalship); all individual initiative and ideas, and all debate, must be stifled (and their originators sometimes punished); its constitution entrenched the notion that no election would ever take place and ensured that all properties and monies were under the sole control of and invested in the name of the General. Thus did most commentators make autocracy seem an essential ingredient of Salvation Army government. William Booth, they suggested, was being exalted by his followers and was, in his Sunday journals, elevated to the status of a demigod.

"The whole movement," wrote Leopold Katscher, "is incorporated in the person of the general; he holds all the threads in his hands. His influence extends from the highest to the lowest grades. He is an absolute monarch, and the monarchy is his own creation; the organization, and the whole construction of the 'Army,' are mainly the offspring of his own brain. He superintends the most minute details, manages the expenditure, appoints the officers, degrades and cashiers them at pleasure. He draws up all the order books, and decides all quarrels. In short, he is an unconscious plagiarist of the General of the Jesuits." One of the obvious dangers, Katscher thought, was that such a system tended to "automatic routine and servility of mind. The servility of the discipline may gradually become intolerable, and make people recede from it with repugnance."[15] And the public utterances of disaffected, dissident officers (not to mention the newspaper reports of the dismissals of popular officers such as F.S. Machin, Gipsy Smith and Frank Smith), substantiated such a view.

John Hollins' was one of those voices. "The military system," he wrote, "has certain advantages as a working method. It ensures economy of time, dispatch, punctuality. But the multiplicity of regulations inseparable from it in a great organization like the Salvation Army tends to mechanical action. Where so much is done by rule there is little room for personal initiative." Taking the unidentified case of Gipsy Smith, who had [so the public believed] been forced to resign because he had accepted a farewell gift from his soldiers, Hollins astutely argued that "autocratic government may do fairly well in calm weather, but when storms arise there is only one step between autocracy and anarchy." When even a minor dispute arises, when "authority always carries the day," and members are unable to defend themselves, there will always be mass defection (as there was in the Gipsy Smith case). It was Hollins' opinion that the Army could only be successful if there was a "very judicious exercise of power on the part of authority" and "a wise recognition of the rights and privileges naturally associated with the voluntary element."[16]

Other dissidents were less sanguine than Hollins. Ex-officers such as Cudmore, Sumner, and Redstone were adamant in maintaining that autocratic despotism would be the ruination of the Army and offered graphic descriptions of its pernicious influence. Take J.J.R. Redstone's *An Ex-Captain's Experience of The Salvation Army*, a book which went through two editions and gained considerable public notoriety. It offered transcriptions of the numerous forms, with their petty questions; samples of the statistics demanded by headquarters; letters from superiors seething with autocratic jargon and orders, the genuineness of which could not be denied by Army officials. And Redstone finally described a dismissal —one among many, so Redstone claimed— that was unfair, arbitrary, "without trial, without formulated charges, on the strength of secret complaints." The conclusion of the press, in its reviews, was that "the Pope is a constitutional monarch compared with Mr. Booth," and that nepotism was second only to despotism in the organizational control of the Army:

> The Salvation Army is open to the remark that it is emphatically a family concern. Mr. Booth, senior, is general; one son is 'Chief of the

Staff,' and the remaining sons and daughters engross the other chief positions. It is Booth all over; indeed, like the sun in your eyes, you can see nothing else, wherever you turn. Even the married daughters retain the illustrious name before that of their husband's, who themselves also adopt it. The most sounding titles have been appropriated by the illustrious household. One daughter is 'the Maréchale'; another is at the head of the 'Indian missions,' as joint-apostle with her husband, beyond the Indus. Mr. Bramwell Booth figures as 'Chief of Staff,', ruling, as such, over all peoples, nations, and languages, Nebuchadnezzar-like, so far as they are connected with the Salvation Army. Nor does it seem too much to say of the officers of the Army that they tremble and fear before him; or that in a metaphorical sense, 'whom he would he slays, whom he would he keeps alive, and whom he would he sets up, and whom he would he puts down'. . . .

Such a state of affairs is inevitably unwholesome. No one, I should suppose, would for a moment imagine that any member of the family fails in zeal, or is other than strictly upright and clean-handed, but too much power in one family can never be good. Mr. Booth and his children are very great people in their own world; indeed, the only great people it knows. Wherever they go they are objects of noisy ovations. Their names are continually before the public in grandiose displays or announcements. Even so strictly private an affair as the marriage of a daughter is made the occasion of an immense gathering, and, of course, of a huge collection; no less than £5,000 having been raised in connection with the last event of this kind, as a gift to the happy couple for their work in Hindostan. Such light-foot publicity, so distasteful to most people, seems dear to the members of the favoured household; at any rate, to be the heads of a widely-spread sect carries with it many advantages —not all exclusively spiritual.[17]

Thus it was that, along with despotism, "the cult of the Booths" became a topic of much debate in the early commentaries. The two would, in fact, become matters for more intense debate at various times, and in specific contexts, in later years. Indeed, as subsequent essays will show, concerns regarding despotism and Boothism became motivating factors in several *causes célèbre*, most notably in the Philpott, Ballington Booth and Bramwell Booth affairs of 1892, 1896 and 1929.

For the moment, however, it is enough to note that the main impression of The Salvation Army created by early journalistic descriptions was of an organization with the superficial appearance of a military unit —as evident in its uniforms, ranks, brass bands and frequent marching— but which, in its forms of worship, could best be described (as Thomas Huxley later did) as 'Corybantic' —resembling a style of religious frenzy supposed to have been practised by the priests of Cybele. The latter aspect —the irreverence and rowdyism— occasioned great consternation amongst its critics who were often at pains to convince the public that they should not support such indecent and indecorous religious behaviour. To add strength to their argument most painted a picture which looked very much as if they were describing a Jesuit order and drew on Jesuit writings to support the case: a supreme leader demanding blind allegiance, making his officers virtual slaves to his 'rules and regulations,' in sole control of all property and assets. The Canadian ex-officer Arthur Sumner, put the matter this way:

> Gradually the cords have been drawn tighter and tighter, and the liberty of the individual conscience has been more circumscribed, and so what was once an organization that appeared to offer what some thought a dangerous liberty of thought and action to its members, has been developed into a sect of the most exclusive and rigorous description, governed by military despotism, the supreme and entire control of which is placed in the hands of its chief officer, who makes its laws, promulgates its creeds, defines its dogmas, and enunciates its faith, and that too without any advisory council, and against whose will and fiat there is no possible appeal.[18]

Left at that, the public's perception of early Salvationism seems overwhelmingly negative. That would be a mistaken conclusion. For, though the dominant view was negative, there were both a number of wholly positive commentators or some who, like Cardinal Manning and Archdeacon Farrar, while deploring the excesses, nevertheless saw some value in the organization's methods. Thus, while the dominant impressions of Salvationism were not significantly altered, the more positive commentaries offered a better understanding of the

Army's motives.

Take the accusation of 'irreverence,' for example. Could it not, some argued, be the case that the Army's critics had no acquaintance with the "language of the people"? And might not 'rowdyism' be, if one cared to look closely, be more properly rendered as 'joyousness'? Such were the counter arguments offered by such influential voices as Archdeacon Farrar and the reverend Randall T. Davidson. "I have seen," wrote Davidson in 1882, "no single account of the Army's work in which its *irreverence* has not been held up to condemnation or rebuke. And not always, as it seems to me, quite fairly. I have heard addresses given at crowded Army meetings, both in east and west, which it would have been easy, by the mere report of a shorthand writer, to represent as irreverent in the extreme. And yet, when spoken in plain bold words by an earnest man to a rough audience, whom he had hushed into silence by his manner and his voice, there was no irreverence about them, but a solemn and heart-stirring appeal to his hearers' consciences in a way —perhaps the only way— that they would understand."[19]

The point was reinforced by the well-known Church official, Archdeacon Farrar: "No objection against the Salvation Army is more common on the lips of superfine people than that which complains of its shouting and howling and blaspheming and vulgarism. Well, but though there may be at times real vulgarism, which should be seen to and checked, and often is seen to and checked, at headquarters, it is well for us all to make up our minds that the people of the slums will never be won by a rose-pink religionism. The Salvationists have a right to say that the Father, 'who desireth that all who worship Him should worship Him in spirit and in truth,' may be worshipped by one of His street children in street English which may be 'quite shocking' to the female mind."[20]

Some observers, rather than rebutting the negative commentaries, chose simply to describe the Army in action, hoping that an objective, firsthand account would do more to dispel false notions than would reasoned debate. In *Sleeping Christianity* (1882), for example, an anonymous supporter tried to do just that by describing a typical outdoor congress gathering:

Mr. Booth's followers on Monday were emphatically a 'jolly party.' In joy lies their strength. Joyful hymns, joyful tunes, joyful cries, joyful exhortations, were everywhere prevalent.

In different parts of the grounds more than a dozen groups were to be seen, each composed of three or four hundred people, engaged in a Salvation Army service.

A Captain or Captainess would exhort for a few minutes, and then lead off a chorus, which was taken up with great gusto, and repeated again and again by the rest of the company. Occasionally one corps would wave their handkerchiefs to another, and a loud volley of 'Amens' would be answered by an equally boisterous shout from the next body.

One large group we passed were engaged in a prayer-meeting, all kneeling in the deep, unmown grass, while one after another, in rapid succession, offered brief and hearty petitions, in which there was little, indeed, to offend taste. . . .

From first to last we failed to see the least impropriety of behaviour. As for the processions themselves, the vast majority were of the lower working-classes —the very class which makes a walk uncomfortable on Sunday night along High Street, Islington, the very class which in its juvenescence is a nuisance to all our great towns, and which in its maturer age largely recruits the ranks of the drunkards, the wife-beaters, and the women home-destroyers. If General Booth can permanently lay hold of these, we are not at all particular to inquire into his *modus operandi*.

Similarly, Mrs. Charles Garnett in *The Eclectic Magazine* (1885) wrote one of the best descriptions of an Army meeting on record, setting down in fascinating detail, without personal interpolation, every moment of that meeting. Some earlier readers would no doubt still have been shocked by the seeming 'irreverent language' of the preacher and those who 'testified', but no one would have doubted the sincerity of the believers. "So ended what was to me a deeply interesting and touching evening," concludes Mrs. Garnett. "I leave the reader to draw his own conclusion."[21]

It was, in fact, the informality and spontaneity of Army meetings that impressed most of the supportive commentators and which they thought was one of the secrets of the Army's astounding success. In her *Red Cross Knights of the Salvation Army* (1884), Agnes Maule Machar marvelled at the "unconventionality" of an Army meeting and how adept the leaders (often young women "thrilling with electric energy and personal magnetism") were at keeping things "red hot" with an appropriate chorus after an 'impromptu' testimony, a pithy remark between songs, and "hymns appropriate to the testimony." But the greatest "charm of these meetings," she felt, "and that which secures for them perpetual freshness and attractiveness, keeping their halls filled, night after night, is contained in their personal testimonies of the converts in the 'great salvation' from sin and its bondage. After the singing has had its effect on both the audience and the 'soldiers,' the latter are desired by the 'captain' to 'fire away,' these testimonies being considered, in Army phraseology, the 'red-hot cartridges'. . . . That young men and women, but a short time before as careless and giddy, as reckless or dissipated, as any of their companions, should have the courage to and power to stand up before a crowded assemblage of their own class, and declare what a change the accepted love of God has wrought in their own hearts and lives, appears to most of the hearers little short of miraculous" (p. 21).

The wonderment expressed by Machar in her last sentence had also been a matter of contention among Army critics and supporters. The Salvation Army believed strongly that new converts should become immediately involved in its evangelizing mission —testifying (as soon as converted), marching, pub-booming, preaching even full-time ministry— and they even had a little song about it:

> They grumble at the way our converts testify;
> They say we ought to wait a year to give them a good try;
> But we believe they ought to speak of what they now enjoy,
> Before the devil gets a chance to damp their new-born joy.

As one observer wrote: "Every man, woman, and child accepted as a recruit is supposed to become from that moment [of conversion] a centre of evangelizing work. One who has entered the hall out of sheer curiosity, or perhaps to scoff is brought, it may be, before long, to kneel with bowed head at the 'penitent's form.' Half-an-hour later he is bearing public testimony to the fact of his conversion, and that night or the next day sees him with the great 'S' upon his collar selling *The War Cy* in the streets and public-houses, among the companions of his former life."[22]

In the minds of some critics, mainly clergy, this so-called 'shallow conversion' had all the marks of inhumility and smacked too much of egotism. As A.F. Marshall pointed out in *The Catholic World* (1890):

> A convert may have been ignorant of even the natural proprieties when he accidentally strolled into a Salvationist hall; but he issued forth two hours later an exemplar of that Christian spirit which eager audiences claim is quite typical. Now this is, of course, exciting, and perhaps interesting, but what it means is complacency, not conversion. So that when the new "saved one" immediately gets into the "Salvation lift" (the slang, perhaps, is excused by the fatuity), and is urged by his spiritual captain to become a "boomer" (here again we recognize appropriate language), we feel naturally inclined to suggest a little modesty, a little shrinking from the applause of the young women . . . But then, as we have said, when the conversion is all emotion, consequent on the tickling of the natural ears, it is only consistent that the emotion should be "passed on" and "preached upon" as a moving text to the emotionable. Thus spiritual vanity takes the place of all reality; in short, conceit is the main gospel of the penitent.[23]

Most observers, however, believed that "the immediate use to which the Army put it converts" was both salutary for the convert and practical for the Army's work. Archdeacon Farrar suggested in Booth's defence that "many of the wavering might have been lost forever if they had not been from the first taught and encouraged to come out of their evil surroundings, and boldly take their side with God and the work of God."[24] Others noted the Army's "watchful care" over its new converts, the "sense of belonging" which every convert experienced, and the astuteness of Booth's notion that his best witnesses were other people's newly-converted neighbours. Nor could they deny that, when all the shouting was set aside, there was indeed a great joy evident in all Army events. "The overpowering joy which some poor creature shows who has been rescued from the neglect of the respectable, who have only shrugged their shoulders at him, and left him to the tender mercies of the publican, is one of the characteristics of these humble converts." And, in the final analysis, whatever the criticisms, most commentators felt constrained to confess that "These people have got something that I have not."[24]

For, when everything had been said that could be said —when all the grievances had been aired and the few praises lavished— there was a single characteristic of Salvationism which could not go unnoticed. It was this: The Salvation Army was more attractive to the common people than any other religious movement of its day. For not even the staunchest critic could deny the fact that, in the first four years of its existence (1878-1882), almost fifteen thousand converts were enrolled as 'soldiers' and about eight hundred others had committed themselves to full-time officership. In 1883 these officers were holding more than 6000 services each week, at some of which (on Sunday evenings, especially) they could expect as many as two thousand people to hear their "salvation" messages. Some who came to listen may, no doubt, have been drawn by the publicity, seeking perhaps to find out for themselves the truth of the matter. And a few of them may have been so favourably impressed that they, too, became a part of the newest religious experience in Britain, enlisting as soldiers in The Salvation Army.

Public Processions and Public Protests: The Army's Right to March

In the pleasant autumn months of 1884, when the seaside resort of Worthing, England, should have been basking in sunshine and visitor largesse, riots and mayhem ruled its streets. Its tradespeople complained that "one of the finest seasons ever known at Worthing" was "utterly ruined by the noisy parades." The parades about which they complained were the stock-in-trade 'open-air warfare' of The Salvation Army, recently come to Worthing. The 'noise' emanated not from their singing but from the organized mobs —often more than a thousand strong— which marched counter to them, matching Army glory songs with their ribald parodies, beating home-made drums, pelting the Salvationists with stones and rotten fruit, and planting saboteurs in windows of empty buildings to drop bags of dust and lime on their heads.

The physical assaults began on Sunday, August 17, when, according to *The Illustrated London News*, members of The Salvation Army marched through the town —"men and women, boys and girls, singing their hymns and carrying a banner inscribed 'Blood and Fire, 458', the leaders being attired in flaming red uniforms." Along the route they were heckled and harassed by an unfriendly mob, part of which seemed to be an organized Skeleton Army whose "hideous black banner [bore] the figure of a human skeleton painted in white." At Bath-place, near their barracks, the Salvationists were attacked, several being "severely beaten and kicked," escaping into their hall only when the police interfered and arrested some of the mob's ring-leaders.

On the Monday, angered by the summonses issued against them, members of the Skeleton Army renewed their attacks, marching through Worthing, "shouting and singing," to the Army hall where a meeting was being held. "Showers of large stones were hurled through the windows, to the great danger of the congregation, some of whom sought shelter under the benches." Growing tired of throwing stones at the barracks, the mob turned its attention to the nearby shop of Mr. George Head, an Army supporter and ironmonger:

> For some time the mob contented themselves with hooting, but at length assailed the shop windows with stones, and finding themselves unmolested in their work of destruction [no police having been dispatched], they at length tore down the sashes and broke all the lamps exposed for sale in the window. Garden and other implements, with which the shop was stocked, were seized when the windows had been destroyed and they were used to break open the door. . . . After forcing the door the shop was entered, and the mob began to destroy the goods; but got outside again when they found Mr. Head in front of them armed with a shovel. After a while another rush was made, and amid the din a pistol shot was heard, and one of the leaders of the party was wounded in the wrist, but it was afterwards found this was done by broken glass. The pistol, it was thought, had been charged with blank cartridges. The shop was cleared again but another attempt to enter the premises was made, and this time there was no doubt as to the efficacy of the pistol-shots, for a lad named Eldridge was shot in the face, a man named Reed shot through the hand, and Mr. Head's own son was wounded. Seeing how serious matters had become there was no further attempt to wreck the house, although stones were freely thrown at the building. The house was first attacked at 11, and it was 2 o'clock before the mob was finally dispersed (*Times*, Aug. 21).

Though the riot act was publicly read by the presiding magistrate, and the Worthing police force was augmented by a troop of the Royal Irish Dragoon Guards, the riots continued —abetted, so newspapers declared, by several hundred "roughs" from Brighton, Portsmouth and other towns. Incensed that three of their leaders —Messrs Reed,

Standing and Eldridge— were handed a month's hard labour for "demolishing the premises of Mr. Head," the hardcore rioters, amidst a crowd of curious idlers, continued to molest the determined Salvationists at every opportunity. On September 7, the riots were repeated with increased animosity and physical abuse:

On Saturday information was given to the police that the Salvation Army would undertake their usual parade and particulars of the route were furnished. The special constables sworn in on Friday were summoned on duty and the local police were reinforced. Captain Drummond, Chief Constable of West Sussex, was in command. As early as 10 o'clock vast crowds assembled outside Montague-hall, the barracks of the army, and hissed and groaned at the Salvationists as they entered. After a short service in the hall the Army came forth joining fours up the road. They were at once pressed by the Skeleton Army, and a dense mass of people followed. The hymns shouted by the Salvationists and the yells and hooting of the rabble which followed were something terrible. . . . . Soon after starting, the Salvationists were pelted with flour and then by bags of lime. One of these, thrown from a garret window, fell upon the Salvation Army Captain Ada Smith. Loud cheers came from the Skeletons each time the bags were thrown. . . . The mob returned into Montague-street, and, after stoning the barracks, collected opposite Mr. Head's shop, the lower part of which is still barricaded. Two or three stones were thrown at the upper windows, when Mr. Head appeared at the window on the first floor, and, pointing a revolver through one of the holes in the glass, deliberately fired twice or thrice at the crowd. A young man, named Edward Olliver, fly driver, was shot in the neck, while a woman narrowly escaped. A bullet struck the wall close to her, and, rebounding, struck a man on the foot. Olliver was taken to the Worthing Infirmary. Fortunately the injury was not of a serious character, the bullet having glanced off. The crowd was terribly excited. Some clamoured for revenge, but Mr. Head stood at his window with a gun as well as a revolver, and no one had courage to go near the house. The police and special constables were at once called out, and remained on duty for some hours in Montague-street. Later on a warrant for Head's arrest was issued, and he was removed to the police-station, followed by an excited crowd (*Times*, Sept. 8).

It was well into November —after the riots had infested nearby Shoreham and then Brighton, and after nearly twenty of the rioters had been fined and/or jailed— that the authorities finally brought peace and order to Worthing. When it finally became clear that The Salvation Army would not be suppressed, that it was not as offensive as some critics claimed, and that the courts would defend the Army's right to march, the opposition was forced into quiescence. But not before the citizens of Worthing had experienced (and many had participated in) some of the most ferocious street riots in its history and The Salvation Army had undergone one of its severest trials by fire.

The riots at Worthing represented only a single segment of a vast network of violence directed against The Salvation Army in the first decade of its work in England. At Bath, Guildford, Basingstoke, Weston-Super-Mare, Whitchurch and many other cities Salvationists were set upon by 'mobs' bent on suppressing what many considered, and what many newspapers told them was, a 'common nuisance.' In 1882, the Army recorded a total of 669 soldiers (251 of them women) as being "knocked down, kicked, or brutally assaulted; 56 barracks were wrecked; and eighty-six Salvationists were sent to jail for 'disturbing the peace' with their singing, preaching or drum-beating. "Perhaps the worst of the riots," writes Booth's biographer, Harold Begbie, was that which occurred at Sheffield [in 1882], when a procession led by General and Mrs. Booth was attacked by a numerous and savage multitude armed with sticks and stones. The procession arrived at its destination with bruised and bleeding faces, with torn and mud-bespattered garments, cheering the general who had passed unscathed through the rabble."[1] That would be a familiar story, reported both in English newspapers and in the Army's *War Cry*, for many years to come. What was the public's reaction?

Though some early commentators offered simplistic explanations for the widespread outbreaks of violence associated with Army marches —attributing them to Army stubbornness and a hardcore opposition mounted by publicans— one soon learns from the diversity of opinion that there is a sufficiently complex attribution of cause-and-effect to suggest that such riots —more than a hundred in the Army's 'invasion' years— were themselves as multi-faceted as the society which bred them.

It is, of course, quite clear, as a number of Army historians have shown, that there were deliberate, locally organized, attempts to demoralize and eventually 'put down' The Salvation Army. Some of these originated with publicans whose 'immoral trade' was threatened; or they were organized by opportunistic rabble-rousers who then solicited the financial support of 'disreputable' publicans. Self-styled 'Skeleton Armies,' they were composed mainly of young men (some ex-military), many of them seeking excitement and free beer. They parodied Salvationist practices, adopted a black flag with a white skull, sang ribald parodies of Army songs, and intentionally marched against Army marches in order to disrupt and assault its soldiers. Some branches of the Skeleton Army had their own newspapers, collectors and collecting sheets (just as Salvationists had theirs) and, perhaps with some intimidation, solicited fees for services rendered.[2]

Looked at realistically, Skeleton Armies, though sometimes highly organized and often allied with publicans, were simply groups of young malcontents —at odds with society, bored with their lot in life, and always on the lookout for thrills: they were, in a sense, the 'motorcycle gangs' of the late nineteenth century. They were by no means unique, just better organized and more focussed than most gangs, for the century saw a great deal of mob activity. As Gavin Thurston points out in *The Clerkenwell Riot* (1967), earlier in the century well-known agitators became professional mob-inciters who, for various reasons and clients, would arouse a mob to looting and burning, a thing easy to do when there was so much "hunger and poverty among the masses." And though, by 1884, social control was not as fragile as in the first half of the century, it was still easy to incite a segment of the populace to mob violence. This the Skeleton Armies did quite often. For they could always count on a following —a feature of the riots acknowledged in nearly every report by the terms 'roughs,' 'rowdies,' 'riff-raff,' 'roughnecks' and 'rabble'; a contingent of idlers, 'consummate loafers,' thrill-seekers and so forth, who, though not actual members of the Skeleton Armies, were only too "fond of a row, and glad of any plausible excuse for making one."

It is, then, fair to conclude (as many have done) that some attacks on Salvationists were intentional, Skeleton Armies deriving their *raison d'etre* and their sport specifically from Salvation Army activities; but just as fair to insist they often attracted to their 'attacks' many other people who participated offhandedly, committing unpremeditated acts of ruffianism in an uncontrolled manner. It seems most unlikely, however, that either of these two groups —The Skeleton Armies and the 'roughs' they attracted— knew or cared much about Salvation Army theology or methodology. They were not, in any philosophical sense, opposed to Salvationism. The Army attracted them merely by being so obvious in their open-air witness. As the *Saturday Review* put the matter, "the rough is quite undiscriminating in his choice of those whom he attacks. The same sort of men as those who assailed the Salvationists. . . are in the habit of insulting, knocking down, and kicking harmless people whenever they themselves are sufficiently numerous and exhilarated with alcohol and the passer-by is sufficiently defenceless. The rough who makes the thoroughfares in London impassable at certain hours is not determined in his choice of a victim by anything else than the convenient opportunity" (Oct. 20, 1883:492).

Victorian society was, to put the matter mildly, in a state of turmoil (or 'flux', as some historians like to call it); it was a society full of boils waiting to erupt. Democratic aspirations (especially among the poor), trade-unionism, late industrialism, fast urbanization, and a population that had doubled in Victoria's lifetime, all contributed to a social ferment that was almost impossible to contain. The lower classes, now no longer shackled to the aristocracy, were venting their anger at every public opportunity. It was this element, suggested Catherine Booth, that was responsible for the 'Army riots' —that "vast mass of our population entirely untouched by any civilizing or Christianizing influences." George Scott Railton, supporting Mrs. Booth's view, further believed that all the trouble had been caused "by the weakness of the authorities in giving way before ruffianism" and felt that there were, "in every locality, plenty of men who can be led to acts of violence against anyone who is not likely to be defended efficiently against them." And there were many citizens who also shared this view, one 'eye-witness' stating his views in the *Times* of London:

Sir:— On Sunday, by accident rather than design, I was a visitor to Worthing, and not only witnessed the extraordinary scene described in your columns on Monday, with regard to the movements of the Salvation Army and their opponents, the Skeleton Army, but attended two of the meetings held by the Salvationists in Montague-hall. It did not appear to me that, either in their marchings or their services, the Salvation Army did anything to justify the extraordinary violence to which they have been, and still are, subjected. . . . The singing of the Army on the march was decorous, and there was no show of bravado. Those who wore the well-known red guernseys were not more than 14 in number, and no one carried weapons of any kind, not even an umbrella, though showers fell during the progress of both marches. The Salvationists did not number 100 in all, but several hundreds assembled at the service held in their hall. What surprised me most was that the 'Captain,' Miss Ada Smith, and the 'Lieutenant,' Miss Alice Griffin, who had been in charge of the work for the past four months, were extremely young women, the elder certainly not more than 22, both of them modestly dressed, quiet-mannered young women, with good voices, and fluent and sensible speakers. They have been subjected to so much serious violence that on Monday they marched in the second row, not the first; four young men wearing the red shirts walking before them. One of these was the Rev. E. Piggot, late of St. Jude's, who was attired like the others. Notwithstanding the efforts of the gentlemen on horseback, Captain Drummond, the Chief Constable, Superintendent Henderson, Colonel Wisden, and others, and the assistance of about 150 special constables, a very noisy crowd of Skeleton Army men, without leaders, tacked themselves unto the Salvationists, and not only shouted out ribald songs, but kicked and cuffed the men and women repeatedly. I saw the marks of the kicks on the legs of the Salvationists after they reached their hall. Flour and water mixed was also thrown from windows as the armies passed along the streets. The hymns sung by the Salvationists were quiet and appropriate; and in no instance throughout either march did I see a blow struck by any of them. . . . There does not seem to be any apparent reason for the outbreak of violence which has disgraced the town; and there is ample testimony borne by very many to the good effect resulting from the evangelistic work of the Salvationist (Aug. 24).

That many observers (and later historians) should attribute the mob-violence against the Army to either Skeleton Armies or to simple-minded ruffianism is therefore quite understandable. It is clear, however, that the opposition was more complex than that: in the very large crowds that often shadowed the Army marches there were many people, ordinarily law-abiding citizens, who were voicing a conscious antipathy to the organization or at least to its public demonstrations. The *Saturday Review* was certainly of this opinion. There was, its writer argued, "a noisy, not to say brutal" element in every town, and it was possibly this which attacked the shop of the unfortunate Mr. Head. But there were also, the writer maintained, many 'respectable' people who found "the tramping and parading and processionizing of the Salvation Army through their quiet streets an intolerable nuisance" (Aug. 23). Rowdyism might 'man' the riots; but 'popular feeling' tolerated and possibly approved them. There was, as the London *Times* argued, "something in the constitution and aims of the new movement" that provoked "exceptionally bitter animosity in the neighbourhoods they successively patronize[d]." It was not merely the fact that "martial accoutrements and magnificent titles" created envy but that Salvationists attached to themselves a "superior piety" which offended other Christians. There are plenty of letters by leading citizens, in various newspapers, to show that in Worthing and elsewhere the Salvationists were not welcome and deserved to be driven out. The Salvation Army was, as Dr. John Goldsmith averred in the *Times*, the "fons et origo mali," perambulating through the streets "singing and shouting at the top of their voices, and beating tambourines, &c, to the great annoyance of the peaceable citizens" (Aug. 24). The time had arrived, he argued, for 'special legislation' to put an end to the Army's uproar.

But the problem was, for any British person with a sense of justice, just this: how could the 'noisy processions' of Salvationists be curtailed without infringing on their inalienable right to freedom of movement and of 'public meeting'? Those opposed to Salvationism, just like those opposed to socialism (very often one and the same), felt that the solution was a simple one —that people who created a 'public nuisance' (as they defined it) forfeited their right to protection on such grounds as 'religious tolerance.' In this opinion, they were often supported by local magistrates who jailed so many Salvationists for seemingly inocuous acts such as 'beating a drum' in a public thoroughfare. They felt, moreover, that some legal experts were simply muddle-headed when they insisted that the law must reconcile the right of the public to be protected against "outrageous annoyance" with the right of individuals to "comport themselves in the manner which their religious views dictated." More preferable to practical-minded citizens were the opinions of Mr. Justice Manisty who, late in October 1884, tried the principal participants in the Worthing riots. Though he was forced to find members of the Skeleton Army guilty because they had committed acts of violence against Salvationists and Mr Head, he found the Army at fault, stating that the organization should not be allowed "to conduct their proceedings in such a way as to cause serious annoyance to many of Her Majesty's peaceable and liege subjects." The law, he concluded, was clear: the "scandalous, disturbing, annoying, and vexatious processions" of The Salvation Army should be stopped.

In an article on "The 'Salvation Army' as an Index of Public Opinion" published in *The Nation* (1883), A.V. Dicey suggested that Justice Manisty's view was one with which the public largely agreed. "One would have supposed," he wrote, "that the violence of a disreputable mob bent on interfering with the right of public meeting would have aroused the indignation of respectable men of all classes." But such was not the case. While many citizens remained apathetic —leaving the two opponents to "battle it out"— most felt (as did Justice Manisty) that if 'blackguards' objected to Salvationist hymns and sermons and threatened to dissolve General Booth's prayer-meetings by force, then it was the Salvationists who were causing a breach of the peace, and "the duty of respectable magistrates was to hinder a meeting which, though perfectly legal, was likely to excite the anger of ruffians to break the law. To put the matter in the plainest terms, the popular view (which was to a certain extent countenanced by Governments) is that assemblies otherwise perfectly legal become unlawful if they are held in places where they are likely to offend the feeling of the populace" (77-78).

From a legal point of view, however, the matter was not that simple and, in overturning several magistrates' decisions against the Army, Chief Justices had highlighted a very important point of English law. For example, in the Weston-Super-Mare appeal (1882) Justices Field and Cave had ruled that magistrates at Weston-Super-Mare had no right to prohibit Army processions simply because they *might* lead to a breach of the peace. An Army procession was not in itself unlawful; it could not be proven that it was organized for unlawful purposes; and it could not be called a "tumultuous assembling with others to the disturbance of the peace."[3] What right, asked the Justices, "have others to resort to force to prevent persons from doing that which is lawful? It would come to this, that persons were to be punished for doing lawful acts merely because it led others to act unlawfully and create a riot. Was it a crime in this country for persons who had strong religious convictions and a strong desire to do good by inducing others to attend religious services to hold assemblies with that object and walk through the streets to their place of worship in order to attract others to go there? Was that to be termed criminal? [Justice Field] hoped not, for he hoped that when the opponents learned —as they would now learn— that they had no right whatever to interfere with these processions of the Salvation Army, they would abstain from disturbing them" (*Times*, Je 14, 1882).

The force of the 1882 decision, then, was that any public act (e.g. an Army procession) should be judged by its intention and acknowledged purpose rather than by its tendencies. "Very few reasonable men," declared the *Times*, "will quarrel with this decision." The London *Standard* went even further: "The decision will commend itself to general approval, on grounds alike of equity and common sense. It is intolerable that individuals, or a society of individuals like a Skeleton Army, should take the law into their own hands and should create a riot for no other purpose than to involve the Salvationists in the discredit of the disturbance."

There was then, a significant difference of opinion between what the

The 'Skeleton Army' attacking The Salvation Army barracks in Worthing.
From J.J.R. Redstone's *An Ex-Captains Experience* (1888)

The Sheffield 'riot' of 1882.
From Robert Sandall, *The History of The Salvation Army*, Vol. II.

public thought should be done (in which they were supported by some Justices such as Manisty) and what most legal experts felt could be done. The expectations expressed by the *Times* and *Standard* were, if not naive, somewhat unrealistic. For, there was, even as the various legal experts debated the issue, a strong public feeling that the 'loud Salvationist' was enough of nuisance to be at least restricted to his barracks. As A.V. Dicey suggested, it was not certain, even after the 1882 court decision, whether the British public or civic officials were convinced of "the justice and the necessity of insuring to the members of the Salvation Army, as to all other citizens, the free enjoyment of their lawful rights." It might seem clear that English law protected Salvationists' right to outdoor assembly, but it was not quite so clear that "the Government ought not to possess the power by law of occasionally restricting, on grounds of general policy, the unlimited right of public meeting." That is, it could be argued that an act, though lawful, might not be expedient.

The gist of that argument lay in a nice point of common law, one which Justices Field and Cave had acknowledged. Their decision rested on the argument that The Salvation Army was not acting unlawfully nor was it causing a "tumultuous assembly" or being a public nuisance. For even the law, as Lord Bramwell suggested, could be used to prevent public processions: "if any one or more, either by stinks, noises, or otherwise, make the neighbourhood unwholesome or distressing to its inhabitants, a public indictable nuisance is committed, and the offender may be fined or imprisoned. But it must be a sensible grievance, and not one to fastidious people only; and it must be one affecting not one or two people only, but the neighbourhood generally."[4] There were some voices which made no bones about it —the people who "profanely call themselves the 'Salvation Army' constantly do commit nuisances" and the police ought to put a stop to their processions just as they would "to any other offence openly committed"[5]

There were, however, many others, perhaps more judicious, who acknowledged that it would be nearly impossible (especially in a court of appeal) to secure charges against Salvationists on those grounds. Only two options semed to be open: either the public could endure the 'noise' of Army marches and open-airs (with their accompanying rowdysim) until they died a natural death; or towns could pass by-laws (or resurrect long-forgotten ones) which, if approved by parliament, could prohibit Army open-air processions. It was this latter strategy —the final major public attempt to suppress Salvationist street marches— that was employed by the towns of Torquay in 1888 and Eastbourne in 1891, resulting (in Eastbourne) in the longest series of riots ever encountered by the Army in Great Britain, and in a tense public debate that ended with parliamentary action.

Unlike the Worthing riots, where The Salvation Army was not breaking any law but was being harassed for being the unintentional cause of public tumult, those at Torquay, and later at Eastbourne, were the result of the Army's deliberate defiance of what they felt were unjust laws. Both towns, in fact, had, in anticipation of the Army's invasion, inserted clauses into their Corporation statutes —the Torquay "Harbour and District Act" and Eastbourne's "Local Improvement Act"— approved by Parliament in 1886, aimed (as was later admitted) at preventing The Salvation Army from marching in their streets: "No procession shall take place on a Sunday in any street or public place in the borough accompanied by any instrumental music . . . [excepting] Her Majesty's naval, military, or volunteer forces."

The Torquay affair was a mild one, and only need be mentioned here because the result should have instructed other towns in how to treat the Army's open-air mission. Shortly after the Army arrived, and at regular intervals from August of 1886 to July of 1888, more than forty Salvationists (officers and soldiers) were arrested, fined and/or jailed for contravening Torquay's by-law. Though little mob violence was experienced, there was a large public outcry against police abuse and against the by-law itself —much of it from the citizens of Torquay— and in July, 1888, the by-law was repealed on the advice of a select committee of Parliament. Eastbourne, therefore, should have been instructed.

But it was not. Motivated by what was correctly described as an "unreasoning, implacable animosity" on the part of certain city officials, Eastbourne Council moved quickly to enforce its by-law and to 'put down' a movement which Mayor Morrison described as being "opposed altogether to the spirit of true religion."[6] The Salvation Army just as resolutely defied every official attempt to do so. Thus, for more than a year, beginning in June of 1891, local and national newspapers continuously reported on the riots in Eastbourne, while weekly magazines commented extensively on the political and moral issues involved. Tempers ran high in the streets, in legislative councils, in letters to the editors, and in Parliament. The nature and progress of the public disorder may be gauged by a few selected reports from the *Times* of London:

June 2, 1891: The Eastbourne borough police, under Chief Constable Fraser, had some difficulty in preventing rioting in the streets of Eastbourne on Sunday, by reason of the scenes of tumult caused by the resumption of the musical processions of the Salvation Army. Feeling on the matter of Sunday bands in Eastbourne is divided. The bulk of the inhabitants desire the suppression of the practice, but there were many among Sunday's crowd who showed practical sympathy with the members of the Army by interfering to protect them. The tumultuous scenes were confined to the east-end of the town, and away from the part most occupied by visitors. The Eastbourne magistrates yesterday heard summonses, taken out at the instigation of the corporation, against 'Captain' Robert Bell, W.H. Nicholas, George Loadsman, Henry Baker, and Louise Clark for taking part in the musical procession, and a second summons against Bell for inducing others to join the procession. Each defendant was ordered to pay £5 and costs, or go to prison for a month, and, acting on instructions from head-quarters, they all chose the latter alternative.

June 15, 1891: The Salvation Army bands dispute again caused some exciting scenes in Eastbourne yesterday, chiefly at the east end of the town, which is remote from the portion frequented by visitors. The Salvationist bandsmen who were sent to prison were replaced yesterday by men from other Sussex towns, and thousands of people were in the streets. During the Salvation Army procession the police surrounded the bandsmen and took their names for the purpose of prosecution. But as the Eastbourne Improvement Act allows military music on Sunday, the Volunteer bands from the Cinque Ports annual encampment on Beachy head marched through the streets to St. Saviour's Church without interference by local authorities. Although vast crowds watched the volunteer bands marching through the streets to and from Beachy Head perfect order prevailed. The mob, however, several times attacked the Salvationist band and also the police. The Watch Committee are determined to allow none but military music on Sunday in Eastbourne. The disturbances were renewed in the evening by opponents of the Salvation Army at the east end of the town. Many Nonconformists and others sympathized with the Salvationists, but, despite the efforts of the police, they were in some instances roughly treated.

July 21, 1891: Serious riot. A desperate conflict at the station. Miss [Eva] Booth returning to London. A seething mob surrounded the carriage containing Miss Booth and her suite, and a quantity of red ochre was thrown at the occupants, Miss Booth being also struck on the head with a missile hurled by a cowardly miscreant. Seeing the fair daughter of the General in jeopardy, the Salvationists formed a bodyguard and Miss Booth was practically borne into the station on the shoulders of her supporters. . . . Sticks were flying overhead —heads being split open, and one Boothite had his jaw seriously injured, another was compelled to have his eyes done up, owing to a handful of sand having been thrown into them; several were seen with bleeding and bandaged faces. In such an encounter the women of course fared badly.

Oct. 19, 1891: There was great disorder in the streets of Eastbourne again yesterday at the time of the Salvation Army processions. In the morning the Salvationists met at the east end of the town. They had seven instruments with them, and as soon as they began to play the crowd groaned and hustled them. The police came up and restored order, and the Salvationists recommenced playing. For five minutes they were left at peace, but a rush was then made and the greatest confusion ensued. About a dozen Salvationists and others fell in a heap to the ground and with difficulty regained their feet. The crowd surged about, and in the conflict one instrument was lost and two others very much damaged. The police had a difficult task to restore order, and it was not done until some severe blows had been given. The Salvationists formed into procession as they struggled along and the bandsmen continued to play on the march, but as soon as they reached the highway the police seized them by the throat or took their instruments, and so prevented any further music. Another conflict occurred later on in the morning. In the afternoon the Salvationists met on the beach at the Wish Tower, in the western part of the town. Four instrumentalists and a standard-bearer left the Citadel together, but had not gone far when they were set upon by about 100 roughs, who hustled them, seized their caps, and made a desperate attempt to secure the instruments. They succeeded in getting a cornet, which was smashed to pieces. The standard-bearer was much knocked about. He was stood upon his head and his face was forced into the prickly bushes which form a border to the flower-beds on the front, causing it to bleed.

Oct. 30, 1891: At the Eastbourne Police-court yesterday, George Tobutt, a general dealer, was charged with forming one of a riotous crowd in Langney-road, on the night of October 21, and there damaging the windows of the Salvation Army citadel by throwing stones. Edward Thomas Beesley, commanding the local corps of the Salvationists, spoke of the violence of the crowd and said that while the Salvationists were engaged in devotion at their meeting, stones came flying through the windows. Three of the stones came onto the platform at the other end of the building, and thereby panes of glass were broken. Police-sergeant Burr deposed to the violence of the crowd all along the route and said that at the end of Bourne-street the procession was completely broken up, and that two women belonging to the Salvation Army were knocked down.

Feb. 1, 1892: On few occasions during the long controversy between the Eastbourne local authorities and the Salvation Army have the conflicts between the Salvationists, the police, and the crowds been fiercer or more prolonged than the series of struggles which took place yesterday afternoon. A large crowd had gathered at the Wish Tower, and when the Salvationists emerged from their Citadel shortly after 2 o'clock, four of their number carrying musical instruments, they were greeted with groans. Escorted by 20 policemen, the Salvationists marched in procession singing through the streets to the Wish Tower, the crowd accompanying and responding to the hymns with snatches of popular songs and other noises. A gang of 50 or 60 roughs marched on ahead, and, forming a ring at the position on the beach usually occupied by the Salvationists, they began to sing, 'We never, never, never will give in,' to the amusement of some thousands of spectators assembled on the parades. Finding their stand already appropriated, the Salvationists marched further eastward, and halted in a kind of valley with a high embankment of shingle on either side. The roughs congregated on the backs of the shingle and from these points of vantage made rushes upon the Salvationists and police huddled together below. The members of the army were unable to form a ring, according to their custom, but they endeavoured to carry out their meeting. Owing, however, to the noise, the constant struggling with the mob and the showers of shingle rained upon them little progress was made. 'Captain' Jackson, who has charge of the operations of the army at Eastbourne, and Mr. Felix Wilson, Wesleyan local preacher, were set upon and hustled, and, having been deprived of their hats, they were pushed down the embankment. In spite of the inconvenience to which they were subjected, the four bandsmen tried to play, but before the instruments reached their mouths they were seized by the police, who proceeded to disperse the Salvationists. The crowd closed in and, amidst great clamour, hustled both the police and the Salvationists. A scene of disorder ensued. The police had to make a way for the Salvationists up the incline to the roadway, and a number of people were thrown into the mud. The efforts of the Salvationists to form a procession were frustrated by the crowd. The police worked hard, but, owing to insufficient numbers, they were practically powerless. Blows were exchanged, and the crowd managed to wrench two instruments from the bandsmen and, after subjecting them to considerable ill-usage, threw them into the area of houses in Lascelles-terrace. All the way down the Grand-parade the disturbance continued. The Salvationists by degrees got into some sort of marching order and unfurled the flag. Opposite the Burlington Hotel, however, a dead set was made at the flag. The scuffle was of a violent nature and lasted five or six minutes. The police struck out, but were quite overpowered. The Salvationists clung desperately to their banner, but only a few shreds remained to them. Nearly every man in the procession lost his cap.

Although there was not at Eastbourne, as at Worthing, an organized Skeleton Army orchestrating the disruption of Army processions, there was without doubt a similar element of 'ruffianism' encouraged by civic officials and respectable citizens. It was Bramwell Booth's opinion that many of the so-called 'roughs' were, if not planted, at least openly encouraged by the town's mayor and aldermen. In one letter to the *Pall Mall Gazette*, a Mr. John Hubbard intimated that this opinion was not far wrong. "By what I heard said by well-dressed men standing on [my hotel's] front doorsteps, they seemed fully aware of what was about to be enacted on certain occasions." Mr. Hubbard went on to recount how a hackney-carriage driver seen in the company of those gentleman later attempted to drive his carriage through the Salvationist procession, subsequently to be rewarded with a drink. Whatever the truth of that claim, it seems clear that the Eastbourne crowds were consciously supporting a cause —defending their council's decision to enforce the by-law; a contention borne out by the facts that much of the physical abuse was restricted to those occasions when the band actually played and was directed against the instruments themselves. It became almost a matter of pride that the town, not the Salvationists, would win the contest. As one citizen told Mayor Morrison, "'Out with them' is what everybody hopes for."

It was hardly likely, however, that any civic official would openly admit condoning such outrages.[7] Indeed, Mayor Morrison and others made a great show of amazement when Bramwell Booth suggested that the by-law was enacted deliberately to get rid of the Army and when he also suggested it was unjust that they were prosecuted for breaking it. The Salvation Army, Morrison maintained, "was well received by the people of Eastbourne, and neither by word nor action would have been interfered with had the leaders refrained from breaking the law by insisting on their Sunday meetings being accompanied by instrumental music." But now that they had broken the law, 'popular feeling' had been roused against them, and the various devices adopted by Salvationists had begun to "irritate and annoy the populace." When Bramwell Booth pleaded "Let all laws be just," G.F. Chambers, one the framers of the by-law, insisted that that was "precisely what we at Eastbourne want and, in point of fact, have —a law reserving our streets and highways for the peaceful use of her Majesty's subjects at large on the day set apart by Divine Authority, not for brass bands and Salvation Army rowdyism, but for peace and rest of mind and body" (*Times*, S 18, 1891).

As might be expected, there were a number of newspapers and

magazines which agreed with Eastbourne's crusade. *The Saturday Review*, an unrelenting crusader against Salvation Army 'rowdyism,' was to the vanguard of support. "If [the Army] can force its uproar upon Eastbourne in defiance of an explicit legal prohibition, it will have put its privilege to commit nuisances in the streets beyond dispute. . . . [The people of Eastbourne] are acting wisely in their own interests, and in the interest of all. It is highly desirable that there should be one town in England where decent people, whether they wear frockcoats or the fisherman's jersey, are protected from insult by the 'Army' with its advertising fanatics and its paid ranters" (Aug. 15).

> We suppose [the editor continued later] it is idle to repeat the very simple facts of the case to the persons who consider this religious persecution. If they are capable of seeing these facts, they may learn [that] there is no wish on the part either of the authorities or the townspeople to exclude the Salvationists from Eastbourne. They may hire buildings, hold meetings, preach, screech, and rant at will, as long as they do not insist on making themselves a nuisance, and on breaking the law. . . . It is mere hypocrisy to talk of persecution in this case at all. What is at stake is the right of any scamp or semi-idiot to suspend the law and to outrage his neighbours under pretence of worship. There is not a single argument used on behalf of the Army which might not be equally used to justify any dirty rogues who chose to set up obscene images in the streets on the plea that they were religious symbols" (Sept 12).

More surprising, perhaps, is the vehemence with which the London *Times* denounced the Army's role in the whole affair. "The Salvationists," it argued, "were the guilty cause of all [breaches of the peace]. If they had been content to act within the law, they would have escaped unmolested and unhurt. As it is, they have not only been law-breakers in their own person, but they have provoked other people to break the law by breaking the Salvationists' heads. . . . Their 'stripes and imprisonments,' or, in plain English, the fines which they had to pay, have not only been the very proper penalties which they have incurred as law-breakers, but they have had choice on each occasion to be let off without a fine, if they would but promise not to

repeat their offence. This promise they were not pleased to give. . . .
Mr. Booth has been so flushed with his triumph over the local law at
Torquay, that he has resolved to add Eastbourne to the list of places
at which he can do as he likes. But at Eastbourne he has to deal with
a more determined body of opponents. The whole town is in arms
against him, and he will do wisely not to persist in breaking the law,
with no better excuse than that he thinks it ought never to have been
passed" (Sept. 14, 1891).

Acknowledging the usual exaggeration of such a claim, it was
nevertheless true that a majority of Eastbourne's citizens supported
their council's actions. Not only did they re-elect Alderman Morrison
a mayor for a third time, but, when in November they were asked by
plebiscite to endorse the council's opposition to a repeal of the by-law,
they did so by a vote of 5,331 to 738.[8] Judging by newspaper report,
however, it was equally true that the people of Eastbourne were not
supported by the country at large —they were, so some thought,
being manipulated by a "small body of political enthusiasts," in
perverse defiance of England's common law, of several legal verdicts
against similar by-laws, and in opposition to a decided national
sympathy for the Salvationists.

> Sir,— I am a clergyman of the Church of England, but I have no
> hesitation in saying that the mob law being now virtually acquiesced in
> at this beautiful watering-place will, like all evil principles, come home
> to roost. It is hard for those who have read Church and Bible history not
> to perceive that the way in which the authorities of this town are
> treating the Salvation Army in no way differs in principle from the
> ancient persecutions of the Early Christians or the more modern
> persecutions of the Dark Ages. Here it is not the evangelistic work and
> fervour of the Salvationists which is objected to, but only the simple
> and trivial matter of playing a band of music. If they will only make that
> small concession, say the authorities, no obstacle shall be put in the way
> of their otherwise good work. But an important principle is here at
> stake, which it would be unpardonable for the Salvationists to yield —a
> principle on which the Church bells themselves depend— and that is
> the right to do what a military band is allowed to do, to parade the
> streets on the way to service, and that for the far higher purpose of

calling in the wanderers and careless to hear what God shall say. If this right were yielded there would speedily be an end to all outdoor Christian effort, and in time to free speech itself. It is for this cause that the Salvationists are contending, and not at all to disturb the peace or Sunday quiet of the town in which they work. Where individuals are molested, or obstructions caused, we have abundant laws to meet the case, and redress can always be sought. That the authorities are sincere in the course they are taking, and that they honestly hold that the Salvation Army are disturbers of the public peace, need not surely be doubted. But the same opinion has always been held by religious persecutors in all ages. It would seem, indeed, as if the Eastbourne authorities have sadly reckoned without their host; and if they do not beware in time they may yet have to prove by painful experience that it is impossible to fight against God.

> Another Visitor. (*Times*, Sept. 1, 1891)

Eventually, national sympathy won the day. In November of 1891 The Salvation Army announced that it would seek a repeal of the Eastbourne by-law; the motion would be put as a matter of private business by Mr. H.H. Fowler and seconded by Sir John Kennaway. The announcement was met by the Eastbourne officials with a pledge to "oppose the Bill," by some of its residents in increased violence against Salvationists, and by one of its sensational pamphlets in the form of a caustic satire:

> It is probable that every M.P. who supports the Booth Bill will be promised by Booth a free pass to Heaven. A promissory note, however, of which he is the maker, is more likely to be honoured in hell. And M.P.s need not hug themselves with the belief that by supporting this fraudulent religious organization they can wipe out as with a sponge their enormous sins and iniquities.[9]

But the writing was on the wall. In spite of concerted attempts to sway parliamentary opinion in their favour, and in spite of a 'splendid fight' by Eastbourne's member in the House of Commons, on March 10 the by-law was repealed (becoming law on September 1). The vote, as the *Pall Mall Gazette* put it, was "122 for Eastbourne and 269 for the Salvation Army." And, though many members of parliament tried to base their arguments on the pro's and con's of 'local options' bills, and not on the merits of The Salvation Army, the *Gazette's* description of the vote was a pretty accurate one —the Army's actions, many times judged legal by the courts, had indeed been vindicated by the British Parliament. Next day, in the *Times*, one of the parliamentarians who voted 'aye,' gave his reasons for doing so:

Sir,— As one of the members who voted for the repeal of the too famous 169th clause of the Eastbourne Improvement Act, 1885, perhaps you will permit me to explain the reasons which led me, and I believe many others, to take that course.

"It is," you remark in your leading article today, "an evil admission for Unionists to make that the law is to be altered in deference to wilful lawbreakers." But who have been the law-breakers in Eastbourne? The Salvationists were not breaking the law when they marched out last Sunday afternoon without their band and were assaulted by a ferocious mob, the police doing little or nothing for their protection. The men were struck and kicked, the women were knocked down and grossly insulted. The Salvationists were strictly within their rights under the law in marching through the streets without music. Yet they were exposed, not by any means for the first time under the same circumstances, to the grossest ruffianism and violence.

The Court of Appeal has decided they were not breaking the law when they were fiercely attacked on another occasion and some of them were dragged to the police-station. Mr. Justice Hawkins has stated from the Bench, in reference to the riot of last July, that the Salvationists were not at fault, and that from 'first to last there was not a single act or word on the part of these young men which could be construed into a determination to defy the law.'

Who would have believed, if there were not overwhelming evidence of the fact, that an Englishman would deliberately walk up to a woman in the streets and pour a torrent of foul obscenities in her ear? That is one of the favourite methods of insulting a Salvation Army woman in Eastbourne, even when she is alone. Mable Brown, a hospital nurse, has stated that the roughs have 'accosted her and poured filthy language into her ears.' Miss Edith Maynard says, 'The language used by the men to myself and other women has been of the vilest character.... You have only to be known as a Salvationist in Eastbourne to have the filthiest language used to you. Whether in uniform or not, or whether in the marches or going about town on business, makes no difference.' Are these women the lawbreakers?

. . . The mayor and his friends are evidently disposed to look upon the whole business as a huge joke. It is a screaming farce, well fitted for performance by the seaside. In your own columns last Monday it was reported that the Salvationists gave no kind of provocation on the previous day, when the mob fell upon them like savages, making special examples of the women, as usual. One poor girl was obliged to be taken to hospital. Other women were assaulted in a way that cannot well be described. On the following evening the Eastbourne Town Council held a meeting, and these infamous proceedings afforded them immense amusement. An alderman proudly boasted that the mob had only shown 'young English blood,' and it was 'a very good thing for them' (the Salvationists). The mayor, according to the report, 'created roars of laughter by detailing his adventures with a lassie on Sunday.' He spoke of the men as 'male animals on two legs,' though why their having two legs instead of four should be an offence is not very clear. The women 'flopped down' of their own accord. Is this the spirit in which the Corporation of Eastbourne should treat occurrences which undoubtedly have created a very painful feeling in various parts of the country? Is this a body that is entitled to be left in the possession of exceptional powers, which are used only for the maintenance and exercise of mob law? The position of the Mayor of Eastbourne in the matter is not improved by the act, stated by the Solicitor-General in last night's debate, that he gave his sanction to the 'Skeleton Army' which used to make war upon the Salvation Army at Folkestone, until it was suppressed by the authorities. The mayor, though, doubtless, very amusing at a council meeting, when describing his 'adventures with a Salvation lassie,' is not the sort of man to act impartially between the Salvationists and their cowardly assailants.

Where the local authorities are left to deal with the Salvationists under the ordinary law of the land, these disturbances do not take place. We wish to put Eastbourne in that position, and to repeal a local law under cover of which a turbulent and brutal mob work their will every Sunday on a small band of defenceless men and women. I am, Sir, yours obediently,

L.J. Jennings, House of Commons, March 11

Those views, though somewhat ardently stated, represented the majority opinion in Great Britain. There still remained, and there would remain for some time, considerable animosity towards the Army —many people would not forgive nor forget, and many more, who cared little about Eastbourne, were busily debunking William Booth's 'Darkest England' scheme— but most were grateful that the Army had struck a momentous blow for civil and religious liberty, and were much impressed by the courage displayed by the Salvationists of Eastbourne. As the London *Star* stated, "Everyone must admire the heroic tenacity with which the men and women of The Salvation Army have striven quietly and peacefully to maintain their position against the force of bigot-made law and disorder."

Did the physical intimidation end abruptly with the happy resolution of the Eastbourne affair? Not at all. In Eastbourne itself, the Army ceased its processions long enough to allow tempers to cool and then resumed its open-air ministry, with a full band, without further molestation. Having made their point, however, and with a more decorous set of onlookers, Salvationists could not only show just how melodious an Army band could be but also took steps to ensure that their marches did not unduly interfere with either the peace of the community or its business thoroughfares. In other parts of England, too, mob violence all but disappeared. In many towns, London included, there continued to be individual attempts to charge Salvationists with obstruction and minor offences. In 1893, for example, the Chelsea police charged a female cadet for having annoyed a resident by singing in public. But more often than not, the judges were dismissing the cases. And, by the turn of the century, physical violence against Salvationists was a rarity.

The Worthing and Eastbourne riots —only two of many such encounters between the English public and Salvationists throughout the 1880s— illustrate several aspects of English history that are almost unknown to modern readers of that history and, obviously, to historians as well. To begin with, if they have any acquaintance at all with the Army, they are surprised to learn that this organization

—now held in almost universal esteem— was so reviled and spat upon in its early days. Equally surprising is the enormity and ferocity of the mob violence directed against Salvationists, the organized nature of such violence by the Skeleton Army and by local councils, and the result of those encounters in terms of legislative action. But, most surprising of all is the degree of public interest in and awareness of The Salvation Army manifested in the newspapers and journals of the day. In 1890, 1891 and 1892, for example, Army activities —the Eastbourne riots, the 'Darkest England' affair, the resignation of Frank Smith, William Booth's visit to India (from which he returned to a welcome of some 8,000 Salvationists)— commanded as much journalistic space as some royal events. To put the matter another way, while many historians are aware of the importance of The Salvation Army as a social-welfare organization, they are much less aware of how it achieved such prominence in English society and just how hard fought that achievement was.

W.T. Stead's 'Maiden Tribute': The Salvation Army and the Criminal Law Amendment Act

It would not be unfair to say that in some instances, early in its progress, The Salvation Army courted —or (to put it more mildly) took advantage of— public confrontation as a means of furthering Christianity among the English poor. To stand behind a pulpit, Booth reasoned, to stay within four walls and merely preach against the evils of alcoholism, would be totally ineffectual. It was necessary to confront the publicans, outside their gin shops, and shame them and the English public into an awareness of the problems caused by drink. Place your 'barracks' as near the 'penny gaffes' as possible; compete for souls. Take your music to the streets; let people know, by whatever bizarre means available, that God was alive. Those were Booth's methods, and they were successful. So much so that, by 1886, the Army had attracted more than 3,000 volunteers, from England to India, to engage full-time in its service; and was ministering each week to as many as 300,000 people throughout the world.

We might, for want of a better term, describe that kind of public engagement as the Army's 'intentional' warfare. It was initiated by the Army, sometimes to promote its work and sometimes as the only means of accomplishing that work. It certainly drew, as we saw in the first three essays, a great deal of hostile commentary, even physical abuse, but it did bring thousands into the Army's fold and eventually gained many outside supporters for its work.

There was also a second kind of public engagement, which might be called the Army's 'unintentional' warfare. Rather than being initiated by the Army, this kind represented a Salvationist response to what was, to all intents and purposes, an existing social need or emergency. In short, the Army, having obtained the respect and confidence of the public, was sought out to help tackle 'national' problems. Two instances that come immediately to mind are the First and Second World Wars, when The Salvation Army was asked to lend special assistance to the Allied troops. But the first involvement of this kind occurred many years before, back in 1885, when the Army came to the aid of the British nation in its effort to deal with a national evil known as the 'white slave trade.'

Our story begins with three scenarios, each played out at various times before the 'Maiden Tribute' affair became a national *cause célèbre:*

Scenario I: Exposed is an inadequate law and a British Parliament without the will to change it. Under British law the 'age of consent' —the age at which a girl's consent to sexual intercourse or seduction is legal— was set at thirteen. Partly for that reason, and partly because of rampant poverty, juvenile prostitution was a major social problem, the most evil adjunct of which was the 'white slave trade,' the often illegal procurement and marketing (mainly to European brothels) of young girls for sexual exploitation. In 1881, at the urging of concerned citizens, a Select Committee of the House of Lords was established to investigate the problem. It not only confirmed that indeed there was a monumental problem, but that it was on the increase; the Committee's findings became the foundation of a Criminal Law Amendment Bill, the chief clause of which would raise the age of consent to sixteen. In 1883 it was passed by the House of Lords but dropped by the House of Commons. In 1884 the same thing happened. And in 1885 the Bill, now revised to the lower age of fifteen, again passed the House of Lords, but once more met with little support from the House of Commons. "On May 22, as Parliament was preparing to rise for its Whitsuntide recess, Sir William Harcourt, the Home Secretary, moved the second reading of the bill in the Commons. Only about forty members were present, and in an atmosphere of apathy mixed with hostility the measure was debated until adjournment and no vote was taken."[1] It seemed certain that efforts to curtail the 'white slave trade' were doomed to failure.

Scenario II: In the town of Darlington in 1879, we find William T. Stead, who had just commenced his journalistic career as editor of the *Northern Echo*, making his acquaintance with The Salvation Army. His curiosity piqued by the fact that two young 'Hallelujah Lasses' were drawing crowds of 2,000 to 2,500 every night to their meetings, Stead went to see the thing for himself. "I was amazed," he later wrote. "I found two delicate girls —one hardly able to write a letter; the other not yet nineteen— ministering to a crowded congregation which they had themselves collected out of the street, and building up an aggressive church-militant out of the human refuse which other churches regarded with blank despair."[2] Confessing a prejudice against noisy religion, Stead was nevertheless faced with the 'stubborn fact' that a material and moral change had taken place in the lives of these people —a change he would have declared to have been impossible. "And the only visible means by which this result was brought about, was these two girls, neither of them well educated, both delicate, and without any friends or material resources whatever."

Won unreservedly to the Army's cause, Stead was soon corresponding with William Booth, becoming one of his staunchest non-Army supporters. This was far from being an insignificant thing, for by 1885, the year the Criminal Law Amendment Act was debated and then ignored, W.T. Stead had become one of the most influential men of his time: England's leading crusading journalist and editor of the prestigious London daily, *The Pall Mall Gazette*.

Scenario III: At seven-thirty in the morning, in May or June 1885, the housekeeper of The Salvation Army Headquarters on Queen Victoria Street, London, arrives to find a young lady, cold and distraught, and waiting for sanctuary. After a hot breakfast, she is taken straight to the Chief of Staff, Bramwell Booth himself, where she tells an incredible story. Her name is Annie and she is seventeen years old. The previous year, she informs Bramwell, while living with her grandparents, she saw an advertisement for a domestic position:

'Wanted a girl to help in the general work of the house.' My grandmother wrote about the situation, and as it seemed satisfactory, it was decided I should go. My mistress had to meet me at Victoria station and take me to my new home. I arrived all safely, and at first I thought everything was going to be all right. Mrs C---- was very kind, and let me go to bed at ten. After a time, however, I began to see something was wrong. The ladies in the house used to drink very much and keep very late hours. Gentlemen were coming and going till three and four o'clock in the morning. I began to see that I was in a bad house. But when I mentioned it to my mother, who is living a gay life in London, she scolded me and said she would give me a good hiding if I left my place. Where was I to go? Besides, I thought I might be a servant in a bad house without being bad myself. By degrees Mrs. C began to hint that I was too good to be a general servant; she would get another girl, and I would be a lady, like the others. One night Mrs. C brought me a red silk dress and a new hat, and said she was going to take me out. She got into a cab with me and took me to the Aquarium. There she walked me about and brought me home again. She became more pressing. She showed me a beautiful pink dress and promised me that also if I would do as the others did. And when I would not, she called me a fool, and used awful language, and said what pleasure I was missing all from stupidity. Sometimes she would tell the gentlemen to take liberties with me, but I kept them at a distance. One night after I had come in with her from the Aquarium, a gentleman tried to catch hold of me as I was outside the bedroom. I ran as hard as I could downstairs. He came after me, but I got into the kitchen first, and there I barricaded the door with chairs and the table, so that he could not get in. I was nearly distracted and did not know what to do, when I found in my box the back of an old hymn-book my grandfather had used. It had on it the address of General Booth, at the Headquarters of the Salvation Army. I thought to myself Mr. Booth must be a good man or he would not have so many halls all over the country, and then I thought perhaps he will help me to get out of this horrible house, as I never knew what might happen any night. So I waited quietly all that night, never taking off my clothes. It was usually four o'clock before the house was quiet. As soon as they all seemed to be asleep, I waited till nearly six, and then I crept to the door, opened it, and stole softly away, not even daring to close the door. I only knew one address in all London —101 Queen Victoria-street; where that was I did not know. I walked out blindly till I met a policeman, and he told me the right direction. I walked on and on; it was a long way; I was very tired. I had had no sleep all night, and I feared at any moment to be overtaken, and brought back. My red silk dress was rather conspicuous, and I did not know if, even if I got there, whether Mr. Booth would help me. But I felt sure he was a good man, and I walked on and on. The bad house was in Gloucester-street, Pimlico, and it was nearly half past seven when I got to Queen Victoria-street. The headquarters were closed. I stood waiting outside, wondering if, after all, I might have to go back.

Of course she did not. Her story was, as Bramwell Booth knew well, but one of many that could be told, most of which did not have this happy ending. So angered was he that he made this resolve: "no matter what the consequence might be, I will do all I can to stop these abominations, to rouse public opinion, to agitate for the improvement of the law, to bring to justice the adulterers and murderers of innocence, and to make a way of escape for the victims."[3]

Three scenarios: a national problem, a crusading journalist, and The Salvation Army. Though there will always be some dispute about who actually engineered their momentous conjunction —enough for Stead and Booth to believe it was God alone— what is beyond question is that when the conjunction occurred the world took note. Burdened for many years by the need to do something about 'enforced prostitution' (even of writing a novel about it), and always pressured to do so by the great reformer, Josephine Butler, Stead shared both Bramwell Booth's repugnance of the evil and his determination to suppress it. Now, as a thirty-five year-old editor of the *Pall Mall Gazette,* his time had come. When the elderly anti-prostitution campaigner, Benjamin Scott, pressed him for journalistic action, Stead went to see his friend, Bramwell Booth, to dispel his lingering doubts by interviewing some of the girls whom the Army had 'rescued.' Having heard enough, Stead uttered an un-Army "Damn!" bringing his fist down on Bramwell's desk. "All very well," replied Bramwell, "but it will not help us. The first thing to do is to get the facts in such a form that we can publish them."[4]

From that moment (early May 1885), Stead's mission was clear. Without delay, he immediately set up a 'secret commission' to investigate London's prostitution 'labyrinth' —with himself the tireless leader, prowling the brothels in a variety of disguises, aided by two or three young journalists, Mr. Sampson Jacques, a Greek freelance journalist, and an unnamed young Salvation Army officer who spent ten days living the undercover life of a prostitute. "Let me state as a matter of simple justice to the Salvation Army," Stead later wrote, "that our commission would have been almost helpless without the aid which was extended to us without stint at any hour of the day or night, at any sacrifice, personal trouble, or risk of personal danger, by the intrepid soldiers of that admirable organization. . . . In the elucidation of facts, in the investigation of obscure cases, in the furnishing at a moment's notice of men and women ready to do anything and go anywhere, the aid we received from Mr. Bramwell Booth and his devoted workers was of incalculable value and far exceeded that rendered by all other existing organizations put together."[5]

Where The Salvation Army became inextricably involved —in an action that eventually led to criminal charges against Stead and Booth— was when Stead realized that to *prove* his case he would have to purchase a child and take her to the continent. He had to show that this was easily done.

Protecting himself by bringing several leading citizens into his confidence (among whom were the Archbishop of Canterbury and Cardinal Manning), Stead again went to Bramwell Booth for help. This time the name of Stead's 'coadjutor' did become known —Rebecca Jarrett, one-time brothel-keeper and now a confirmed Salvationist. Though reluctant to return to her old haunts, Jarrett was persuaded to help Stead 'procure' a *pure* child, just over thirteen years old. This is pseudo-fictional way Stead reported the 'deal':

> At the beginning of this Derby week, a woman, an old hand in the work of procuration, entered a brothel in ----st. M----, kept by an old

acquaintance, and opened negotiations for the purchase of a maid. One of the women who lodged in the house had a sister as yet untouched. Her mother was far away, her father was dead. The child was living in the house, and in all probability would be seduced and follow the profession of her elder sister. The child was between thirteen and fourteen, and after some bargaining it was agreed that she should be handed over to the procuress for the sum of £5. The maid was wanted, it was said, to start a house with, and there was no disguise on either side that the sale was to be effected for immoral purposes. While the negotiations were going on, a drunken neighbour came into the house, and so little concealment was then used, that she speedily became aware of the nature of the transaction. So far from being horrified at the proposed sale of the girl, she whispered eagerly to the seller, "Don't you think she would take our Lily? I think she would suit." Lily was her own daughter, a bright, fresh-looking little girl, who was thirteen years old last Christmas. The bargain, however, was made for the other child, and Lily's mother felt she had lost her market.

The next day, Derby Day as it happened, was fixed for the delivery of this human chattel. But as luck would have it, another sister of the child who was to be made over to the procuress heard of the proposed sale. She was living respectably in a situation, and on hearing of the fate reserved for the little one she lost no time in persuading her dissolute sister to break off the bargain. When the woman came for her prey the bird had flown. Then came the chance of Lily's mother. The brothel-keeper sent for her, and offered her a sovereign for her daughter. The woman was poor, dissolute, and indifferent to everything but drink. The father, who was also a drunken man, was told his daughter was going to a situation. He received the news with indifference, without even inquiring where she was going to. The brothel-keeper having thus secured possession of the child, then sold her to the procuress in place of the child whose sister had rescued her from her destined doom for £5 —£3 paid down and the remaining £2 after her virginity had been professionally certified. This little girl, all unsuspecting the purpose for which she was destined, was told that she must go with this strange woman to a situation. The procuress, who was well up to her work, took her away, washed her, dressed her up neatly, and sent her to bid her parents goodbye. The mother was so drunk she hardly recognized her daughter. The father was hardly less indifferent. The child left her home, and was taken to the woman's lodging in A----- street.

The first step had thus been taken. But it was necessary to procure the certification of her virginity —a somewhat difficult task, as the child was absolutely ignorant of the nature of the transaction which had transferred her from home to the keeping of this strange, but apparently kind-hearted woman. Lily was a little cockney child, one of those who by the thousand annually develop into servants of the poorer middle-class. She had been at school, could read and write, and although her spelling was extraordinary, she was able to express herself with much force and decision. Her experience of the world was limited to the London quarter in which she had been born. With the exception of two school trips to Richmond and one to Epping Forest, she had never been in the country in her life, nor had she ever seen the Thames excepting at Richmond. She was an industrious, warm-hearted little thing, a hardy English child, slightly coarse in texture, with dark black eyes, and short, sturdy figure. Her education was slight. She spelled write "right," for instance, and her grammar was very shaky. But she was a loving, affectionate child, whose kindly feeling for the drunken mother who sold her into nameless infamy was very touching to behold. In a little letter of hers which I once saw, plentifully garlanded with kisses, there was the following ill-spelled childish verse:—

As I was in bed
Some little forths (thoughts) gave (came) in my head
I forth (thought) of one, I forth (thought) of two;
But first of all I forth (thought) of you.

The poor child was full of delight at going to her new situation, and clung affectionately to the keeper who was taking her away —where, she knew not.

The first thing to be done after the child was fairly severed from home was to secure the certificate of virginity without which the rest of the security-money would not be forthcoming. In order to avoid trouble she was taken in a cab to the house of a midwife, whose skill in pronouncing upon the physical evidences of virginity is generally recognized in the profession. The examination was very brief and completely satisfactory. But the youth, the complete innocence of the girl, extorted pity even from the hardened heart of an old abortionist. "The poor little thing," she exclaimed. "She is so small, her pain will be extreme. I hope you will not be too cruel with her" —as if to lust when fully roused the very acme of agony on the part of the victim has not a fierce delight. To quiet the old lady the agent of the purchaser asked if she could supply anything to dull the pain. She produced a small vial of chloroform. "This," she said, "is the best. My clients find this much the most effective." The keeper took the bottle, but unaccustomed to anything but drugging by the administration of sleeping potions, she would infallibly have poisoned the child had she not discovered by experiment that the liquid burned the mouth when an attempt was made to swallow it. £1 1s. was paid for the certificate of virginity —which was verbal and not written— while £1 10s. more was charged for the chloroform, the net value of which was probably less than a shilling. An arrangement was made that if the child was badly injured Madame would patch it up to the best of her ability, and then the party left the house.

From the midwife's the innocent girl was taken to a house of ill-fame, No.--, P---- street, Regent-street, where, notwithstanding her extreme youth, she was admitted without question. She was taken upstairs, undressed, put to bed, the woman who bought her putting her to sleep. She was rather restless, but under the influence of chloroform she soon went over. Then the woman withdrew. All was quiet and still. A few moments later the door opened, and the purchaser entered the bedroom. He closed and locked the door. There was a brief silence. And then there rose a wild and piteous cry —not a loud shriek, but a helpless, startled scream like the bleat of a frightened lamb. And the child's voice was heard crying, in accents of terror, "There's a man in the room! Take me home; oh, take me home!"

And then all once more was still.[6]

The girl "Lily" (later to be known by her real name, Eliza Armstrong) was not harmed but, after the transaction to prove Stead's case was confirmed, she was handed over to The Salvation Army, taken to France by a female officer, Mrs. Captain Combe (a Swiss Salvationist), and lodged in the home of a French Countess. In the eyes of Stead and Bramwell Booth, everything had gone smoothly; nothing remained but to write the exposé, awaken society to the truth, and force (they hoped) a positive decision with regard to the Criminal Law Amendment Act.

When "The Maiden Tribute of Modern Babylon" broke on an

unsuspecting public on the morning of July 6, 1885, the British were, on the whole, shocked by what they considered one of the most sensational pieces of journalism —told in the most graphic language— ever to be published in an English newspaper. In four successive issues of his *Pall Mall Gazette* W.T. Stead recounted, in minute detail, how he had gone 'underground' to investigate the 'labyrinth' which nightly sacrificed "not seven maidens only, but seven times seven" to London's Minotaur of sexual lust. "Within that labyrinth wander, like lost souls, the vast host of London prostitutes, whose numbers no man can compute, but who are probably not much below 50,000 strong. Many, no doubt, who venture but a little way into the maze make their escape. But multitudes are swept irresistibly on and on to be destroyed in due season, to give place to others, who will also share their doom. The maw of the London Minotaur is insatiable, and none that go into the secret recesses of his lair return again."

In vivid and sometimes lurid detail, Stead told how brothel-keepers lured young girls from their homes or purchased them from willing parents; how they were seduced and "made fit for service"; how, when demand dictated, doctors were ready to issue a stamp saying "virgo intacta"; how young girls, barely into their thirteenth year, were drugged with laudanum or chloroformed and left to the clients' pleasure —clients whose names would have been well-known to anyone who read the leading papers of the day. "The system of procuration," Stead wrote, "is reduced to a science. The poorer brothel-keeper hunts up recruits herself, while the richer are supported by their agents. . . . . Against their wiles the law offers the child over thirteen next to no protection. If a child of fourteen is cajoled or frightened, or overborne by anything short of direct force or the threat of immediate bodily harm, into however an unwilling acquiescence in an act the nature of which she most imperfectly apprehends, the law steps in to shield her violator. If permission is given, says 'Stephen's Digest of the Criminal Law,' the fact that it was obtained by fraud, or that the woman did not understand the nature of the act is immaterial."

Public reaction was largely one of outrage. On the day after the first instalment, the offices of the *Pall Mall Gazette* were flooded with letters, many of them denouncing Stead's prurience, but many more complimenting him on his courage; in the afternoon the streets surrounding the *Gazette's* offices were crowded with people awaiting the next issue, afraid they would not get a copy because W.H. Smith, who had a monopoly on the news stands, had refused to sell the paper. "The pressure was so great that men were pushed through windows, and eventually it took forty policemen to restore order."[7] That evening in the House of Commons, Mr. George Cavendish-Bentinck, who was to become one of Stead's fiercest critics, called attention to the *Gazette's* 'objectionable' contents, suggesting that they were now being sold by underage children displaying 'indecent placards' at twice the normal price. Surely, Cavendish-Bentinck argued, obscenity charges should be brought against the *Pall Mall Gazette*; Stead maliciously replied that he would welcome such charges since "we might subpoena almost half the Legislature in order to prove the accuracy of our revelations."

For several weeks after his initial onslaught, W.T. Stead continued his journalistic campaign, amidst great public uproar and strong criticism from other journalists and politicians, but morally supported by many of England's religious leaders. Many members of the House of Commons, now debating a third reading of the Criminal Law Amendment Act, were loud in their denunciation of Stead's tactics, characterizing his articles as 'foul slander' and a 'disgrace to civilization' and labelling Stead a 'filthy editor of a filthy production.' But most knew that a shocked public was now aroused to the full horror of the white-slave trade and was insisting, with Stead, that the new law be passed. Thus, on August 7 the bill was given its third reading by the House of Commons and on August 10th received its final approval from the House of Lords. In essence, the age of consent was raised to sixteen and legal action could be taken against anyone procuring a girl under sixteen or any woman by force.

In much of the initial public furore (during which London's City Solicitor banned the sale of the *PMG*), The Salvation Army received only sporadic attention. From the *War Cry*, of course, it could be learned that the Army actively supported Stead's efforts (though

Salvationists were not encouraged to read the lurid details). In early August the Army placed a petition in every Army barracks throughout Britain, eventually signed by more than 390,000 people and ultimately presented to the British Parliament. It was also known that Catherine Booth had written to Queen Victoria on the subject, and though Her Majesty could not publicly comment, her sympathy was expressed and that was enough to lend considerable support to the cause. In Stead's exposé, however, except in one or two instances (notably the 'Annie' story), little was said of the Army's involvement; as Stead would later make clear, both at public rallies and in his court testimony, Bramwell Booth, Rebecca Jarrett and Mrs. Combe had only become involved after he had made his plans to abduct Eliza Armstrong. A majority of England's newspapers believed Stead and made little of the Army's involvement. But not all.

Again, as in so many other sincere attempts to right perceived wrongs, The Salvation Army was branded as an interfering busy-body. This time the accusations came from two London newspapers, *Lloyd's Weekly* and *St. James's Gazette*, each striving to retain readerships in the midst of a 'Maiden Tribute' monopoly on news. In a campaign designed to bring about a prosecution of Rebecca Jarrett, they attempted to 'smear' Bramwell Booth and The Salvation Army by suggesting that they, not Stead, had initiated the whole affair for publicity purposes. It should come as no surprise, they told their readers, "that the revivalists who call themselves the 'Salvation Army' should have gone shrieking into this 'crusade'"; for was it not well known that "religious hysteria and sexual excitement have ever gone hand in hand." What they could not understand was why the Church of England should countenance such activity: "How does it come, then, that they are assisting a most disorderly and most reckless kind of religious fanaticism to discuss in the open street and in the foulest language practices which it was thought intolerable to debate with women and girls in the secrecy of the confessional? . . . Are they jealous of the sensationalism of the Salvation Army and resolved to compete with it even in the gutter?" (*St. James's*, Aug. 4).

In articles with headlines such as "A Mother's Search for Her Child: A Salvation Army Mystery," *Lloyd's* ignored Stead's exposé altogether and tried to pretend that the Eliza affair was a pure case of abduction by The Salvation Army. Its writers conducted Eliza's mother on a tour of Army establishments to see if her daughter were sheltered in any one; gave tearful accounts of how distraught she was to learn how she had been duped out of her daughter's affection; and how Rebecca Jarrett was nothing more than a *poseur* Salvationist.

Eventually, by August, those newspapers had convinced Mrs. Armstrong, who had willingly 'sold' Eliza to Rebecca Jarrett, that Stead's 'Lily' story was about her daughter and that she should force Bramwell Booth to return her to her home. Their focus, at this point, was to show just how Rebecca Jarrett had carried out the transaction:

Within the last two months a young girl was met and stopped in the streets of Winchester by a woman who was an entire stranger to her. The woman asked the girl whether she should like a nice situation in London. The child said 'yes,' and the woman at once made a bargain with the girl to accompany her. A neighbour heard of the incident, told the girl's mother, and gave her a clue to where the child was —namely, at a certain Hope Cottage in that town. The anxious mother went off to find her child. A fly was standing at the door ready to convey the girl off to London. By this time the girl's surname had come out; and then the woman who had "engaged" her remembered an assistant of the same name (Brewer) in a certain Home. The woman now began to hesitate; and it presently appeared that the child she proposed to decoy was a sister of the person she had known in the Home. The mother of the decoyed girl, in her excitement, said that her elder daughter was about to pay her a visit, whereupon the decoy exclaimed, 'Oh, I should like to see her.' Early in June Miss Brewer (the assistant) went to Hope Cottage to see the decoy, who admitted her at once. After a brief introduction the woman said, referring to her attempt to lure away the sister of her visitor, that 'she would not have had it happen for the world!' The subject of conversation then turned from the sister, and the woman made the following statement:— She was employed by the Salvation Army, by the wife of a clergyman in Winchester [Josephine Butler], and others to get girls to prove that 'a mother would sell her child; that the child could be afterwards sent right away, and that no inquiries would be made for the child by the mother.' This woman —the decoy— also stated that she had secured a young girl who was in

Jersey, and that in a few weeks she expected to fetch it back again. Further, that she had been up to London to see some gentlemen, and that what she had done would 'soon come out in the *Pall Mall*.' What she has done did come out —but not by her arrangement in *Lloyd's Weekly Newspaper*, under the heading of "A Mother Seeking a Lost Child," —a story well worth the reader's careful study— in which the decoy figures as Mrs. Jarrett. But when she appears again in the *Pall Mall Gazette* she is presented to the reader in the character of a 'procuress,' and since that time she has appeared as a 'Salvation Army lass.'

What have General Booth, and Mrs. Booth, and the Archbishop of Canterbury, and Cardinal Manning to say to this? Do they hear of it for the first time? Can they say whether it is true or not? (*St. James's*, Aug.. 4).

In this newspaper's opinion, Mrs. Armstrong was "anything but a person who would be a party to the disgraceful bargain attributed to her." Speaking affectionately of her children, she told her tearful story of how (though the trial showed she was clearly drunk at the time) she had been misled by Rebecca Jarrett and of her near "distraction" on reading the sordid story in the *Pall Mall Gazette*:

Some fresh characters now come upon the scene. Having ascertained that General Booth of the Salvation Army [this is how the newspaper always wrongfully referred to Bramwell Booth] knew something of her daughter's whereabouts, Mrs. Armstrong called upon him on Saturday week. He, however, refused to see her, but promised to write to her. Being determined to leave nothing undone to recover her daughter, and wipe a cruel imputation from her own character, Mrs. Armstrong, acting on friendly advice, resolved to lay her case before the committee of prelates and others who were engaged at the Mansion House in examining the contents of the cesspool set under their noses by the genius of Northumberland-street [W.T. Stead]. These grave and learned seigniors listened to the poor woman's story with dumbfounding stolidity, and when she had finished they allowed her to depart without expressing a word of sympathy or of indignation; and not many hours afterwards the advertisement of the "Gutter Gazette," which they were constituted to frame, was published with a fitting flourish of trumpets.

In the beginning of last week Mrs. Armstrong was surprised to receive a letter from her daughter bearing French post-marks; but having neither date nor signature. It was to the effect that her mother would, no doubt, be thinking about her; but that she must not fret. The writer said she was now in France and doing well, being employed in nursing a baby. She added that the woman who left her there was a long time in coming to take her back. On Saturday last Mrs. Armstrong, accompanied by the police-officer who has been investigating the case, again called on General Booth. That person granted her an interview on that occasion. He began by demanding in surly tone what she wanted. She told him that she wanted her child, and was determined to have her. He said she should not, and refused to answer her question as to how he had got possession of Eliza. He stated that he had spent £100 over the child, but declined to say in what manner. She showed him the letter that had come from France. After reading it, he said the girl was doing well, and asked her mother if she did not think it would be a pity to take her away from a good situation. Mrs. Armstrong pleaded with him that he should bring Eliza back to England that she might go before a magistrate with the persons who were present when it was arranged that she go with Mrs. Sullivan [Rebecca Jarrett], so that she (Mrs. Armstrong) might be put right in the eyes of the public. The General replied that he could not comply with this request; but he put his hand in his pocket, and, turning to the police-inspector, asked him what he thought would be a sufficient wage for a girl of thirteen —would not 3s. or 4 s. per week do? The inspector thought that question could be answered best by Mrs. Armstrong. The General then asked Mrs. Armstrong if she would take her daughter's wages, to which she replied, 'No; I want my child.' The General threw down a slip of paper on which was written an address in France, which he said would find her daughter. This Mrs. Armstrong took up, saying it was all she wanted. The address was this —"Eliza Armstrong, care of Monsieur Th. Berard, (Drôme), France." As Drôme is a province with nearly half-a-million inhabitants it will be evident that a letter so addressed would be as likely to find its destination as one addressed— 'Eliza Armstrong, Westminster.' The General then went on to remark that it would be absurd to bring the child back, as she would not recollect what had occurred. He added something about a certificate of virginity which he had obtained with reference to the girl; but I cannot expect you to print such particulars. I have only to add that the general has had the streets in which Mrs. Armstrong lives watched by some of his 'soldiers,' with the object no doubt of finding out what manner of persons are interesting themselves in the poor woman's misfortune (*St. James's*, Aug. 5).

In his next issue the editor of the *St. James's Gazette* was confronted by a letter from William Booth's solicitors stating that the preceding article, so far as it was "calculated to cast a stigma on our client's action," was entirely false: "Mrs. Armstrong has never had an interview with General Booth, although she has seen his son, Mr. Bramwell Booth, who, however, informs us that he made none of the statements attributed to General Booth in the interview referred to. He, however, assured her of the child's welfare, and gave her its full address —not the mutilated one given by your informant." The most the editor would acknowledge was that the story had come from Mrs. Armstrong, attested to by several gentlemen, and seemed confident that the Booths had more to answer for than did Eliza's mother. "How did he [Mr. Booth] come into possession of the child? In whose hands did he find her? By whose means was she taken away? Does Mr. Booth know who the woman was who decoyed her? Is that woman now, or has she since been in the Salvation Army? Will Mr. Booth produce her? Who sent the child over to France without her mother's knowledge and consent? Why is the child not produced when her mother demands her restitution? Is the child called 'Lily' in a certain sensational newspaper? If so, does Mr. Booth maintain that Lily's story, there told, is true, or is it a concoction? Other questions remain. Is Mr. Booth willing to answer these?" It was really necessary, the editor continued, that General Booth should explain to the public why it should not believe the whole affair to be a "shameful fraud: a fraud committed for the purpose of sustaining the system of sensationalism by which he and his organization thrive. It is now pretty evident that the Salvation Army is at the bottom of the great scandal of the time. And it is charged against the Salvation Army, and the literary persons employed with it, that, in order to present the public with startling and shocking cases of depravity, they have in fact been guilty of concocting their cases: and that this has been done in a cruel and most immoral and mendacious way."

As for Mrs. Jarrett, whoever she was, the newspapers alleged that she "was lately seen in or near a certain committee-room at the mansion House in the costume of a 'Hallelujah Lass.'" But certain other people were sure that she was the same woman "of odious character who lately broke her leg in falling through a skylight while engaged with a man in burglary. If it is the same woman she was at that time dressed not like a Hallelujah Lass but like a labouring man" (Aug. 8).

What is difficult to understand at this far remove from 1885 is just why the *St. James's Gazette* —and indeed many other right-wing newspapers— were so intent on deflecting attention away from (or denying the truth of) the main issue, the rampant prostitution and the blatant exploitation of children for immoral purposes. Its attacks were focussed not on the problem but on the 'scandalous' revelations about 'pretended' social evils. Perhaps it was, as W.T. Stead predicted, trying to protect men in high places, for, as he suggested, many of the clients of the brothels were well-known politicians, civil-servants, businessmen and lawyers. In any event, it was clear that such newspapers, unwilling to face reality, were looking for a scapegoat and out of a natural antipathy to sensationalism singled out The Salvation Army. In doing so, it was willing to pervert even the best of intentions.

Thus, when Bramwell Booth made it known that The Salvation Army would launch a "scheme for the better protection of young girls" which would include a "central office of help and inquiry," refuges in London and, possibly, "receiving houses" in Canada and the Western United States, the *St. James's Gazette* ridiculed the scheme. How could one, it asked, support the scheme of a man and an organization which (it was strongly suspicioned) had "feloniously" abducted and "submitted to infamous treatment" a child so that a "loathsome fabrication might be published in a newspaper." Unless one didn't object to an organization which could "destroy the soul of here and there an innocent child in order to forge sensational stories for the work of Salvation." And, in a ludicrous (though not facetious) conclusion it suggested that Booth's scheme might lead to further abductions: "A stolen child might be hidden in 'the Western States' even more effectively than in France, and the indefinite multiplication of Hope Cottages would be a grave public misfortune."

The 'natural antipathy' already referred to was made explicit when the *Gazette*, reiterating a theme already expounded, began to decry the increasing popularity of the Army and William Booth. "Thanks to Mrs. Butler and Mrs. Jarrett on the one hand, and to Cardinal Manning, the Archbishop of Canterbury, and the Bishop of London on the other; thanks also, beyond and beneath these, to a most corrupt susceptibility to sensationalism, which is one of the worst diseases of civilization; the individual who styles himself General Booth is now a person of considerable notoriety and importance." Maddened by such possible acceptance, the editor launched into a virulent attack on the Army hardly equalled even by the *Saturday Review*. Referring to the 'backwoods' conversions of 'lowbred' people, which were commonly accompanied by body spasms called 'the jerks,' the writer suggested that "if you go into a Salvationist meeting, you will see the same sort of thing, the 'jerks' or something like it, differing not one whit from the convulsions that mark the rites of Guinea negroes." It was precisely by such "senseless, sensuous, pagan methods that Mr. Booth and his functionaries proceed," with the result that his converts had "no more religion than the yelling contortionists at a negro sacrifice of 'the goat without horns'."

> And if the reader will reflect a moment upon the enormous power which such an organization *could* give, the instruments it could furnish; the means of espionage or false witness it could supply; the 'information' some of its members could impart, or might wickedly or hysterically invent for purposes of sensationalism or what not; —when all this is considered it will be seen instantly how dangerous such an organization might become. We are speaking of what might be; and in justification point again to the 'Lily' case. Here it is manifest that either some well-meaning but shameless persons have been imposed upon through love of sensation, or they have themselves been led to commit or countenance an infamous fraud; in either case the thing was done for the purposes of sensationalism and its profits. . . . And all has been done on behalf of a 'work conducted with so reckless a resolve to get

up a grand sensation that the very air we breathe seems tainted by obscenity (Aug. 19, 1885).

Single-minded in its perversity, ignoring all the evidence to the contrary, and pretending never to know the real reason for what Stead, Jarrett and Booth had done, the *St. James's Gazette* continued its battering of The Salvation Army until it had won a major victory —that is, until it had convinced legal authorities to bring charges against Booth, Stead, Jarrett and their accomplices. After that had been accomplished (the arraignment being held on September 7) the newspaper, not being able to comment while the case was before the courts, ceased its misinformed attack on the Army. Its last article, on August 25, was a reiteration of its claim that the whole 'Maiden Tribute' exposé was trumped up for the promotion of salvation sensationalism. It did not matter in the least that Bramwell Booth had not been involved in the abduction, that Eliza Armstrong had not been tampered with, had been well-treated, and "was better fed and clothed" than she would have been at home. "It may be a good thing," the writer continued, "that all very poor children should be taken out of the slums and put into Salvation Army 'homes'." But General Booth did not have the right to abduct such children, "conceal them in foreign countries," in order to promote his religious aims. It was, in this newspaper's view, a case of "conversion by kidnapping," and it would do its best to "convince General Booth that the Salvation Army is not to be recruited by methods which savour strongly of kidnapping and fraud."

Though these grave distortions did not (as we later suggest) represent a majority public opinion regarding The Salvation Army, and did not seem to impair the Army's reputation, the editors of *St. James's Gazette* and *Lloyd's Weekly* could at least take some satisfaction from their efforts. It was largely through their advocacy (which even consisted of raising funds for the Armstrong family) that charges of abduction were laid against the principal 'commission members' —first against Rebecca Jarrett and subsequently against Stead, Bramwell Booth, Mr. Jacques, Madame Mourez (the midwife who had certified Eliza's virginity) and Madame Combe (a Salvationist who had taken Eliza to Paris). And it was, perhaps, with relish that they could report that Bramwell Booth would be charged for having contravened the 'new' Criminal Law Amendment Act, for which he had so ardently campaigned. As the *Saturday Review* rather spitefully remarked, "The Salvation Army has good reason for knowing that the Criminal Law Amendment Act was required. The Salvationists falsely boast of having procured the passing of the Act. They are at least showing that, when they talked of the need for it, they knew what they were talking about."

The actual trials themselves began on October 23 and concluded, after twelve sessions, on November 7 with verdicts of "guilty of abduction" against Stead and Rebecca Jarrett, while Bramwell Booth and Sampson Jacques were found not guilty (the charges against Mrs. Combe had been dropped earlier). Subsequently, on November 10, Stead and Jarrett were tried on separate charges of "aiding and abetting an assault" and were again found guilty. Rebecca Jarrett was sentenced to a six months' jail term and W.T. Stead to three. The zealot had indeed bowed to the law but was no less a zealot for that.

During those trials, public attention on The Salvation Army diminished, partly because it was considered improper to comment on a 'trial in progress.' And when reporting the trial transcripts, newspapers were forced to focus on what trial solicitors and judges deemed most important: the personalities, in order of popularity, were Eliza Armstrong, W.T. Stead and Rebecca Jarrett. Her association with the Salvation Army, though known, was not a central issue, though the fact that she had been an unreliable assistant was seen to be the chief reason for the 'guilty' verdict. As Bramwell Booth later stated, "Rebecca Jarrett broke down under cross-examination. She had kept a house of ill-fame, and certain things were brought forward relating to her past which she had not the courage to admit. It was a cruel ordeal for her, and I repented while I sat in the dock that I had allowed her to embark on such an adventure. Yet I am satisfied that the evidence we obtained through her was an essential link in the chain, and that without it we should never have enforced the need for raising the age [of consent]."[8] As for the organization Bramwell Booth represented, little was said about it during the trials: Booth himself refrained from bringing Salvation Army affairs or philosophy into the proceedings (perhaps on the advice of his mother) and did not seek to benefit from the publicity. He was, with justice, acquitted after an admirable speech by his solicitor, Mr. Waddy. In the court reports printed in leading newspapers, therefore, apart from knowing who Bramwell Booth was (mainly through such newspapers as the *St. James Gazette*), The Salvation Army gained little publicity.

Outside the courtroom, the Salvationists were subjected to the same insults, though no more serious than those directed against W.T. Stead. Large and hostile crowds greeted them daily, among which were the merely curious, but many angry at what they believed to be the Army's involvement (even complicity) in Stead's 'pornographic' exposé in the *Pall Mall Gazette*. They rushed at Bramwell Booth as he left the courthouse, aiming " a succession of blows at his head and face, battered his hat, tore his coat to pieces, and otherwise severely maltreated him before he could reach a cab standing near Drury-lane."

This episode, however, like the distortions printed in *Lloyd's* and *St. James's Gazette*, did not represent the majority view or actions of the British public. Indeed, it was generally conceded that The Salvation Army's prestige —its growing reputation as a reliable social-reformer— was enhanced by what W.T. Stead kept referring to as their public 'unselfishness.' Most public commentators sided with the Archbishop of Canterbury, Cardinal Manning and their beloved Queen Victoria in believing that The Salvation Army had only the good of the nation at heart and had acted purely out of Christian love. Given such generosity, it might be suggested that the lies perpetrated by *Lloyd's* and *St. James's Gazette* were more efficacious than damaging.

Bramwell Booth, in fact, believed that the 'Eliza Armstrong Affair' did the Army a great deal of good. "It made us known," he later wrote, "and put us at one stroke in the very front rank of those who were contending for the better treatment of the lost and the poor; and while it roused some powerful enemies, especially in the Press, the enmity lasted only for a time, while the sympathy which was generated remained and remains a permanent possession. Our work for women was greatly furthered by these strange circumstances. We gained friends in political circles, won recognition from the Government then existing, and from its successors, and were brought into touch with Queen Victoria and with some of her Court who ever since have been interested in what we have been doing."[9]

That may have been so, in hindsight. And some facts seem to support Booth's view. By 1888, for example, the Army's contingent of 'Rescue' officers had increased from four to forty, and its Rescue Homes for Fallen Women from two to ten. But, during the affair itself (and especially during the trials), it was clear that this first experience of 'unintentional warfare' —of becoming involved in social reform rather than initiating it— was a worrisome one for the Army's chief. Control of the progress and outcome of all former engagements had been entirely in the hands of William Booth; this time Bramwell had made all the decisions to become involved —and to become involved in a campaign controlled by and carried out in manner not always to the liking of the General. It is known that he did not wholly trust Stead's judgment, and that he and his wife, Catherine, decided to stay out of the affair as much as possible. Letters between the two indicate that they were genuinely worried —not merely by Bramwell's actions but by the possibility that, for the first time, public opinion was against them to such an extent that their eldest son would be jailed and the Army brought into some disgrace just when it was beginning to branch into serious social work. They therefore cautioned their officers (Railton in particular) not to hold public meetings in support of Bramwell's cause, lest they might exacerbate conditions and turn the public more thoroughly against them.

The greatest test of the 'Maiden tribute' affair was that of learning to compromise when it was necessary to do so. It was one of those compromises which The Salvation Army, engaging in social work, had to face many times during its history and over which William Booth often agonized. In World War II the Army had to agree to military policy and offer canteen services (cigarettes, for example) which had been totally forbidden to its own officers. In the 'Maiden Tribute' affair the compromise involved tacit approval of the language of an exposé which (in an age when Salvationists were forbidden to read novels) no Salvationist would ordinarily read.

Again hindsight teaches that such lessons were valuable ones.

Though William Booth, the autocrat, was not always willing to accept public interference (and rarely asked for advice from within), it was clear that the public was not always to be distrusted; that, though playing a supporting role could be dangerous (the public mistaking the parts being played), there were times when the Army would have to do just that in order to gain a foothold in some aspect of social work. It was the general consensus of public opinion that, in the 'Maiden Tribute' affair, The Salvation Army had indeed done the British nation a 'yeoman service.'

Essay Four

A Lamb Among Wolves:
Catherine Booth in Switzerland

La Marchale

The British public —like most families— could be very contradictory in its familial behaviour: at one moment, severely critical of a family member (even to the point of ostracism) and, at another, highly protective of that member when non-family pressures threatened. It was the usual natural phenomenon, "I have a right to beat up my sister, but don't you dare lay a finger on her." Let The Salvation Army stay in Britain, and it would always be at the mercy of some 'big bully' brother; but let it go abroad —to India or the United States— and it was sacrosanct. To attack The Salvation Army abroad was to attack the British flag. The British were also very fond of martyrs. So, when patriotism could be brought to the support of a Britisher abroad who was fighting for right against insuperable odds —a veritable Joan of Arc— the indignation back home was nothing short of righteous.

In 1883, a year in which public assaults —verbal and physical— on Salvationists in Britain were commonplace, The Salvation Army experienced this curious form of familial behaviour when its emissaries to (or, as the Army put it, 'invaders' of) Switzerland, encountered an opposition both unexpected and bitter —more intense and brutal than any its members had yet endured, culminating, in 1886, in the death of a young Salvationist. Denounced by public officials, harassed by court orders, denied police protection, the *salutistes* risked serious injury, even death, to bring their message to the Swiss people. At their head, splendidly courageous, was the General's nineteen year-old daughter, Catherine.

Catherine Booth —La Maréchale. From everything one reads about her, she was an unforgettable person. Strikingly beautiful, gifted with platform personality, she had the special magnetism of an actress which not merely awed her listeners but transfixed them. At just seventeen, her eloquence and her eyes would silence the noisy crowds when even her father failed to do so. As a travelling teenage evangelist throughout England her platform power was so great that rival events were cancelled, unable to compete with her spiritual campaigns. Her "control of an audience," wrote one observer, was extraordinary. "Often, when in the early part of a meeting before she rose to speak, some unruly disturbance made it extremely doubtful whether there would be anything like good order, I have seen her rise, and fixing her eyes upon the culprits literally quell them into silence and attention in her first dozen sentences, and in as many more, entirely secure their sympathy."[1]

The French called her 'La Maréchale,' describing her as "une tragédienne instinctive, la belle salutiste." To them she had gone, at her father's request, in February of 1881, and in France, as Carolyn Scott, her brilliant biographer, relates, Kate's personal magnetism became a Paris legend:

'Tel que je suis, pécheur rebelle,' they sang on their knees, *'Jésus, je viens à Toi,'* while Kate came down the stairs from the platform and walked up and down the aisles among the people, going first among the rowdiest and singing to them, her eyes dwelling on them one by one, and then walking on a little, singing and speaking, standing still or climbing on a chair so that they could all see and hear her.

A pastor, disgusted by what seemed to him to be no more than showmanship, and blatant emotive sensationalism, left a graphic description of the scene:

'The Maréchale,' he said, 'her body leaning forward, arms extended with ecstatic countenance, her look immersing anyone who saw it in a strange flame, with a supplicating manner, slowly called "Come, my friends, come my sister, come my brother, come, come!" and a man rose, his captive eyes attached to her, dragging himself forward on his knees, cast himself violently down, and in a series of inarticulate cries, threw his soul in a disorderly way at the Saviour's feet.

'Once more the Maréchale rose, once more she advanced. You could see her concentrate on one point the powerful fascination of her look, open her arms as if to enwrap and bring back to herself a friend whom the devil was trying to take from her. You might have heard her push her cry of "Come!" with such a vibration of anguish, terror, and compassion, that every eye sought to find out which way she was looking. The answer to this explosion of divine, irresistible and devouring love had not long to be waited for. Breaking away from her husband, who wished to hold her back, a woman rushed out, mounted the steps of the platform and fell at the Maréchale's side.[2]

But Catholic France, though making a heroine of La Maréchale, was a difficult assignment for an English girl, and only mildly receptive to this strange form of Protestantism. Not only had there been physical opposition (knives and stones being favourite weapons of the crowds), but by the end of 1882 French authorities had closed most of the Army's buildings. Catherine had, her doting father felt, accomplished miracles; but, clearly, the fatigue was beginning to sap her strength and it was to Switzerland, for rest and respite from French abuse, she would go. Geneva, the most tolerant city in Europe, would no doubt offer a refreshing change.

"In Geneva," wrote George Railton, "there was liberty. No difficulty was to be apprehended. We had, we were told, many friends in that city, and there could be no doubt that not only there, but throughout Switzerland, we should receive a welcome, and find, comparatively speaking, an easy sphere of labour." Sent ahead, Arthur Clibborn, a young Irish ex-minister of The Society of Friends, who had joined The Army in France in 1882, prepared the way by holding some private meetings at which he explained the Army's mission. He found, Railton continued, "every sign of favour [with only a slight prejudice against the ministry of a woman], and nothing that indicated any other but an easy victory for The Army."[3]

But Geneva was a wolf in sheep's clothing. Outwardly liberal, its Calvinist church still held great power and, given its doctrine of salvation by election, would naturally be antipathetic to Salvation Army beliefs. More than that, however, the tolerance of political extremes for which Switzerland was famous was itself a problem for

Salvationists. For the *demi-monde* of Geneva, ignored by most of its prominent citizens, was composed not merely of the usual 'submerged tenth,' but of a great many of Europe's exiles —anarchists and nihilists— to whom religion was a hated thing. Therefore, when Catherine Booth, in her enthusiasm, tried to reach them, she and her followers were subjected to the roughest kind of physical abuse.

Inside, the meetings were riotous affairs; outside, Salvationists were attacked by mobs while the police refused to interfere. The former were full of "students shouting anarchist slogans from the boxes in the galleries and criminal and political refugees fighting in the pit. Among them, Genevan Christians said they were seeing the city as it really was for the first time in their lives. Prayers were laughed at and hymns shouted down."[4] In the city Army offices were vandalized, officers were openly attacked with stones, those who joined lost their jobs, and the authorities publicly denounced the crazy Salutistes. If, stated one journalist, the 'two J.C.'s' for whom Geneva was famous —Julius Caesar and John Calvin— had appeared in the flesh on Mont Blanc, "the one calling his perished legions from the tomb, the other rebuking his degenerate successors for their heresies and backslidings," they could hardly have created more excitement than the Salvationists. On February 1, the London *Times* correspondent from Geneva thought the whole affair worthy of English attention:

> The proceedings of the Salvation Army in this part of Switzerland are attracting considerable attention and provoking serious disturbances and much angry controversy. Here at Geneva, where their meetings have been interrupted and their processions attacked by organized bands of rioters, M. Héridier, head of the department of Justice and Police, has peremptorily refused them the protection of the law. When questioned on the subject in the Great Council, he declared that he would not move a single gendarme to help people who were so stupid as to give themselves military titles and seek to obtain converts by talking about blood, battles, and fire; and his declaration was warmly applauded by a majority of the members.

This brief report was followed on February 6 and 13 with longer, more detailed and more critical analyses, by which time the Maréchale and her chief assistant, seventeen-year old Maud Charlesworth, had been expelled from the Canton of Geneva. To the *Times'* correspondent, the outburst of fanaticism which greeted the Army in Geneva was "a strange and almost inexplicable phenomenon."

The Salvationists, with unwonted discretion, did not, as they are in the habit of doing in England, begin operations with grotesque processions and blatant music; they simply hired a building for their meetings and announced them by posters couched in their usual blood and thunder style. The attitude of the public was at first one of astonishment and amused curiosity. It seemed so droll that anyone should want to convert Geneva. "Ils tomberont sous la ridicule" said people to each other. But, somehow or other, they were not killed by ridicule. Their meetings were well attended; everybody said that 'Colonel' Clibborn spoke extremely well *pour un Anglais*; Miss Booth was declared to be a *très belle fille*; she charmed her auditors —especially those of the male sex— by the sweetness of her voice and the gracefulness of her gestures, and converts began to enlist under the Salvation banner. Then opposition arose, the meetings were disturbed by brawlers, who sang ribald songs and drowned the voices of the speakers in yells and groans. The authorities refused to interfere —at any rate they did not interfere— and as a measure of self-protection, the Salvationists allowed to be present at their meetings only those who were furnished with tickets, which could be obtained at the headquarters in the Longemalle. This insured quiet inside, but did not insure quiet outside. The building in which the Salvationists met was beset every night by bands of rioters who hustled, bespattered with mud, and even stoned the audience as the latter went in and came out. The head of the police department, as I have already informed you, flatly refused to protect them, on the ground that people who hold the doctrines they hold and use the language they use do not deserve protection. The mob, naturally encouraged by this declaration, renewed their attacks, and on Thursday last the strife culminated in an onslaught on the Army's headquarters in the Longemalle and a general riot, which the police hardly so much as attempted to suppress. On the next day appeared the *arrète* of the Council of State ordering the suspension of the meetings, and the meeting which it was intended to hold the same evening had to be abandoned. Gendarmes were stationed about the building to prevent the entrance of the Salvationists and the attacks of the rioters. The Salvationists appear to have few friends in the press. Even such papers as the *Journal de Genève* and the *Tribune*, though they demand for them justice and fair play, disapprove their doctrines and denounce their practices, and tell them plainly that they cannot possibly make any permanent impression on the population of Geneva. The *Genevois*, organ of the local government, the *Bund*, and some other papers are more actively and more bitterly hostile, not hesitating even to resort to coarse vituperation and gross misrepresentations.... The Salvationists are declared to be more dangerous to society than the Anarchists; one day they are charged with obtaining recruits by bribery, another with making them pay for their conversion.

Most Geneva newspapers branded the Salvationists as *schwindel-gesellshaft* and applauded officials for having the courage to forbid their meetings. "We congratulate the Department of Justice," wrote *La Scène*, "but what would have been still more effective would have been expulsion in regular form. People do not spare the parasites who live and fatten on public credulity; why spare those who open a shop to sell righteousness just as formerly indulgences were sold; persons from whom are not even demanded the necessary pass-ports and papers, and who did not pay for their permit of residence, nor for the police license to exercise their trade of public cheats?" (Feb. 6, 1883).

It was this kind of 'foreign' attitude —one linked to the rights of British citizens abroad— that began to irritate English news correspondents. One might think, in fact, when reading the *Times* for example, that it had suddenly become a staunch supporter of The Salvation Army. But when ones looks closely at its reports (primarily from its Genevan correspondent), one detects a great deal of British patriotism and self-interest. Thus, it is not so much the safety and well-being of Salvationists that is of primary concern; rather, it is the reputation of Britain and the welfare of its foreign citizens. There is, first-of-all, an implicit claim which, in effect, says to the Swiss "they are ours and you have no right to mistreat them." It is a slightly hypocritical stance which insists that, though we may not think much of Salvationists, those in Geneva are British and that makes all the difference. A second stance, closely related to the first, has a political motivation —if foreign (i.e British) Salvationists are mistreated in this manner, other foreigners (i.e. other Englishmen) may be similarly mistreated, and this is something that simply cannot be allowed.

As the early reports all make clear, other British citizens in Geneva had been mistaken for Salvationists and had been assaulted. What the treatment of The Salvation Army represented, then, was a refusal of the Geneva police to "protect English subjects from the attacks of the mobs." Therefore, in nearly every report there was a mention of other English citizens being mistaken for and being mistreated like Salvationists: "An English midshipman, whose uniform was mistaken for that of the Salvation Army, was savagely attacked by several of the rioters;" "an Englishman, wrongly suspected of belonging to the army, was hunted through the streets and seriously maltreated. Similar scenes have been enacted at Chaux-de-Fonds and Bienne." As far as its own citizens were concerned, the *Times* correspondent maintained, Switzerland might be the "freest country in Europe; but foreigners live here only on sufferance. . . . Inoffensive persons (including friends of my own), have been hustled, insulted, and chased through the streets, to the cry of 'Throw the mummers into the lake,' merely because, being English, they might be Salvationists."

There was little doubt, the correspondent concluded, "that the expulsion of these ladies [Catherine Booth and Maud Charlesworth] was a violation of international law and of the treaty rights of British subjects residing in this country. There has long existed a convention between England and Switzerland whereby the natives of each State in the territory of the other are placed by that other upon the footing of citizens —that is to say, an Englishman domiciled or merely travelling in Switzerland enjoys precisely the same rights as a Swiss, and *vice versa.* . . . It is of great importance to British subjects living in this country that their position in relation to the police should be exactly defined, for if the expulsion of Miss Booth and Miss Charlesworth can be justified, nobody is safe from one day to another" (Feb. 22).

Added to all this was the feeling that a chivalric code was being ignored —that the maltreatment was being directed primarily against females. On the one hand there was a tone of derision when speaking of how backward the Swiss were in their expectations regarding a woman's place (as if the British were any further advanced!):

> The expedition was commanded by a *jeune fille*, a young girl, who called herself *la maréchale*; she had under her orders two other young girls and two men (one of whom with two of the ladies has since gone to Neuchatel) and she appeared on a platform and spoke in fluent French with all the self-possession and more than the eloquence of a veteran pastor of the National Church. The horror of all this may be imagined when it is remembered that at Geneva it is not considered *comme il faut* for a young girl to take the shortest walk unaccompanied by her *bonne*, to shake hands with a male cousin in the street, or speak in society without first being spoken to. I cannot put into words the verdict a Genevan matron passes on young girls who travel about with men who are neither their fathers nor brothers, while the sight of a *jeune fille* in uniform distributing pamphlets or canvassing for converts seems to her something more and worse than a gross violation of propriety.

On the other hand, there was a definite sense of pride in the fact that British pluck —especially praiseworthy when demonstrated by women— was rising above tyranny. Catherine Booth and Maud Charlesworth were veritable Joans of Arc, defying great odds, even death, to bring the truth to Geneva. It was a story too good to resist, and when the *Times* and the *Daily News* related Miss Charlesworth's courageous confrontation with the Geneva police, all London was talking about the Salvation Army's 'lamb among wolves.' The *Spectator* called Miss Charlesworth's account "one of the most charming bits of narrative which we have come across for a very long time." (Feb. 24). Here is the *Times'* version of that story:

> Miss Charlesworth, who is now at Coppet, has been good enough to give me the following account of her expulsion and events which preceded it. Her artless narrative is both interesting in itself and valuable for the vivid light which it throws on the ways of Genevan justice to foreigners. According to the *Journal de Genève*, M. Heridier, Councillor of State charged with the Department of Justice, was present at Miss Booth's and Miss Charlesworth's examinations, but behind a curtain, 'after the manner of all Grand Inquisitors.'

"On Saturday afternoon," says Miss Charlesworth who, it may be well to mention, is just 16 years old, "a man came to the house of M. Lenoir, where we were staying, and said that Maud Charlesworth, aide-de-camp to Miss Booth, was to go at once and see the Chief of Police at the Hotel de Ville. I went at once, taking M. Lenoir with me as I did not like to go alone. When we arrived M. Lenoir sent in to ask the Chief of Police, M. Heridier, if he might be allowed to accompany me. We waited half an hour, and the answer was that I must go alone. So there was nothing else for it, and I had to follow a savage-looking magistrate upstairs into a very small and hot office, where I was asked to sit down. I suppose they thought that the exceedingly cross-looking officer was not enough to question me, for two others, with equally unsaved (sic) unshaved? looking faces, came in to help him. I had been with Katie (Miss Booth) both the times when she had to appear before police, so I was quite prepared for the sort of questions they were going to ask me. The last thing Katie said to me was, 'Do not sign anything,' and I answered that I would rather let my right hand be cut off; and when I got into that little room I made up my mind that when they came to the end and asked me to sign I would refuse unless they would allow M. Lenoir to come up and read the paper through.

"Well, they began and asked me about the private meeting at which I had been present. They said it was a public meeting, because three detectives had got in without being asked at the door for their cards of invitation. I denied the false statement, and made them write down my answer plainly. The point on which I laid the most stress was that we, the four Salvation officers, had been invited to a private meeting in a private house, to which others (strangers to us) had also been invited; that we spoke, prayed, and sang, as did others who did not belong to the Salvation Army, and that if people who were not invited made their way in, it was not our fault; we were only guests. Then they asked me how I dared to wear my uniform at the meeting when I had been told of the law forbidding the wearing of religious dress. Now, I know this law by heart. It says that no one is to wear a religious dress on the public highway. My answer was that I did not think the words 'public highway' could apply to the kitchen of a cottage in which a private meeting was held. I must here tell you that my questioners, or rather persecutors, of whom most of the time there were five, were very unsaved and possessed very quick tempers. Their object was evidently to frighten me so as to make me answer unwisely, and catch me in my speech. But they were disappointed, for they had never had to do with a Salvationist before, and could not make out why I was so calm and answered so clearly. They were also disappointed to find that I understood their language, and no matter how fast they read I was always ready with an answer. Every now and then one or another went into a passion. But the worst was to come.

"'Have you got a passport or 'leave to stay' in Geneva,' asked one of the crossest of the examiners, with whom I was now quite alone, and I could see by his manner that he thought I had not got my papers. I answered that I had my leave to stay; and that my passport was in the hands of the police. You should have seen the rage he got into. He rose, threw down his chair, stamped out of the room, shouted for some under officer, and asked the man what he meant by saying I was not provided with a passport. This man also lost his temper, went off to look for the passport, and in a few minutes returned and saw I was quite right, that they had my passport and I my 'leave to stay.' The inspector then flew into a greater rage than before, and scolded the man who had misled him. When he was more composed he continued. But now he came to personal questions, which I told him he had no right to ask, and I inquired what law authorized him to ask them. He said that was not his affair; he had been told to ask these questions, and I must answer. He asked if I had my father's leave to remain at Geneva, and when I said "Yes," he wanted letters to prove it. I asked him how he dared to doubt my word, and told him to write down that Miss Booth had letters from my father authorizing me to stay. A little later he said that I had prayed in a private meeting, according to the form of the Salvation Army. I insisted that the Salvation Army had no form of prayer, and asked him in what way their prayers differed from other prayers. He said they differed very much, but he could not tell me how; he repeated that we had a form of prayer, and began to storm and rave so loudly that an inspector ran in from the next room, saying 'Gently, gently, there is somebody outside.'. . . At last, after a great deal more questioning, my paper was finished. I knew all my answers were true, and that there was no harm putting my name to it; but then I remembered my promise to Katie, so I refused, unless I might go down and fetch M. Lenoir, and I said I would not sign the paper until he had read it. Of course they raved at me, but it had no effect; so they went for M. Lenoir, but unfortunately he had gone away, as they came back in triumph to tell me. I still refused to sign, and said I would not sign until 'Captain'

Bouillat, a member of the Salvation Army, had read it through. They were angry, and tried to frighten me, all talking as fast as they could at the same time. Then they said they would read the paper all through again, which they did three times; but nothing could move me. I said I would go with Zitza and fetch Bouillat. They answered that I might go, but not with Zitza, a Salvationist, who was waiting to be examined; but I said I could not think of such a thing —that it would be very improper for a young lady to walk through the streets after dark, especially as I knew there was a plot on foot to do us harm.

In the end two gendarmes were sent for Bouillat, Miss Charlesworth and Zitza waiting meanwhile in the little hot office.

"All at once it struck me," she continues, "that we would have a prayer meeting. 'Zitza', I said, 'we will pray. Let us go down on our knees and pray for these people, for if ever we wanted the Lord with us it is now.' So down we went, and prayed out loud for about ten minutes, and it did us good. The inspector was very much surprised; he cleared his throat, grunted, and finally got up and went to the door of the outer office. Then four of the men came back. I said to Zitza that we would tell the Correspondent of the *Times*, and that I wondered what the English would think of the way in which their country-women were being treated. This was overheard, and seemed to make an impression, for two men came and said I was quite free to go if I liked, or if they could fetch me anything they would do so. I wanted to fetch Bouillat, but when I found that I should either have to go alone or walk between two policemen I preferred to wait.

At length Bouillat came, and on his recommendation she signed her deposition.

"The great fun was," she goes on, "that all these cross magistrates and inspectors were kept from their dinners. So were we; but as I told them, that was a very secondary consideration to us. We left that office at half-past 7 singing 'Glory to His Name.' I had been there four hours. The whole town knew it. A lawyer at once took down all that had passed in French, because he was so indignant.

"On Sunday I received a paper which told me that before 6 o'clock I was to be out of the Canton, because, first, I had broken the law by speaking in a public meeting (lie No. 1); secondly, because I had nothing to show that my parents consented to my being with Miss Booth (lie No. 2); thirdly, because that morning I had not appeared when sent for by the police. (We sent a letter to say we could not go on

Sunday.)

"Before the man who brought me this letter went away I made him tell me who else was expelled, and I found that Bouillat, Zitza, and Emile, all foreigners, had shared the same fate. We sent for them to come up that we might arrange where to go, but they did not come, and we found that they had been fetched out of their room, put into a cab with a policeman, and driven away without a moment's notice. So those three are gone, I know not whither, and Miss Booth sent a Swiss lass with me, as of course, I could not go alone.

"If the Salvation Army has many such officers as Miss Charlesworth," commented the *Spectator*, "we do not wonder that it makes converts." Though still not persuaded that The Salvation Army was anything more than a passing fad, the editor of the *Times*, had nevertheless to concede that Miss Charlesworth was a courageous woman, worthy of Booth's confidence: "she displayed the self-possession of a veteran in the trying cross-examination to which she was subjected by the police authorities. There is, indeed, in her tale a quaintness almost Puritanic when she dwells upon the 'cross and unsaved' faces of her examiners, and on the way in which they lost their tempers while she remained imperturbable. The Salvationist 'General', as we all know, has a keen sense of humour, and it would seem that he possesses the art of imparting it to his lady disciples."

Such praise was, however, given rather grudgingly. *The Times*, especially, while applauding female heroism and protecting British interests, did not want to seem to support the Army as a whole. And, in its final analysis of the situation, it was still fairly negative: "We English cannot entirely plume ourselves upon the mode in which we treated Mr. Booth and his followers when they first came into prominence. But experience has taught us that the function of the authorities is to preserve the peace, and insure that the 'Army' shall not be the butt of lawless violence —and, that insured, to leave the movement to run its course. This policy will, it may be hoped, ultimately be adopted by the Genevese. To treat the movement seriously, as a sort of State conspiracy, is only to endue it with vitality; but, left to itself, the Salvation Army is probably destined to grow and die as so many other religious movements have grown and died before" (Feb. 20).

It was rather to the *Times* delight, therefore, that the current popularity of the Army —stemming from the persecution of two young English heroines— was somewhat checked by a small controversy concerning the seventeen year-old Maud Charlesworth. Her father, it seems, on reading her story in the *Times*, was "greatly distressed" by being reminded of how the Booths had, in his opinion, 'alienated' his daughter from the true Church and from his affections. On February 21, therefore, the Reverend Samuel Charlesworth of Clapham Common, apprised the British public of the inconsiderateness of William Booth. Some two years earlier, he stated, he had taken his only daughter to Army meetings where she was introduced to some of the Booth children. "Being of a very impressionable and excitable nature," she became fascinated by the Army and the Booths, until "she was so absorbed in the movement that all other interests seemed entirely to merge in her conception of the importance of the Christian work carried out by the Army." Nothing Mr. Charlesworth did —gentle persuasion, parental rebuke— would dissuade Maud from her unwise devotion to the Army; she was so "wrought up" that no other form of worship "satisfied her spiritual cravings."

> Mr. Booth's family were entirely unknown to me. I wrote to two of them with whom my daughter seemed most associated very earnestly, appealing to them not for the present, while she was so young and a schoolgirl, to do anything which would tend to encourage the excitement or the all-engrossing fascination of the Army meetings and work. I regret to say that my appeal met with no responsive sympathy; indeed, I must add that, both with respect to my child and to other young persons of whom I have heard, I fear the Army influence has a direct tendency to wean the converts from home associations and interests, under the idea that its work is paramount in importance to all other pursuits and obligations, and even to the known wishes of parents. At all events, I then discovered, to my deep sorrow, that one of the most loving and devoted children had found stronger interests and more absorbing pursuits in the arena of the Army than in her own home.

In the very painful dilemma in which I was placed with a motherless daughter to watch over, feeling that my child's happiness, and health of body and mind, probably depended upon her continuance in the Army work, and yet dreading the excitement of the work as carried on in London, I took her to Paris, having the impression that the work among the Parisian poor was of a less exciting character. I attended several meetings, and was greatly pleased with the earnestness of all the workers, and the moderation and propriety which pervaded all the proceedings under the superintendence of Miss Booth.

By my daughter's desire I arranged with Miss Booth to leave her for a time in Paris, that she might assist Miss Booth in her arduous work among the poor; but expressly stipulating that she was only to be regarded as a young friend and visitor, and that she could not become an officer of the Army or wear the uniform.

Shortly after, Miss Booth went to Geneva to open a station there, and took my daughter with her. Thus she has been most injudiciously and to me most lamentably placed in the very forefront of an aggressive movement in a foreign land; not only in direct contravention to both the letter and express spirit of my own express stipulations, but also opposed to the course which ought to have been taken even if unexpressed, with reference to one of such tender age and so inexperienced. Any judicious parent reading the statements contained in *The Times* on the Geneva proceedings must have felt what a sorrowful and unwise position that young Christian girl had been drawn into.

I am most deeply pained and grieved to write this letter, but the publicity given to my young daughter's position and proceedings in the Army operations, at Geneva, seems to me to demand such an explanation, if it be only as a caution to other parents.

William Booth seemed justified in asserting (in a letter to the *Times*) that the Reverend Charlesworth's accusations were placing him in an awkward position. Since it was clear that Charlesworth was using his daughter's willing involvement in the Army's work as a means of "condemning the Army," it was impossible to answer the charges (and to protect the Army's reputation) without setting out the truth of the matter —the truth being (as letters proved) that Maud Charlesworth did have her father's (reluctant) approval to be where she was and to do what she was doing. As the *Spectator* put it: "It is fair to Mr. Booth to acknowledge that Mr. Charlesworth has evidently been more willing to allow his daughter to take part in the work of the Army than he now cares to remember. . . . Mr. Charlesworth has evidently found that his daughter's connection with the Salvation Army has brought her into greater prominence than he wished, and in the irritation of the discovery he seeks to throw the blame on Miss Booth." The moral of the story, the *Spectator* concluded, was

> that parents who do not wish their children to become officers in the Salvation Army, had better forbid them attending the meetings in the first instance. When once the flame is kindled, there is nothing in the rules of the Salvation Army which forbids them to fan it by every means in their power. The part which the Army assigns to women has extraordinary attractions in these times. They can be in every way rivals of men, they can take an absolutely equal part in the establishment and building-up of the new organization. By the side of such experiences as this career opens to them, the ordinary routine of home must appear intolerably dull. . . . Where, in Clapham, can Mr. Charlesworth hope to offer his daughter any career that will stand comparison with one that admits of such possibilities as these? It is undoubtedly hard upon him to lose a daughter; but if he now takes her back, he will receive but a shadow of her real self. Her heart will probably be with the Army, no matter where her body may be. . . . For a nature of this ardent and excitable type to be disillusioned is no common trial, and we could almost wish that she may never be disturbed in her conviction that she belongs to that chosen band which embraces great Missionaries and the founders of religious Orders, and generally, all those who have ardently loved and deeply-moved their fellow-men" (F 24, 1883).

The *Times*, however, was not prepared to be as charitable and, as William Booth predicted, interpreted Samuel Charlesworth's complaint as a criticism of The Salvation Army, calling Maud Charlesworth "but a Protestant reflection of many a Catholic maiden who has taken to the cloister as the place where she can best satisfy her religious fervour," both being "alike in their remoteness from the life of the family." One should therefore sympathize with the Reverend Charlesworth whose wilful daughter had made such a poor choice of religious vocation (if choice there were):

> The religious passion is so strong and so incalculable that it is always rash to prophesy a speedy end to any 'movement,' however extravagant. Mr. Booth's Army, however, is a phenomenon in which there is so very little essential novelty that its horoscope may be drawn with tolerable certainty. In so far as it is called an Army, and has grades, titles, and regulations, it is new; but in so far as its object is 'conversion,' it does not differ from the thousand revivalist schemes that have been started in England and America from the days of Whitefield downwards. It may safely be said that a short time will suffice to wear out the fantastic externals of the scheme, and that what is vital in it will remain. As far as concerns the outward organization, indeed, there is much to be urged in dispraise of its latest manifestations. Of the processions and hostile feelings which they arouse enough has been said already; but for the rest, its success has been too sudden and too personal to last. A City missionary, who had for a dozen years carried on services in the East-end with mediocre success, all at once dubs his congregation an Army, and works out the metaphor into elaborate detail. In a short time he has shops in prominent thoroughfares for the sale of his newspapers and uniforms, his own bust, a score of times repeated, occupying a prominent place in the window. Simultaneously the financial side of the organization assumes great proportions, and large purchases of premises are made in great thoroughfares. How long will all this last? . . . Mr. Booth's fantastic parody, which could not have succeeded for a moment among any people except the English, will have its day, like other extravagances, and all that will survive of it will be the genuine devotion to the good of others which in many of the performers unquestionably underlies the disguise in which they choose to masquerade.

It was, as some might see it, a near thing: the *Times* was, in an emotional acceptance of the 'Lambs Among Wolves' story out of Geneva, almost lulled into a toleration, even support, of The Salvation Army. Only at the last moment had the rational (though some say it was an insane) voice of the Reverend Charlesworth intervened and brought it back to reality. Not even an appeal to patriotism —the protection of English citizens in foreign countries— found any sympathy with the *Times*; in its opinion, then and thereafter, The Salvation Army, not the Swiss authorities, were at fault. That seemed to be the end of the argument.

But it was not the end of the Army's trouble in Switzerland; in truth, it was just the beginning. Every appeal of her expulsion from Geneva being denied, Catherine Booth continued her preaching just over the border in France. To a mountainside near Savoy hundreds of Swiss Salvationists flocked to hear La Maréchale and continued to do so in spite of police attempts to prevent them. Meanwhile, in Neuchatel, where Captains Becquet and Kate Patrick were valiantly fighting, the agitation against them was, as the *Times* reported, "assuming formidable dimensions, and the peace of the town is seriously threatened. The Salvationists are stoned as they pass through the streets, and a few nights ago the windows of a house in which they had assembled were broken. At a public meeting held last week resolutions were passed denouncing the Army as a nuisance, and calling on the authorities to expel foreign Salvationists from the canton" (May 15).

The upshot at Neuchatel, as at Geneva, was a prohibition against Army meetings, either in public or private places. And when, in a bid to test the constitutionality of the decree, Kate Booth conducted a meeting in the forest just outside the city, she was finally arrested, precipitating the now-famous trial at Boudry —a trial whose significance is still discussed by Swiss legal historians.

Treated as a political prisoner —considered a danger to public peace— Catherine Booth spent the two weeks preceding the trial in a Neuchatel jail, "a child in prison for Jesus' sake," as her mother phrased it. Though largely criticized by her own compatriots, and sometimes ridiculed, she was strengthened by the prayerful support of the thousands who packed the Exeter Hall in London. Thus, while *Punch* might chide

> Hey for our Catherine, blushing so feminine,
> Rousing the Swiss to conviction of sin;
> Out on their 'beak' who, the tide of grace stemming', in-
> Sisted on brutally running her in!

> List to dear Catherine's fervent beseeching,
> Even for prefects, policemen and all;
> Poor old St. Paul rated women for preaching,
> Catherine knows rather more than St. Paul (N 10, 1883).

Commander Railton might boast that he had, in La Maréchale's behalf, just attended a "tremendous prayer meeting, one of the biggest and best this world has ever known. . . . God knows what is coming next, but anyhow, we shall win."

The trial, which took place on September 29 and October 1, was, as the *Times* asserted, one of "great interest and importance." The former was proven by the presence of the British ambassador, an independent observer from the British Foreign Office, hordes of journalists, curious lawyers and leading citizens from all over Europe. The latter was so by virtue of the fact that it was the first time in history that "a Swiss tribunal has been called upon to try persons accused of meeting for prayer, an act which though imputed to them as a crime by the cantonal authorities is authorized alike by the Cantonal and Federal Constitutions."

> The question is [the *Times* went on] can the sworn guardians of the law annul by decree the most solemn guarantees of the Constitution. The authorities of Neuchatel, like those of Geneva, might have expelled Miss Booth and Captain Bequet by administrative order and justified the proceedings by reason of State, but having chosen to arraign them together with two Swiss citizens on a criminal charge the issue must be decided on purely legal grounds by judges and jurymen who take oath to respect the liberties of the people. On the other hand, the organs of the Governments of Geneva and Neuchatel, both of whom belong to the school of authoritative Radicalism, are exhorting the jury to render a verdict in accordance with public opinion. The *Genevois* argues that, although the prohibition of a religion by a despot is an act of tyranny, a similar measure taken by the elect of universal suffrage is perfectly legitimate, and on this principle only can the local authorities defend their treatment of Salvationists. They have even gone the length of forbidding the sale of their books of devotion in the kiosk Albert. . . . It is remarkable that the cantons which so far have taken measures

against the Salvationists are the so-called Protestant cantons of Geneva. Some Swiss members of the army who are now conducting a campaign in Fribourg meet with no opposition either from the people or the authorities. This only proves that Catholic dislike of Protestantism is less intense than the dislike of authoritative Radicalism for any religious manifestation whatever (Oct. 2).

Though some of the spectators may have been interested in the legal precedent, most were there to see and hear *la belle Salutiste*, Kate Booth. And she did not disappoint them. Sitting placidly (masking her fatigue), she endured the public prosecutor's depiction of Salvationists as fanatics threatening to fill the asylums with those they duped and listened with patience to his misinterpretations of their Orders and Regulations. But, finally, it was her turn. "I have no need," she began, "to enter upon the legal aspect of this question. Yet, as le Procurer-Général himself went off the ground of law to discuss at great length the doctrines and methods of the Army, I feel I cannot for truth's sake be silent."

If the Consiel d'Etat had any doubts or misgivings concerning the methods and end of the Salvation Army, the honourable members should have sought information from competent judges, that is to say, from those who know us, who had both seen and heard us, before accepting the opinions of persons who have done neither one nor the other. . . .

Our only message has been 'Repent, and turn ye to the Lord that your sins may be blotted out.' We want to see the drunkards, the thieves and the outcasts washed in the precious blood of Jesus and changed into peaceful, loyal citizens.

This being our end, it is to the interest of all governments to protect us and in protecting us, they protect themselves.

In our efforts to attain this end we have met with the bitterest opposition in Switzerland, because our motives have been wilfully misrepresented. Lies as absurd as untrue have been circulated about us; and we have been bitterly persecuted —first by those who resent the light, and secondly by those who have been misled and will one day regret their action.

The great accusation against us is that we have disturbed the public peace; in a word, we were the cause of scandal. If to preach the Gospel, to denounce sin, and to pray over the masses is a scandal, then do we even as Christ and Paul. The Procureur-Général has attempted to describe in detail our proceedings, yet this gentleman has avowed that he has never attended a single meeting, never put a foot inside Mont Blanc; he cannot, therefore, be considered capable of judging. Monsieur le Procurer-Général has said that we attacked the town with drums and trumpets and other extravagant things. I ask le Procureur-Général how many drums he has seen in Neuchatel, or trumpets? Not one. What is the truth? No musical instrument, with the exception of a piano, has been employed. No flags and no processions. The only bill that has been issued, I hold in my hand, which simply announces that the Salvation Army will have meetings at seven, three, and seven.

Le Procureur-Général has referred to the language of the Salvationists. He says we teach that all that is necessary for salvation is for one to jump on the platform and say 'Je suis sauvé! I am saved!' after five minutes of self-examination. No one in Switzerland has ever heard us declare such an outrageous sentiment. It is not true. Notwithstanding, there may come a day when Monsieur le Procureur-Général and others would give all the world to be able to say 'Je suis sauvé!' The time will come when he will have to face the great unknown future, go before another tribunal, to face another Judge! Then he with others will prove the value of those words, 'Je suis sauvé!'

But what were our proceedings? First, we have sung hymns in a hall that we hired. Second, we read the Bible. Switzerland has not waited till the Salvation Army came to read the Bible. You know this Book. Third, we pray, and fourth, persuade men to leave the road to sin and death.

Is that a scandal? To sing, and speak, and pray in the name of Jesus? It is not we that throw stones, that break windows, that howl and hoot after respectable people in the streets. It is not we who violate domiciles. It is against all logic to say that *we* are the scandal of your country.

Ah, the question of all questions, the question which every intelligent man ought to face is, 'what are we to do with the masses?' If they are not reached by the power of the Gospel, if they are not won from sin and the power of Satan, a day will come when they will turn round against you, occasioning terrible trouble and disorder, and awful will be the consequences. Then, Messieurs, you may have reason to regret your action in this matter. If these disturbers are capable of manifesting such hatred, such rage against citizens who pray to God, they will also be capable of manifesting the same rebellious spirit against any other opinion, or any other law, which may not please them.

Further, we have broken no law since we entered your country. We have submitted and submitted again and again, until you have taken away from us the right to meet and pray. We have now no more choice. We must obey God; we must be in harmony with the laws of Heaven. We are not here to plead 'Not Guilty'. No! Like the early Christians, we weighed this matter. I weighed it in my room on my knees. We have all told you that we did violate the decree.

We have no wish to hide it. I note, however, that the devil has full liberty. He can lead to perdition thousands of victims. He is permitted to drink, and shout, and sing, and dance, and make all the noise he likes without the least interruption on the part of the authorities, while we are made prisoners for praying in a wood!

Although we have suffered terribly through lies and misrepresentations that have been wilfully circulated about us, we are not discouraged; we know that truth and justice will soon triumph. I love Switzerland all the more for what I have endured. A little while and Switzerland shall know us, a little while and Switzerland shall love us. We shall win thousands to righteousness, peace and Heaven.

All we demand is that which is guaranteed by your Constitution —religious liberty. But there are people in Switzerland who are interested in, and gain by, sin, and they fight against us. . . .

As he had once or twice before, Monsieur Cornaz, the Prefect of Neuchatel, perhaps fearing the enchantment of Kate's voice (as well as her argument), demanded that the judge bring the proceedings to a close. "She has spoken long enough —tell her to be quiet." But to no avail; hers was a captive (and captivated) audience, and Kate continued:

Monsieur le Procureur-Général referred to the Queen, saying that even she was subject to the decrees of Parliament, but that I placed myself above her in refusing to become subject to the decrees of the Grand Council. There is no parallel between Her Majesty and myself. No Act has been passed to forbid her praying in a wood, or I think Her Majesty would have something to say on the subject!

Monsieur le Procureur-Général has spoken in a way that has astounded me on public opinion, which, he says, he cannot afford to take lightly. Let me remind Monsieur le Procureur-Général and all here that it was public opinion that crucified Christ. Do you justify this action? That was *public opinion.*

One word in conclusion. You can punish us; you can imprison us; you can persecute us (as long as you are permitted). But what you cannot do is stop this work, to suppress us. I warn you. Beware what you do, for your country's sake. . . . Take care that in banishing us, you don't banish the light, that you do not banish Jesus Christ. . . .

You can laugh at me, you can mock me, but you cannot deny what I have said. God is with us!

It was, from one so young and speaking in a foreign language, a magnificent speech —eloquent and cogent— and it did not fail to impress the seven members of the jury. Though they could do no other than admit that the accused had defied the decree, they accepted the argument that the Salvationists had not acted with 'culpable intention.' The judge therefore declared an acquittal. Swiss Salvationists, notwithstanding the fact that La Maréchale was still banished from both Geneva and Neuchatel, were ecstatic. Monsieur Cornaz, on the other hand, bitter to the end, dismissed his gendarmes on the spot, leaving the Salvationists to fend for themselves as they made their way home through an angry mob.

Back home again, in October, Catherine Booth was given a heroine's welcome. Salvationists packed the Exeter Hall to hear her own account of her imprisonment and trial; newspapers likened her to Joan of Arc. And even the *Times* was forced to admire her spirit. Though the editor suggested that "Salvationists expect such treatment, and, if it were not forthcoming, would feel it as a reflection on their work," he nevertheless admitted Catherine's tenacity and dedication: "The authorities have done what they could to repress her, and they have found her irrepressible. She has defied them once and twice, and she will go on defying them to the last. She comes back with a halo of martyrdom and with words of triumph on her tongue to bid them defiance once again." As far as Maud Charlesworth was concerned, her chief attraction to the Army was becoming clear and it was one about which her father could do little. "A more certain intelligence is that Miss Charlesworth and Mr. [Ballington] Booth are about to be married, that the young lady has a good private property of her own, and that her father disapproves of the match. We are not sure how long this attitude will be maintained. Miss Charlesworth joined the Salvationists with her father's approval. He may yet be brought to give his consent to her more close alliance with the order."

Catherine Booth, La Maréchale, preaching in a Paris café.

The Toronto *News* on the Salvation Army: Boothism in Canada

When The Salvation Army 'invaded' Canada in 1882 it occupied a country that was British to the very marrow of its being. She was the eldest daughter of the Empire, settled mainly by British emigrants, and governed by a British system of government and justice. Most certainly, loyalty to Britain and the adoption of British values were things taken for granted by most Canadians. With J. Castell Hopkins they asserted: "[We] are every year becoming more attached to Great Britain and more grateful for the power and liberty which can be obtained within the British realm." And with John A. Macdonald they declared: "A British subject I was born —a British subject I will die." It was, to be sure, a picture of contentment —contentment with the *status quo.*

By the end of that decade, however, smudges were beginning to appear on the political canvas. There were annexationists, like Goldwin Smith, arguing that Canada's future was best assured by either a commercial or political union with the United States. And there were the independentists and nationalists who advocated severing all ties with the motherland. They were beginning to grow tired of 'landlord colonialism' —of the very terms 'colony' and 'colonial'— and they resented the know-all attitudes of English emigrants and the fact that the only power Canada possessed came from a statute passed at Westminster. "It is not unreasonable to assume," wrote J.W. Longley in 1891, "that the period will be reached when her sons will think of Canada *as* Canada and not as a mere dependency."[1]

In Canada, then, the last decades of the century were turbulent ones. A long-lasting economic depression, a Métis rebellion on the prairies, a Catholic-Protestant rift manifesting itself in the Manitoba Schools Question, and an 1891 election fought mainly on platforms that proposed and opposed commercial union with the United States —these were the growing pains the young nation was experiencing. And much of it had to do with its ties with Britain. The pro-British imperialist was in control, but was kept busy maintaining that control by a comparatively small, though vocal, group of nationalists, some of whom were annexationists and some seeking nothing more than Canada's independence. Their voices could be heard, and their influence felt, not only in the political forums of the nation, but in many other places; one of the strangest, and most surprising perhaps, in the ranks of The Salvation Army.

In Canada, The Salvation Army began, as it had in several other countries, in an impromptu manner. In 1882 emigrants such as William Freer, Jack Addie and Joe Ludgate, who had experienced Salvationism in Britain, commenced Army-styled meetings in Toronto and London, and soon had impressive followings. Concerned that the essentials of English Salvationism be maintained, and that control not slip from his grasp, William Booth was quick to place the Canadian wing under the command of English officers, initially under Thomas Moore (then in charge of the United States), and later under Thomas Coombs (1884-89), Thomas Adams (1889-1891), David Rees (1891-92) and Herbert Booth (1892-96).

They found it, however, a difficult task, in a large country, to consolidate their victories and centralize the administration. The Army was simply growing too fast. In its first year, Corps were opened in twelve Ontario cities and, by the end of 1884, had invaded another hundred Canadian towns. Characterized as, and indeed acting as, a 'camp-meeting' revivalistic movement, it rushed pell-mell from town to town, conducting meetings, gaining converts but also paying little attention to permanent residency. Confusion was rampant. Men

People pretending to be SA officers

claiming to be officers of the Army invaded small towns, captured a following and, like Mark Twain's mission man, absconded with the money. "Beware of a young woman named Nellie Beaton," ran one early *War Cry* announcement, "who represents herself as being an officer in the Salvation Army. Has deceived several soldiers and trades people in different towns." When Thomas Coombs assumed command, he found the whole system to be "in a state of utter confusion" and, though he and his successors made progress towards consolidation and control, it was a slow and painful task.

It was especially slow because some Canadian officers, new to the Army, were of the opinion that the organization should be nothing more than a revivalistic agency, untrammelled by bureaucracy, orders and regulations, headquarters' control, and British methodology. Over the years from 1884 to 1888 the number of resignations increased, as Thomas Coombs tightened his control and enforced the Army's regulations. Some of the disillusioned officers continued their free evangelism under such titles as Saved Army or Hosanna Banner. But they rarely made much of a public fuss. Not until 1889.

Throughout that year, beginning in March, Edmund E. Sheppard, editor and proprietor of the Toronto *News*, and a staunch advocate of democracy and Canadian independence, undertook a disclosure of the 'evils' inherent in Salvationism —particularly of the maltreatment of Canadian officers by their English superiors— in a series of interviews with and letters by angry ex-officers. Rarely had the Army been so scathed by journalistic denunciation, an example of which is contained in this July editorial:

> The Salvation Army is sighing for martyrdom, and sings hallelujahs whenever any of its members are arrested for obstructing the streets or otherwise offending against the laws, that it may carry the offenders around the country after they have been discharged from jail and exhibit them as victims of ungodly persecution at so much a head for admission, just as a dime museum manager carries around his freaks. The unfortunate rank and file, who are compelled to buy their English-made clothes in the Army store, who are expected to sell War Crys without extra pay and turn the proceeds in at the box-office, who are not allowed to wear such a worldly and devilish thing as a watch, unless

they buy one supplied by the Army, who are supposed to beg and starve and support themselves, not out of the funds they collect, but as best they can with whatever they may be able to pick up, while the chief pushers, who are here to make money for the Booths, get fifteen dollars a week and 'expenses,' live in houses said to belong to the Army, and lord it over the baser sort as if the latter were slavish lackeys instead of free men. This farce, this miserable travesty on religion, which has been tolerated long by the people, who hesitated to oppose it lest they do something offensive in the eyes of God, has been played to its end. The eyes of the public have been opened to the fact that the so-called religious crusade is but a vulgar scramble for money, which the commissioners and generals and majors and other silly apers of positions of command greedily grasp, that they may further enrich the family which made big drum and penny whistle salvation their stock in trade. The dupes of this selfish and sordid movement are not so pliable as they were, and of late it has not proved the bonanza that it once was. . . . It is said that men like to be humbugged, but they refuse to be humbugged any more by the Gradgrind theology and Pecksniffian morality which pervades the Army. It has seen its best days in Canada and cannot again galvanize public interest to the point of contributing money to keep alive a movement which is almost dead of greed and hypocrisy (July 18, 1889).

To bring the Canadian public to an 'intelligent' state of awareness, the Toronto *News* spared neither effort nor rhetoric. Its front-page headlines declared: "Worn-Out Soldiers Neglected," "Leaders Living in Comfort and Luxury," "Starving Soldiers Suffering and Dying Far From Home While the General's Pets Want for Nothing," and "Base Ingratitude: How the Army Treats its Best Friend." They were supported by graphic, often firsthand, descriptions of the 'heartless treatment' of Canadian officers, 'dispossessed' by Booth's English minions, and left to survive on charity while monies collected went towards the acquisition of property. "Financial success with some of the leaders of the Army," declared the *News*, "is placed higher on the program than spirituality":

Former Salvation Army officers, and even some who still retain a connection with the organization, tell interesting incidents of how money is wrung from the needy corps in the towns to fill the coffers at headquarters in Toronto, and keep the highest dignitaries in palatial city residences, surrounded by every luxury that people of affluence could desire. Many a broken down and almost destitute Army man feels the truth of this, and knows that the extensive funds with which the movement has been inflated, and with which the high officers have lived and travelled in royal style around the world, have for the greater part been blood money, squeezed sometimes almost forcibly from the humbler corps, leaving unpaid, unfed, and frequently slowly dying missionaries to their fate.

Behind all the pomp of the Commissioner's visit to the corps of a town there is a final picture which is characteristic of all these demonstrations, when gotten up by order in honor of the visit of any dignitary from headquarters. For weeks before the event it has been advertised by flaring posters everywhere, and the attention of the public secured. Although there are advertising bills to meet and many other expenses, the Commissioner takes charge of the gross receipts and carries them to headquarters. The local officers will perhaps draw his attention to their unpaid bills, incurred solely by reason of the visit, but the Commissioner, with fervent assurance, refers them to the people, and probably suggests 'we all have a word of prayer.' They are told that it is God's will that he should take this money along, and with a closing, 'God bless you, I must now catch the train,' he is gone. This is how the corps outside the city are 'worked' when they are worth it. A corps which is too poor to yield any fair return for a visit from the Commissioner is scarcely ever honored by his presence, or cheered with an encouraging word (March 7 & 8, 1889).

Support for such accusations daily poured in to the offices of the *News*, mainly from ex-officers whose names —Shankland, Thomas, and Joe Ludgate— were familiar to many Canadian Salvationists. The stories they told ranged from simple discontent to serious unsubstantiated charges of neglect, but nearly always involved some sort of criticism of the imported English officers:

Editor *News*: I see you have undertaken to expose the rottenness of the present administration of the Salvation Army in Canada. I simply say that the truth of the statements made cannot be gainsaid. Having been an officer in the Army something over three years, I am able to state many things that have come under my personal knowledge of the avarice and self-seeking of the imported English staff, who have broken the second commandment and are worshipping at the shrine of the 'dear general' and his beautiful family. It has been already said that the English officers obtain all the best appointments. As proof of the statement I would mention the time of the arrival of the first contingent of Hindoos [group of East Indians displayed at Army meetings to raise money for overseas work]. The same train that brought the Hindoos into the city brought about one dozen of English Training Home lads, and out of that number two were appointed to good stations in this city, two were given easy jobs at headquarters, one was sent in charge of Peterboro', a particularly good appointment, and although just now I cannot recollect the other appointments, if inquired into you would find the majority were appointed to flourishing stations, where there were no privations to endure, while in the small country villages and towns officers who had helped at the start of the work were suffering for lack of the proper nourishment to fit them for their arduous labors. For instance, just about that time I myself and family were compelled to live and pay house rent on an average of $1.75 per week, while the above English officers were getting their $6 per week regularly. . . .

Many a time have I got up in the morning and have had to go to some friend in the place and ask them to give me the money to buy a loaf of bread before I could give my family their breakfast. I would not mind this if the staff officers shared the hardships of the fight with us, but when I see them living on the fat of the land, and in many cases getting better livings than they could possibly get in business life, I think that it is time that something was done to open the eyes of those who have been supporting a movement which, at its inception, was doing a wonderful work for the benefit of the human race, in bringing them to a knowledge of the truth as it is in Jesus, but which is today, except in a few isolated cases, a grand scheme of financial salvation (March 8, 1889).

In a similar manner, through editorials, interviews and letters, in almost every issue for three months, the Toronto *News* lambasted The Salvation Army. Naturally, it claimed to do so only for the betterment of the organization. Theirs was, after all, an 'honest endeavour' to expose abuses detrimental to the organization; not to impair its usefulness but to 'throttle wrongs' which must inevitably "swamp the movement" (Mar. 9, 1889).

It would be foolish, however, to believe that such reporting was devoid of self-interest. The very nature of the attacks (in one instance claiming the Army was responsible for the death of an officer), makes the *News'* rationale seem rather weak and falsely pious. More acceptable was the sales-related admission that "the interest of Army people, and also that of ex-Salvationists, is excited and retained from day to day by stories of Army experiences." And, beyond sales incentive, there was the political fact that Sheppard had an anti-British axe to grind and was abetted in his purpose by several ex-officers, notably Albert Britnell, who had become fairly prosperous and prominent in Toronto. They were, in fact, very satisfied that the newspapers had been effective in bringing together many ex-officers, encouraging others to follow their lead. Every week they convened as The Christian League, ostensibly for evangelical worship, but mainly (if the reports were true) to re-hash old grievances:

The recent series of articles in THE EVENING NEWS relative to the abuses and evils which have developed in the Salvation Army during the past few years have not been in vain. A week ago last evening a private meeting of some twenty or thirty ex-officers and soldiers took place at 69 Queen street east, when a committee was appointed to draft resolutions to be submitted at a public mass meeting called for the purpose of discussing and protesting against the wrongs permitted, and the general management which at present characterizes the organization. That committee reported progress last night at another meeting. . . . Although no public announcement was made, the hall was filled with an interested audience. Mr. Albert Britnell presided, and opened the proceedings by explaining what had been done at the previous meeting. The resolutions were read by Mr. Arthur Sumner, and their adoption moved by Mr. George Thomas. The latter said he thought it was only proper to make some public declaration in explanation why so many had withdrawn from the Army, which has of late years developed into a monetary organization. He would not pretend to say that there were not good, earnest people still in the ranks, but in a general way the movement had fallen from its wonted place in the world for the accomplishment of good.

Louis Bell Smith, formerly a prominent Salvation man, then spoke for some time on the future course of those who have left the Army, but desire to continue in evangelistic work. He proposed that they call themselves the Christian League. The idea of the formation of a rival sect to the Army was deprecated. His propositions summarized were as follows: That the movement be styled the Christian League; that all evangelical Christians anxious for the salvation of men shall be eligible for membership. Members can also be connected with other churches; services of the league must not be held at the same hours as in the city churches, in order to avoid any semblance of interference with other religious bodies; all offices shall be held on the elective principle. The organization thus will be conducted on entirely democratic principles. As soon as the leader goes wrong he can be turned from office (April 17, 1889).

As exciting as all this may have been, however, the best (especially in terms of journalistic exposure) was yet to come. While most ex-officers were telling their stories to the *News*, ex-Captain Arthur Sumner, former editor of the Canadian *War Cry*, was hoarding his into a separate compilation called *The New Papacy: Behind the Scenes in the Salvation Army* due to be published by Albert Britnell (now a bookstore owner) in late April 1889. And it was at this point that the whole affair took a bizarre turn, mainly through the ineptness and naiveté of Commissioner Coombs. Fearing that Sumner's 'revelations' would do further damage to the Army's public image, Coombs 'persuaded' Sumner to suppress the book's publication. "It seems," reported the Toronto *Globe*, "that Sumner yielded, and by his assistance 5,000 copies of the book, which were printed and waiting to be bound at Imrie and Graham's printing house, were turned over to, paid for and destroyed by the officers of the Salvation Army."

The Toronto *News*, much less sanguine and objective than its rival, turned the affair into a regular 'cloak-and-dagger' story. In an article with the daring headline "Held by the Enemy: An Ex-Salvationist Captured by the Army," its reporter stated that the Army's printing house on Albert Street had been "turned into an improvised Bastille, and the prisoner of state confined therein was ex-Staff Captain Arthur

Sumner." Intimating that Commissioner Coombs had "some hold upon Sumner" such that, when his intention to publish a book was discovered, he was offered "two alternatives: he could take any sum of money he desired, give up every copy of the book and the stereotype plates, and leave the country, or be arrested on an old offence." Sumner was, the *News* averred, "compelled to take the course most men would have taken." He was confined to prevent discourse with others (i.e. Britnell), and on Saturday express wagons, "captained by the brusque Fred Perry, chief manager at the Army printing house, invaded Imrie & Graham's printing office and secured every published copy and the stereotype plates." From there they proceeded to Blackhall's bindery, where thousands of copies were being bound, seized the lot, took them to the Army's headquarters where they were "burned by the Commissioner and Perry. Some of the hands were given a half-holiday, and the remainder sent on an errand to Perry's farm at Eglington, so that their absence might be secured while the burning was in progress" (Apr. 24, 1889).

The truth behind such a report is indeed difficult to ascertain, and may never be satisfactorily known. What is clear is that ex-Captain Sumner (though never a 'prisoner) had second-thoughts about his actions, made a statement to that effect, and sold (or gave over) his rights to the book to Commissioner Coombs who, rather unwisely, had it destroyed (burning being a logical and appropriate means of destruction). Equally clear and understandable is the fact that it was impossible to destroy every copy, and on April 23 the Toronto *News* was issued with a legal letter cautioning it not to publish extracts from a 'stolen' copy of the book which was solely the property of Commissioner Coombs. With this the *News* complied but took satisfaction in the assurance that the book would be re-published, and that very soon:

> Public interest in the fate or probable outcome of that mysterious book, called "The New Papacy, or Behind the Scenes in the Salvation Army," continues unabated, though the line of proceedings by the publisher and his solicitor has not been altered since yesterday [Britnell was allegedly suing for damages]. The book no doubt will be issued in some form. So

far as is known, only one complete copy remains, and the whereabouts of this is a secret which will be profoundly kept. It is safe to say that if the Commissioner kept on guessing until the next anniversary, he would not strike the secluded location of the one volume among five thousand which escaped, when he and his assistant, Mr. Fred Perry, believed they had cast every vestige of the forbidden work into the fiery furnace (April 26).

Not that it really mattered. For when Albert Britnell sought legal advice he was assured his had been 'prior' rights and that no action could be taken against him if he decided to re-publish. On June 15, therefore, *The New Papacy* was, like a "conflagration bursting from dead ashes," again ready to reveal the "inner history of the Salvation Army."

In reality, however, Sumner's book offered little that had not already been reiterated almost *ad nauseam* in the pages of the *News* over the preceding three months, suggesting that some (perhaps much) of the newspaper's inside information had come from Sumner himself. Thus, as per formula, Sumner denounced the Army's "Orders and Regulations," the officiousness of its leaders, Boothism in general, and the increasing bureaucracy of the organization and its departure from mere revivalism, nearly all of which evils could be attributed to the influence of English staff-officers, acting on instructions from London, and ignorant of Canadian ways. The excerpt below shows the similarity of criticisms already voiced in the Toronto *News* and those appearing in Sumner's book:

Those of us who were acquainted with the professed objects and workings of the Salvation Army during the early days of its existence in the Dominion cannot fail, as we look back upon its six years' history, to be impressed with its wonderful development. Of course it is impossible to ignore the fact that it has gained for itself a position amongst religious organizations that is phenomenal. And yet it is equally apparent that its present position is altogether a different one from that to which it professed to aspire, and from that which at that time had been marked out for it by its leaders. Then, it will be remembered, it professed to be the humble hand-maid of the existing churches; its professed object was the simple evangelization of the masses. It repudiated the idea of building up a separate body, and it denounced the practice of gathering together wealth and the accumulation of property. Men and women other than its own converts gathered around it and threw themselves heart and soul into its work, for the simple reason that it offered, as they supposed, a more extended and widely open field for evangelical effort. Ministers everywhere were invited and welcomed to its platforms, Majors and Colonels were few and far between and the supremacy and power of the General were things unknown. Its members passed in and out amongst other denominations without let or hindrance, and were frequently seen at the communion rails and in the love feasts of the evangelical churches. Care was taken to avoid anything like proselytism; its converts were never coerced into joining its ranks. They were urged to connect themselves with some visible religious body, but only those who promised to be useful workers were asked to consider the question of joining the Army's ranks. In a word, the organization occupied the position of an auxiliary mission and recruiting agency for the various religious bodies.

As long as this state of things continued success was assured, and the confidence of the people in the Army as a means of usefulness daily increased. At the same time the spirit of unity and mutual esteem amongst the workers was perfect. All differences of opinion and all preconceived ideas were cast aside, and each and every one gave themselves up with a whole-souled devotion to the common object, namely, the salvation of the masses. The staff at this time consisted of two individuals, and distinctions of rank were more a matter of convenience than a matter of position, and the deference afterwards exacted towards superior officers was a thing unknown. There could be but one result to such a state of things, and consequently we find at all times that the meetings were crowded, people professed conversion by the score, the public liberally supplied the means to carry on the work in their respective communities, therefore every corps was wholly self-supporting, its officers were properly if not luxuriously cared for, the local expenditure was amply provided and under the supervision of the secretary, a local member, and the officer in charge, the funds were disbursed in the towns where they were collected, and the spirit of satisfaction and confidence was mutual all around. But those who have remained in the ranks, and more especially those who have been daily conversant with the Army's machinery, are well aware how entirely and radically the whole system has changed, and how from a band of devoted and disinterested workers, united in the bonds of zeal and charity for the good of their fellows, it has developed into a colossal and aggressive agency for the building up of a system and a sect, bound by rules and regulations altogether subversive of religious liberty, antagonistic to every branch of Christian endeavour and bound hand and foot to the will of one supreme head and ruler.

How such a state of things have come about is almost impossible to conceive. But as the work has spread through the country, and as the areas of its endeavours has enlarged, each leading position has been filled one after the other by individuals, strangers to the country, totally ignorant of the sentiments and idiosyncrasies of the Canadian people, trained in one school under the teachings and dominance of a member of the Booth family, and out of whom every idea has been crushed except that of unquestioning obedience to the general and the absolute necessity of going forward to do his bidding without hesitation or question.

Of course the *modus operandi* has been gradual, although the result has been rapidly achieved. As the work has progressed in extent the country has been divided up into divisions, and each of these has been placed in charge of a newly imported officer, fresh from immediate contact with the Booth influence, and imbued with the one idea of the Booth supremacy as inculcated at the English Training Home at Clapton. True, some few Canadian officers have been put in like positions, but this only after serving an apprenticeship as assistant under the imported leaders and upon their recommendation as to their fitness in all respects. Other officers, too, have been imported and invariably placed in charge of the larger and more flourishing corps, and the common object of all has been to inculcate the duty of obedience to the general and to establish and strengthen the influence of the Booth *régime*. This favouritism exists in every country where the Army is, and is causing universal complaint everywhere. We desire, however, only to speak of it as it affects the Dominion and as it has come under our own observation. We need not repeat what is the reason and necessity for this favouritism but it is obvious that the leader in the Dominion is not mainly responsible. These people are sent out to be provided for. It may have been necessary in the interests of the institution to remove them from England, or they may be sent more especially to keep the General *au courant* with affairs in Canada. Be that as it may, they must be well placed and kept quiet and comfortable. Consequently they are sent to the larger cities and so have to appear before the most intelligent audiences. For the most part they exhibit much less intelligence than an ordinary Canadian crowd. Their vernacular is such as to be almost unintelligible and their peculiarities of speech and manner are generally repulsive to the Canadian public. They come, too, imbued with the spirit of dominance which is prevalent amongst English Salvationists and with strained ideas as to the prerogatives of a 'commanding officer' and instead of attempting to assimilate themselves with the habits and sentiments of Canadians, they try to coerce the people and those associated with them into their own insular notions. Of course all this is strange and unwelcome to the free sentiments of our people, and the 'Hinglish Hofficer' soon becomes a bye-word and a reproach. In spite of this, all the leading corps are placed almost entirely in their hands, rapid promotion is awarded to them, as being more thoroughly imbued with the Army spirit, and old Canadian workers are superseded and passed over in their favour. Being bound together by sentiment and training, these strangers naturally form themselves into a separate *clique*, and the officers of the two schools are separated by a marked line of division, which breach, growing wide and wider every day, threatens speedily to bring about an internal conflict that must destroy the whole institution.

It would be naive to believe that the single-handed campaign waged by the Toronto *News* (unsupported as it was by other newspapers) did not persuade other officers and soldiers to leave the ranks, and perhaps deterred some members of the public from subscribing to Army projects; it is even possible that the removal of Commissioner Coombs a few months later was prompted by his mishandling of the affair. But evidence suggests that the newspaper exposé and Sumner's book, *marked* (rather than *caused*) a natural turning point in the history of the Army in Canada. The organization had, as it were, reached the end of its 'invasion-by-enthusiasm' period. It could no longer engage in a 'camp-meeting' kind of evangelism —a kind of evangelism that officers like Sumner had wished for. It was, now that a social outreach was also part of the Army's mission, time to consolidate and move towards permanence. It was one thing, as Herbert Booth later said, "to get up a revival in a village and something entirely different to maintain a permanently organized corps of the Army."

To achieve stability, however, was not easy. Throughout 1890 and 1891, though the newspaper campaign dwindled, the turmoil continued. Commissioner Coombs' successor, Thomas Adams, proved unequal to the task and was himself dismissed before his term was completed. The appointment of David Rees, for a very few months in 1892, was a stop-gap measure until someone of the General's own choosing could be sent to bring the colony 'into shape.' That task he entrusted not merely to another English officer but to his own son, Herbert, then just thirty years old.

To some Canadian Salvationists, Herbert Booth's appointment (in July 1892) was a clear message that Boothism —strict control by London, strict adherence to Army regulations, and unquestioning obedience to the General (or his territorial representative)— would be the operative mode for Canada. Many felt, and correctly so, that the General's own son had been sent expressly to establish that fact. He had, in fact, been sent as a response to Commissioner Rees' allegation that certain senior Canadian officers —chief among them being Brigadier Peter Philpott— had been stirring up trouble in the ranks. As in 1889, officers (who had not yet resigned) were again openly questioning certain practices and policies: the inadequate financial care of sick officers, the discrepancy between the salaries of staff officers and field officers, and a perceived misappropriation of Self-Denial funds. Commissioner Rees' reaction was to treat the matter as insubordination, naming Peter Philpott as the leading agitator, asking for a return to London and leaving the matter to his successor.

It was extremely naive, however, and a certain sign of William Booth's ignorance of Canada, to assume that the mere presence of a Booth, like the presence of a redcoat among natives, would bring order to the Territory. Rather, what Herbert Booth's appointment as Commander did was to bring this clash of ideals to the public's attention. Prior to his coming, the newspapers had been silent on the issue —most likely aware of it just not interested. No sooner had the strong-willed Booth arrived to confront the equally strong-willed

Philpott than the 'affair' became public domain, with the private clash
of wills becoming a much larger issue, a struggle between two factions
"Boothism versus Philpottism." The Toronto *Evening News* was again
quick off the mark:

X Philpottism may or may not be a nightmare for Commandant Booth,
but it designates the new dissident wing, and the term is said to have
been coined by the Commandant himself in the course of a conference
when referring to the forces arrayed against Boothism. One or other had
to go, but Boothism is entrenched behind the bulwark of Army wealth
and is the likeliest to stay. The rank and file and the aggrieved officers
say it is Englishism against Canadianism (Aug. 7, 1892).

So, once again, during a Canadian economic depression when The
Salvation Army needed all the public support it could get, Canadian
newspapers were full of 'Army troubles.' Again there were the
sensational headlines —"Soldiers Step Out," "S.A. Torn Up," "Won't
Answer to the Drumbeat," "Divided Into Two Camps," "Philpott vs
Booth"— promising a battle of wills, with stories of corruption and
personal vindictiveness. And, on the whole (a few excepted),
throughout the month of August, 1892, the only kind of newspaper
coverage accorded The Salvation Army was similar to this piece from
the Toronto *Globe*:

During the past week there has arisen within the ranks of the Salvation
Army a disturbance which threatens to wreck the entire organization in
Canada. Briefly told, the trouble is a fight between Commandant Booth,
supported by the officers in the Old Country and a few personal
adherents here, and the subordinate officers in the city. It is an attempt
on the part of the higher officials to remove themselves beyond the
power of the great body of the Army and make themselves practically
despotic. At least this is the way in which the officers in revolt look at
the matter, and they have about decided to leave the Army rather than
submit.

The immediate cause of the present trouble was a communication
addressed to Brigadier Philpott on Thursday last from Headquarters, in
which he was notified that in consequence of disloyalty on his part to
the Army he must either submit to a reduction to the rank of Captain

and to removal from Toronto or quit the service. When Brigadier Philpott received the message he was about to address a meeting at Well's Hill, and he intimated in his speech during the service that it was his intention to resign. The announcement caused great surprise, and when full particulars were learned much indignation was expressed at the action of the commandant.

According to statements of the officers here the alleged disloyalty charged against Philpott consisted in protests on his part made last year to Commissioner Rees against extravagance on the part of some of the higher officers while many petty officers throughout the country were in an almost destitute condition. That Commissioner Rees had resented this interference on the part of a subordinate as an infringement on the dignity of his superior, and when he returned to England he placed Philpott's conduct in the worst light possible. That, in fact, Commandant Booth came to Canada with the fixed impression that Philpott was a dangerous man, one who was making an effort to undermine and destroy the influence and power of the chiefs of the army, and one who must be transferred to some smaller field or removed altogether. That, accordingly, he took the earliest opportunity which offered itself of giving the Brigadier the alternative of 'knuckling under' or 'getting out.' Philpott has decided to get out, and his friends say he will take the greater portion of the army with him, leaving the commandant with but a small and scattered remnant to rule over.

When Brigadier Philpott made his explanation to his colleagues on Well's Hill on Thursday evening they drew up a remonstrance, which they addressed to the commandant, asking him to make his charges against the accused before a meeting of the officers in the city, at which Philpott and Mrs. Philpott were to be present. This remonstrance was signed by thirty-seven officers and sent to the commandant on Friday. A refusal was the reply.

On Monday Captain Pink of the Richmond St. corps and five other officers were selected as a deputation to interview the commandant, and urge him to grant the request they had preferred on Friday. The deputation met with a very chilly reception. At first they were refused a hearing altogether, but after two and a half hours' consultation with his personal attendants, Commandant Booth ordered them to be admitted to see him.

In the name of the officers whom the deputation represented, and in the name of the Army in Toronto, which they claimed sympathised strongly with Philpott, Captain Pink, the spokesman, strongly urged the commandant to make his charges before a general meeting of the officers and in the presence of the accused.

Commandant Booth, it is said, replied at some length and with considerable warmth. He declared it would be a breach of army principles for him to submit to such a proposition.... He must, therefore, emphatically refuse their request.

They returned with the answer, and the officers on hearing it, with one accord said it was unjust and that they would not submit to it. Accordingly, they drew up the following protest, which they all signed (thirty-seven of them):—

We, the undersigned, have heard your explanation and find that it is not satisfactory to us or just to those accused, as it is necessary and right in making the charge that the accused should be present.

This document was given in charge of Captain Pink, who took it to Headquarters yesterday morning (Aug. 18, 1892).

Most newspapers were content to report the affair as it unfolded. The Toronto *News*, however, saw it as a continuation of the Sumner affair three years before. It was manifestly a case of "English-ism against Canadianism." The English 'element' had ruled in all matters, and Philpott was voicing Canadian concerns, especially opposed to sending Self-Denial money to England —money "so much needed by the officers and soldiers at the poor stations" in Canada. "When the series of articles first published in THE NEWS appeared [in 1889], Brigadier Philpott was one of the most zealous defenders of the existing regime, and though possessed of some information that would not have helped Army leaders, kept quiet and would not be interviewed. Since then it seems he has been fighting in the Army councils against the very grievances which were then condemned." The charges of 'disloyalty,' therefore, stemmed from nothing more than Philpott's determination to fight against "rule from England, and the carrying away of money collected in Canada" (Aug. 17, 1892).

By this time, as far as public perception was concerned, the whole affair had become quite ludicrous. At meetings intended to rally his troops, Herbert Booth demanded, as a requirement of admission, that his soldiers sign the following document:

As a loyal Salvationist being anxious to listen with an impartial mind to the commandant's statement, I pledge myself in attending this meeting to the following:

1. That I have not already made up my mind to accept Brigadier Philpott's word before that of Headquarters.

2. If I have without having heard a word of defence or explanation already committed myself to expressions of mistrust and unkind accusations I hereby pledge myself to cease from harboring any such feelings concerning headquarters until I have heard their explanation upon the subject.

A reporter of the Toronto *News*, discovering that his conscience would let him falsely sign such a document, attended such a meeting. Outside the door he met several seceders with placards reading "REMEMBER YOU HAVE NOT YET HEARD BRIGADIER PHILPOTT'S EXPLANATION":

It was nearly 8:30 when the proceedings opened, with a few volleys for Jesus, a prayer and a little singing. There were about 300 present, the vast majority of whom seemed to be loyal to the Commandant without any explanation; a few wanted to hear his side of the case, while a few others seem to have made up their mind in favor of Brigadier Philpott.

Herbert Booth is a chip off the old block. He is clever and shrewd. Nothing showed that clearer than the way he went about getting the gathering to indorse his course. He did not begin with an explanation at all. For one solid hour he appealed to his hearers. He appealed to them by the love they bore the Army, by his loyalty to his "dear father," by the work he had done in the past, and by everything else, and at the same time he incidentally tarred his former brigadier with a good coat of dark, thick pitch. This appeal was stopped occasionally for prayer or singing and when the audience was in a proper receptive frame of mind for the explanation it was made.

The Commandant commenced by telling his hearers how grieved he was at recent events. It struck him to the heart that members of the Army should have brought scandal and ignominy upon it.

'You have seen what was in the papers?' he shouted.

'Amen! we have,' came the response in chorus.

'You have read The News?' he continued.

Everybody seemingly had read The News, and they said so, some cheering, some laughing, and others groaning, and as the latter groaned with an emphasis that seemed to say they held The News directly responsible for all Salvation Army troubles, the reporter felt as if he would be more comfortable breathing freely out under the star lit sky, but he lingered necessarily. . . .

The Commandant dwelt at great length upon all the unpleasant things that had been said and written about him. It was unkind, he declared, to slander the dear old general's son that way. He had been called a tyrant. He a tyrant? A tyrant because he had done his duty in their interest and in the interests of the Army. It was as their representative, as an officer who had their welfare at heart, that he displayed firmness and honesty of purpose in maintaining his and their authority, and that his slanderers called tyranny. Why, he came to this country not for his own but for their welfare, with his heart bursting to serve them, and the events of the past few days had been the most painful in the whole experience of his life. . . .

Another story which the Commandant said caused him great pain was a report that he and the general officers lived in luxury, while the ordinary officers had to subsist under very different conditions. They said that he came out here and took all their best furniture from the other officers to furnish his own house. These slanders had arisen because he had had three rooms of his house carpeted with the very cheapest carpet that could be had. When he came out here, finding the Army was so straitened for money, he would not even put them to the expense of buying new furniture for his house, but took any old articles the other officers could give him. Thus he had come to Toronto from a happy and comfortable home in England. He had taken his wife and child out of the midst of luxury, had taken her away from where she moved in the MOST ELITE SOCIETY where her bosom friend was the daughter of the Minister of Foreign Affairs, to come to Canada and put up with accommodation she had never been used to. And then they said he was selfish.

They all said 'Amen.'

'May I ask a question?' asked a soldier.

'Better tell it to me privately. We are here only in the interests of the Army,' responded the commandant.

'This question is in the interest of the Army.'

'Then come up and tell me privately first; we don't want any trouble here.'

The soldier went up and his question, which the commandant answered later, was as to why this explanation had not been made in the presence of Brigadier Philpott.

'The reason,' said the commandant, 'is because it is directly contrary to military discipline. Why, fancy the colonel of a regiment in the regular army who punishes a lieutenant bringing the man before his regiment to explain to them in his presence why he did so. Such a thing was never heard of.'

But several of those present thought if it was unmilitary to make an explanation in the culprit's presence it was more unmilitary and unprecedented to ask the regiment to vote on the merits of the case. Fancy a colonel in the British army taking a vote of his men as to whether he did right or wrong. That is the way several looked at it and voted accordingly afterwards. . . . [T]hen the Commandant invited everybody to go down on their knees and close their eyes so as they would not see how anyone else was voting. They went down.

'Now,' he said, 'while you pray and keep your eyes shut, all who are satisfied with my action raise the right hand.'

Most of the hands in the audience went up.

The Commandant then called on those who were not satisfied to raise their hands.

About a dozen or fifteen went up.

The Commandant looked surprised and remarked, 'Perhaps you all do not understand what I said. I want those who are not satisfied to raise their hands.'

'We want to hear Brigadier Philpott first,' shouted a lusty soldier.

'Then you are not satisfied. Put up your hand.'

Up went about fifteen hands. The Commandant counted those he saw to the number of a dozen.

A volley was fired for the Commandant, another for the General and others for the Salvation Army and Jesus. Then one of the officers moved a resolution approving the Commandant's action and this, of course, was carried. That ended the proceedings (Aug. 22, 1892).

In the end, the 'Philpott affair' degenerated into a game of public charge and counter-charge. Much to the delight of reporters, both sides seemed to have lost their senses and, in an un-Christian manner, made accusations which exceeded the actual truth. For the public then, as for the historian now, it must have been difficult to decide where the real truth lay. And the matter was probably made no less confusing by the publication, in late 1892, of a full-length exposé by the two ex-officers Peter Philpott and A.W. Rolfe, called *New Light: Containing a Full Account of the Recent Salvation Army Troubles in Canada*. In it the old troubles were re-hashed, and the grievances, now so well-known to most Canadians, were aired again. The public, in Canada as in England, were getting their fill of The Salvation Army.

To what extent, then, did the two newspaper controversies, in 1889 and 1892, affect the progress of The Salvation Army in Canada? In an immediate sense, it is reasonable to believe that the overall defection in 1892 —almost one hundred officers and about two thousand soldiers— would never have been as large had the affair not become a public *cause célèbre*.[2] In terms of numerical strength, some Toronto Corps never fully recovered. The creation of several branches of the Christian Workers' Church, staffed by ex-officers and headed by Peter Philpott, had, for a while, larger memberships than did many Salvation Army corps.

That there was validity in the discontent leading to the accusations can also be substantiated. Herbert Booth, was at best a reluctant dictator; and is later said to have regretted his high-handed actions. Colonel George Mackenzie, Booth's Chief Secretary in Canada (an Englishman who, like Booth, later resigned from the Army), committed his opinion to print: "If one has to judge of God's favour and disfavour towards the actors in a crisis like this by the success and public acceptance and Christian usefulness that have followed, there is no doubt that those of us who as strangers in a strange country sought fearlessly to maintain the military principle in a welter of misunderstanding and suffering, give proof enough to this hour that the Divine disfavour rested upon us."[3]

But, it was also true, as Mackenzie notes, that The Salvation Army did regain much of its lost public favour and recouped its membership well beyond that which defected. As for the nature of the organization itself, while sociological factors would inevitably have brought about a slowdown in its advance and a consolidation of resources, it seems probable that the public exposés carried out largely by the Toronto

News brought home to the Army's leaders the urgency of reform. As Herbert Booth later wrote in a *Brief Concerning Canadian Affairs*, "something drastic required to be put into operation to save us from inevitable ruin, and yet to propose some radical reform with everybody in the touchy state they were might lead us into more difficulty still."

Early in 1893, therefore, Herbert Booth set up a Commission of Enquiry to investigate the difficulties attending the work of officers in small corps. He then initiated a series of vigorous reforms calculated to speed up the already-planned process of consolidation, to allay fears of a retreat and to restore public confidence.

First, Booth initiated a complete revision of Canada's administrative setup by creating five provinces (Manitoba, Western Ontario, Central Ontario, Eastern Ontario, and the Maritimes and Newfoundland) thereby eliminating fifteen divisional commands. The number of staff officers was reduced from one hundred and five to thirty-five, and the money saved was ear-marked for the better maintenance of officers in financially poor corps. By 1894, Booth's program of consolidation was in full swing and the Army on its way to recovery. Celebrating his father's jubilee year (the fiftieth anniversary of his calling), he launched fifty new schemes, among them a social farm near Toronto, a Salvation Navy, a clothing club for officers, new rescue shelters, prison-gate homes. So intense did Army life become that, very soon, the Philpott affair became a thing of the past.

It has been suggested that Peter Philpott and many of the officers who shared his views were mere 'evangelists' rather than Salvationists —evangelists who could not "accept direction from above." They had been attracted to the Army without fully understanding the intention of Booth's military discipline, and therefore could not, temperamentally, become Salvationists. There may be some validity to that argument; but the fact is there were evils inherent in Boothism and injustices caused by extreme adherence to regulations (which have largely disappeared from the organization). In questioning these injustices, officers like Philpott were courageously correct and, helped by public opinion, did much to save the Army from its own worst faults.

The Times of London, T.H. Huxley, and Booth's Social Panacea

It is reasonable to assume —indeed, evidence suggests— that the kind of journalistic comment most appreciated by early Salvationists was that which applauded their mission. The unequivocal praise of W.T. Stead's *Pall Mall Gazette* and *Review of Reviews* was particularly favoured. On the other hand, it is also provable that Salvationists were not entirely dissatisfied with the opposite side of the coin (the vitriolic denunciations of the *Saturday Review,* for example), for they soon learned how to turn such criticism to their own advantage. They knew, as William Booth stated, that 'persecution makes friends.' People who cared little about the Army, would rush to its defence when they saw it being trampled on.

The kind of public commentary that worried Salvationists most was the 'voice-of-reason' variety —those newspaper and journal articles which explored all sides of an issue and tried to approach each in a rational way. These did not call for an emotional response, but demanded a thoughtful consideration of Army policy or methodology. As such, they were difficult to defend against, impossible to use for propaganda purposes and were very appealing to an educated public.

The leading proponent of such journalism in England was the London *Times*. It was not merely that *The Times* could, for good or bad, alter the course of history, even emperors and kings having 'heeded its counsels' and statesmen its 'admonitions'[1]; rather, it was the rational manner in which *The Times* approached each subject. Not always impartial, but always independent, writers of its editorials and 'leading articles' rarely allowed an emotional appeal to cloud their critical judgment. Much of their writing was considered to be free of political and parochial bias. If not, *The Times* allowed ample debate in its "Letters to the Editor," a section which could be a forum for important and history-making discussion. In them, some of England's greatest thinkers influenced public affairs. And it was there that an organization like The Salvation Army could be minutely examined and shrewdly judged; and where many intelligent, middle-class readers could be persuaded to support it or not.

At first, as far as *The Times* was concerned, there was little to worry and much to please Booth's followers. During 1879 and 1880, for example, *The Times* was content merely to report on Salvationist activities —on meetings at the Exeter Hall (London) and Mrs. Booth's lecture on "The Principles, Measures, and Aims of the Salvation Army" at St. James's Hall— and did so, to Salvationists' relief, in a most uncritical, neutral and accurately factual manner. The only interpolation of any note, stemming from *The Times'* contempt for impropriety, was a comment to the effect that some of the speeches were "couched in a language which would be out of place in newspaper columns." On the whole, in these early *Times'* reports, Army meetings seemed no more unusual than those conducted by the Methodists or by temperance movements. Salvationists were content with that. The most prestigious newspaper in England had given them space and had thereby legitimized their mission in the eyes of respectable citizens.

In the decade that followed, in fact, gratification gave way to ecstasy, when *The Times* began to take what can only be called a 'proprietary' interest in The Salvation Army. Not only were its reports longer and more detailed, but they covered a wider range of Army activities than most other newspapers would. Prominent, of course, were the 'invasions' which met opposition —the 'riots' at Weston-Super-Mare, Salisbury, Exeter and Worthing, and the legal skirmishes resulting from those encounters. But, throughout its pages, are decorous descriptions of the Army's 'free-and-easy' meetings and reports on the openings of the Army's 'Rink' on Regent Street and its

Clapton Congress Hall. There are statistics from Booth regarding the Army's finances, notes on Salvation Army hymns, descriptions of Army weddings (particularly of the Booth children), and lengthy reports on the Army's difficulties in Switzerland and India. Among newspapers, only the Army's own *War Cry* was carrying more Army news than *The Times* —though the latter would have denied any intention of promoting the Army's cause.

And yet it most certainly did. In its editorials, where its sympathy is more apparent, one can discern an early support that, though rationally maintained, went against the general tone of public comment. The first of these, published on October 13, 1881, though exploratory, conveyed through intentional under-statement a spirit of tolerance and good-will that remained constant for much of the decade:

> For two years or thereabouts, our towns have had frequent opportunities of witnessing an exhibition not to everyone's taste. The 'Salvation Army,' as far as can be known to the uninitiated, consists of bands of men marching through the streets, generally towards 'church-time,' with banners, devices, and sometimes emblematic helmets and other accoutrements, singing sensational hymns, and by their gestures inviting all whose eyes they succeed in catching to fall in and march with them to some headquarters or rendezvous of those that are to be saved. The worship they conduct under cover is not quite of the sober and monotonous character that finds most favour with English respectability. The confident heirs of a newly acquired salvation sing hymn after hymn, with emphatic refrains, in an ascending scale of devotional energy. At intervals exhortations which are at least simple, intelligible and frequently reiterated, restore their energies for fresh multitudinous utterances.

Most citizens would, in the opinion of this writer, be inclined to let the Army go about its curious business: "they will be neither for it or against it." They should not, however, condone the actions of "irresponsible roughs. It is with them that the Salvation Army is waging its only physical warfare. . . . The faith of the majority, the good taste of the educated, and the universal sense of decency are outraged under the pretence of interrupting the exceptional methods of a few. . . . The fellows who throw stones at the Salvation Army are quite as likely to take offence at anything else that reminds them unpleasantly of a better life and higher aspirations. . . . We must beware how we quarrel with the rude remedies and uncouth methods employed by those who honestly believe there is a great work to be done. If we do not like these singular modes of propagandism and conversion, we need not assist the 'roughs' to put them down. Another course lies before us all. It is to do the work in a better way."

There being no serious objection to such a tolerant view, *The Times*, in its next editorial some months later, became more outspoken and positive. And, in what amounted to an astute sociological and psychological analysis, offered its reasons for the Army's success:

> The Salvation Army with its antics is a reaction on a small scale, as was Methodism on a great scale, against the complacent belief of an age or people in its own prosperity and excellence. It is a reaction, as was Methodism, against the assumption that individual effort is no longer needed for religious enlightenment. It is a reaction against the general monotony of existence. Industrious mechanics and small tradesmen find in its mummeries a protest that much has to be done before humanity has entered upon the road to perfection. If they have suddenly been touched by an instinct of the necessity of religion to temper human life, they welcome in this buckling on of an armour and baptism of fire opportunities of parading their discoveries. In proportion to the modest reserve which prompts alike the deepest and the most careless faith to be mute on theological experiences is the defiant eagerness of the heated novice to proclaim his tenets and challenge antagonism. In working-class or lower middle-class life variety is not so plentiful that the pleasure of masquerading under arms is an unimportant bribe at the disposal of the Salvation Army recruiting sergeants (Jan. 26, 1882).

At this early juncture, *The Times* was so concerned to give the Army a fair hearing that, when the first letter of complaint arrived on the editor's desk, he felt obliged to make it the subject of a lengthy comment. The complaint, by the Reverend Rippon, was a common one, to the effect that the established Church had expected Booth to return his converts to the orthodox fold and perhaps even seek a merger with it. Instead, Rippon maintained, The Salvation Army was taking a line antagonistic to the church, and was setting itself up as permanent institution, acquiring money and property, as well as a 'despotic organization.' *The Times* begged to differ:

> We believe our readers will take a fairer view of the case. General Booth is perhaps the truer exponent of John Wesley's principles. Born in the Church of England, he was converted to Wesleyanism, and in due time became a minister of the Methodist New Connexion. True to his original instincts, he found he could not do all the good he wanted even in the free harness of the New Connexion. He looked round, and thought he saw a world to be conquered. . . . The Salvation Army, it must be admitted, claims to be the true church, marching to Sion. Theoretically the claim may seem ridiculous, but much the same must be said of the very same claim made by many other religious bodies. The real question is one of a more practical character. Is there not a cause for some such movement? Is there, or is there not, as alleged, a very large part of our population that the existing religious organizations have utterly failed to make Christians in any appreciable sense of the word? (April 8, 1882)

The Times had no doubts on that score. "The success of the Salvation Army," a later editorial stated, "is among the most singular phenomena of this generation. . . . [Booth's] style is clear and natural. His views are expressed with laudable simplicity and directness." And, even though the writer felt the Army would eventually "fade away altogether, or become incrusted with traditions and imbedded with ease," at that moment in history it exhibited "a power which is not to be despised, and is not to be insulted."

The only aspect of Salvationism that disturbed *The Times* and slightly diminished its enthusiasm was the Army's public demonstrations —demonstrations which were becoming increasingly violent, leading to numerous court appearances:

> Our quarrel with the Salvationists is not for what they teach, nor for their somewhat too authoritative enunciation of it. They can please

themselves, thus far, and if they are pleased it is no concern of anyone else to take umbrage at their self-satisfaction. But when they deliver their message with too little regard to time and place and manner and circumstances, and raise public disorder by so doing, they go a little too far, and lay themselves open to reasonable censure, and in extreme cases to restraint. At the Royal Grecian Theatre, or at any private gathering on ground of their own, they have a just claim not only not to be interfered with, but to be protected. But when they appear in public places, when they take possession of the squares or parade the streets in uniform, with banging of drums and shouts of Hallelujah, they are less certainly within their right. Such proceedings are a nuisance, and if they raise counter-demonstrations they become a dangerous nuisance (Oct. 23, 1883).

On the whole, then, throughout the 1880s, *The Times*, though sometimes bothered by Salvationist 'antics,' was never highly critical of the organization. It liked to think itself, as it characterized the public, as being 'entirely impartial.' It would be gratified to be "convinced that a fresh and true humanizing agency" was at work for the public's welfare, but it thought it should, in the meantime, be "simply curious as to the battering effect upon vice of the Salvationist ordnance." In actual fact, *The Times*, as we have seen, was more supportive of the Army than that statement would lead one to believe. In its several 'Army' editorials it had leaned farther left than it had done for most other causes.

The opinion of *The Times* began to turn —or was caused to turn— when its readers started to take issue with its editorials. Hitherto that had been desultory at best; but in late December and early January, 1888, its "Letters to the Editor" columns became a debating forum on the general topic labelled by *The Times* "Outcast London and the Salvation Army." More than forty letters were contributed to the debate —attack/reply, counter-attack/rebuff— led by the Reverend Llewellyn Davies, vicar of Christ Church, Lissongrove. In his first letter, Reverend Davies suggested that people gave money to the Army because they believed that it had a unique success in "reclaiming men and women *of the lowest class*" —a belief that simply could not be supported by the facts. In his own parish, perhaps one of the 'wickedest' in England, The Salvation Army had been labouring for several years without any visible evidence of reclamation from the 'lowest classes.' "Speaking for Lissongrove and West Marylebone, I have to say that many persons belonging to 'the churches' have been accepted as members, and that the officials of the Army are unable in these two years to produce a single convert of the 'uncared-for' class to be found within this large and populous area" (Dec. 25, 1888).

General Booth being on tour at the moment, the burden of reply fell to Commissioner George Scott Railton (who signed himself simply 'Railton,' misconstrued by some readers as a silly pseudonym). In a neat bit of evasion, Railton offered an impressive set of statistics to the effect that the Corps in the Marylebone district had enlisted 142 soldiers and 128 recruits "who hold 30 services per week, and 87 of those persons still live in the district. . . . No less than 17 persons converted at this corps have become officers in the army, devoting their whole life to the salvation of the lost." Neither Davies nor *The Times* were impressed. In the opinion of *The Times*, Railton's reply did nothing to clarify the essential question: "the position in life of the classes from which the army draws it converts."

> If it is found that the army is merely diverting, by the superior attractions in the form of excitement which it offers, members of other congregations, or persons who, if there were no Salvation Army at all, would in probability have been led by their natural proclivities to join other congregations, then the popular opinion of the Salvation Army will be considerably altered, and, it is needless to say, not for the better. The only condition upon which rational men can approve of the travesty of religion cultivated by the Salvation Army is that it should not be a competing sect, replacing the sober devotions of Christianity by semi-barbarian antics, but that it should reach by these forlorn hopes a stratum which Church and Dissent seem equally powerless to reach. Disprove the claims of the army to this distinction, and their *raison d'etre* vanishes (Jan. 5, 1889).

In the 'teapot tempest' that ensued over the next two weeks, Railton struggled valiantly to defend his position, but did not succeed. It was clear that many Salvationists, though from the poorer classes, were not from the 'abject' social stratum; and, conversely, many from that group who were helped by the Army, did not always join. Railton's counter-charge was certainly quite ingenious: "The changed form of criticism upon our work is, I must say, rather amusing. For many years we were represented as a sort of fanatical rabble. Now that the army has grown too much in size, organization, and favour for such statements to be credible we are accused of recruiting from the classes who would have been religious if we had done nothing at all; and the decent appearance of our processions, once described as mobs of riffraff, is pointed to as evidence against us" (Jan. 7, 1889). But his claim that the Army never intended its message solely for the 'abject classes' was easily refuted by reference to Army publications which stated that it was God's chosen agency for "conveying salvation to the lowest and worst."

As for the Davies' camp, it was clear, and some readers said so, that their main concern was not so much for London's 'outcast' as for the fact that the Army was enticing some church members into its ranks —a concern which, as the Reverend John Clifford declared, was entirely groundless. As president of the Baptist Union, Clifford had had ample opportunity of observing the Army throughout the country: "So far as I can form an opinion over so widespread a fact, it is that the invasion of the Salvation Army has at first shocked the old-fashioned and quiet piety of many Christians, attracted a few of our Church members, but by no means in great numbers, quickened the apathetic and indifferent to fresh faith and zeal, and by general confession led hundreds of the drunken and vicious to temperance and virtue. In such results (even though mixed with some evils) every patriot and every lover of humanity will rejoice" (Jan. 11, 1889). This opinion, perhaps the dominant one throughout the debate, and most reasonably put by the vicar of Penzance, seems to have reflected (as later events would show) the predominant public attitude towards The Salvation Army:

Sir:— The discussion in your columns on the work of the Salvation Army illustrates the extreme difficulty which good men of different classes encounter when they try to understand each other. The Salvation Army succeeds in England, and still more in India, because the officers throw themselves unreservedly on the charity of those whom they teach, and because they obey implicitly those over them. Our Lord seems absolutely to have assumed that evangelistic effort to be successful must be based upon these principles. St. Francis of Assisi, J. Wesley, and now General Booth have proved the power of this trust in the innate gentlemanliness and humility of men. 'The meek' again 'inherit the earth.' It does seem a grievous pity that good, thoughtful, and cultured Churchmen should fail to see all this, and should write so critically of one of the great movements of our day.

Old Fuller somewhere says that the standard of decency in worship is the public opinion of one's neighbours as to what is becoming therein. To my own feelings the ritual of the army is most unpleasant, but to a very large number of working people it is impressive in itself, and when backed up by the wonderful persistence of its officers, the voluntary poverty they embrace, and the sympathy they therefore feel for the trials and temptations of working people, it is not wonderful that these should 'hear them gladly,' and that they should freely offer the best and most devout of their sons and daughters to help in a work which they feel is likely to bring about an epiphany of the Christ-life in our slums at home, and among our heathen fellow-subjects abroad. I have a somewhat extended experience of the officers of the army, and I am lost in astonishment at the single-hearted devotion of these poor people. They show a love for souls which has often shamed me, a humility and a power of obedience I have admired and would fain imitate. I could, if I cared to, speak just as strongly as Mr. Llewellyn Davies has done of their failure in this and other parishes to accomplish their ends; but, when all Christian workers fail so constantly, and when we try to see in our own failures the mark of the Cross, which is the symbol to us of triumph presently and resurrection, I venture to press upon my brethren of the clergy, and upon all thoughtful students of human life, that, before we criticize very severely the Salvation Army, we had better try to learn the lessons it teaches; and, above all, to find room in our more elaborate systems and nobler ideals for similar efforts of evangelistic zeal.

Faithfully yours, J. Andrewes Reeve.

That issue, then, seems to have settled nicely into the Army's lap. It had, in truth, caused only a mild 'stir,' though by now *The Times*, perhaps persuaded by Reverend Davies' arguments, was much less sympathetic to the Army's cause. So much so that, when the next great 'Army' controversy blew its way, it was decidedly on the opposition's side.

William Booth launched his 'Darkest England Scheme' —one of the boldest social-reclamation schemes in England's history— in October, 1890; and he did so in his usual dramatic fashion by publishing a 300-page book designed to stir the public imagination and generate an awareness that would arouse the nation to action and, perhaps, generosity. Capitalizing on the current publicity surrounding Henry Stanley's search for Dr. Livingstone, and the moral and spiritual abyss pictured in his *In Darkest Africa*, Booth tried to vivify an even deeper abyss right in the heart of civilized England. "[Stanley's] is a terrible picture," wrote Booth, "and one that has engraved itself deep on the heart of civilisation. But while brooding over the awful presentation of life as it exists in the vast African forest, it seemed to me only too vivid a picture of many parts of our own land. As there is a darkest Africa is there not also a darkest England? Civilisation, which can breed its own barbarians, does it not also breed its own pygmies? May we not find a parallel at our own doors, and find within a stone's throw of our cathedrals and palaces similar horrors to those which Stanley has found existing in the great Equatorial forest?"

So, in *In Darkest England and The Way Out*, Booth showed, pretty much as Andrew Mearns had shown in *The Bitter Cry of Outcast London*, just how vicious was the grip of poverty on the nearly one million citizens who lived below what Thomas Carlyle had earlier called 'the cab horse standard.' Booth did so by dramatizing the true stories of London's homeless:

'I'm a tailor; have slept here [on London's Embankment] four nights running. Can't get work. Been out of a job three weeks. If I can muster cash I sleep at a lodging-house in Vere Street, Clare Market. It was very wet last night. I left these seats and went to Covent Garden Market and slept under cover. There were about thirty of us. The police moved us

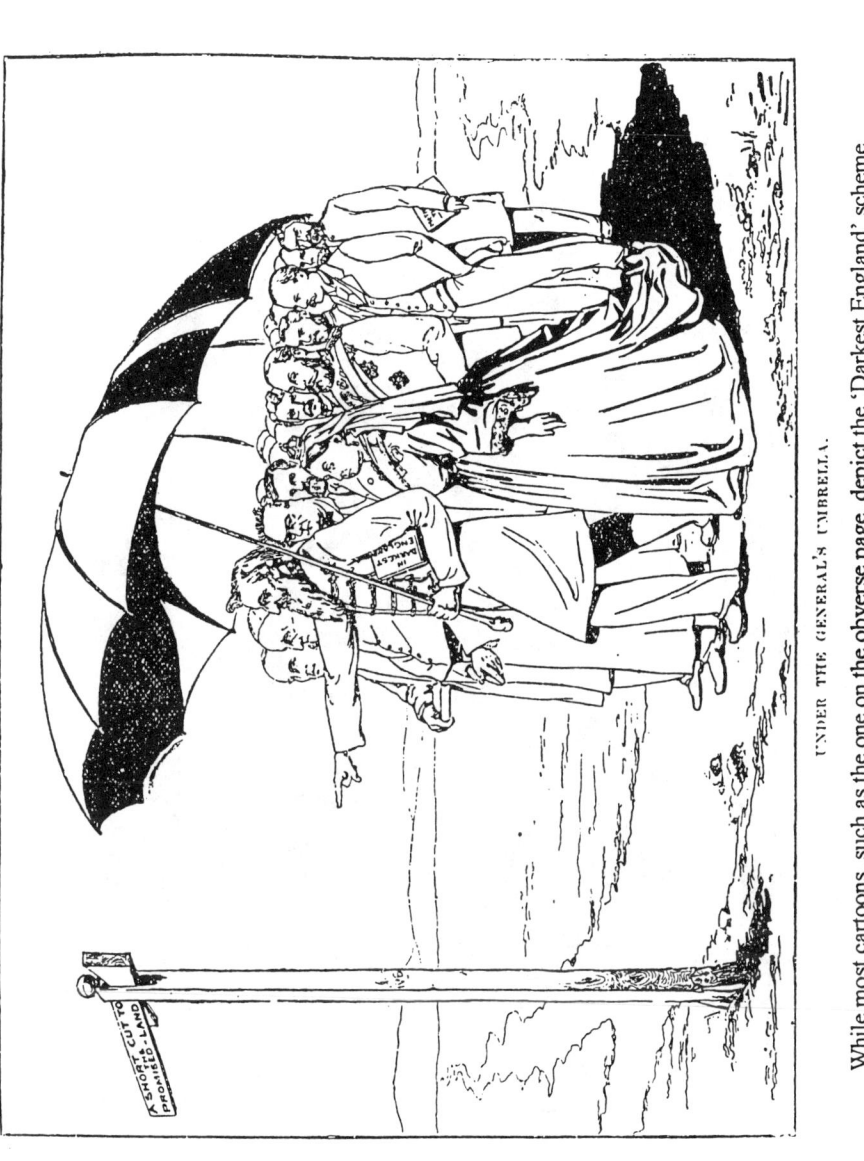

UNDER THE GENERAL'S UMBRELLA.

While most cartoons, such as the one on the obverse page, depict the 'Darkest England' scheme in an amusing or satirical manner, this one from the *Review of Reviews* quite seriously suggests that many high-ranking church officials and even royalty were under Booth's 'umbrella'.

[*Funny Folks.*]

THE FUTURE POLICE FORCE.

[September 27th.

'General Booth said he hoped to see the day when the police would be rendered unnecessary by the influence of the Salvation Army

on, but we went back as soon as they had gone. I've had a pen'orth of bread and pen'orth of soup during the last two days —often goes without altogether. There are women who sleep out here. They are decent people, mostly charwomen and such like who can't get work.'

and he surveyed the "dark and dismal jungle of pauperism, vice, and despair" in which wandered the "dis-homed multitude" —those caught in the net of vice and drunkenness, and the thousands of children abandoned to the streets and the workhouses.

Then came Booth's plan of 'Deliverance.' "For Darkest England, as for Darkest Africa, there is a light beyond. I think I see my way out, a way by which these wretched ones may escape from the gloom of their miserable existence into a higher and happier life." His scheme, simple and uncluttered, consisted of three geographical zones: a 'city colony,' a 'farm colony,' and an 'over-sea colony.' The first would involve "the establishment, in the very centre of the ocean of misery of which we have been speaking, of a number of institutions to act as Harbours of Refuge for all and any who have been shipwrecked in life, character, or circumstances." The institutions themselves would be, in addition to the shelters already in operation, factories, labour bureaus, and re-cycling depots. The 'farm colony' would take unemployed city-dwellers to country 'estates' where they could be both retrained and 'resuscitated in health and character.' When re-trained, they would be sent to an 'over-sea colony,' and with the aid of an Army emigration bureau, resettled in one of several British colonies. It was, Booth felt, a wholly practicable scheme and only awaited public support:

The sign for which I ask to embolden me to go forward is single, not double. It is necessary and not arbitrary, and it is one which the veriest sceptic or the most cynical materialist will recognize as sufficient. If I am to work out the Scheme I have outlined in this book, I must have ample means for doing so. How much would be required to establish this Plan of Campaign in all its fulness, overshadowing all the land with its branches laden with all manner of pleasant fruit, I cannot even venture to form a conception. But I have a definite idea as to how much would be required to set it fair in operation.

Why do I talk about commencing? . . . In this country we have been working on the verge of the deadly morass for some years gone by, and not without marvellous effect. We have our Shelters, our Labour Bureau, our Factory, our Inquiry Officers, our Rescue Homes, our Slum Sisters, and other kindred agencies, all in good working order. The sphere of these operations may be a limited one; still, what we have done already is ample proof that when I propose to do much more I am not speaking without my book; and though the sign I ask for may not be given, I shall go struggling forward on the same lines; still, to seriously take in hand the work which I have sketched out —to establish this triple Colony, with all its affiliated agencies, I must have, at least, *a hundred thousand pounds*.

Booth's 'Darkest England' scheme was soon a major topic of everyday conversation. There have, of course, been many better-written books than Booth's, and some which have been as daring in their social implications, but there have been few so widely-bought —as many as 200,000 in its first year— or so comprehensively discussed. From London to John o' Groats, from Toronto to Bombay, there was hardly a newspaper or magazine that did not have an opinion on the 'scheme,' its author and The Salvation Army:

Review of Reviews: The decision to employ the Salvation Army, with all its trained officers and disciplined soldiers, in a serious, practical attempt to deal with the question of unemployed labour and amelioration of conditions of life among the poor, is the most hopeful fact of our time. No one who reads General Booth's book can venture to assert that the Age of Faith has passed; and, while the Age of Faith remains, the Age of Miracles is still with us.

The Month: We believe that the same impulse which has given the Army its marvellous success may be successful in carrying into effect up to a certain point the scheme. But when we turn to the spiritual aspect of the question, and ask ourselves whether the work carried out by the Salvation Army can be one which of its own nature tends to the glory of God and the salvation of souls, we cannot speak with any confidence in its favour. On the contrary, we are reluctantly compelled to declare our conviction that, as its spirit does not seem to be from God, so it cannot really promote His work in the world. Hence we do not think that as Catholics we can favour the present scheme.

Blackwood's Magazine: Since Robert Owen's time, no Englishman has come forward with such a bold proposal, promising in its realisation —even in its partial success— so widespread and beneficial results; and the courage and self-confidence which have made General Booth stand to the front, are qualities that will stand him in good stead in the desperate struggle in which he proposes to engage. He may go down in the conflict, but the world will even then be the gainer, as it was in the case of Owen before him.

Saturday Review: Mr. Booth may, of course, plead that his scheme is so large and the need is so great. There is no denying either plea. But reasonable men do not ask, of a speculation, is it big; but, rather, will it work? This 'Darkest England' scheme is a great deal too big to be practicable, too complex to be worked under one head and centre, too cumbrous to be disciplined with the discipline of the Salvation Army.

Spectator: 'We suppose, from figures given elsewhere, that General Booth will get the money he asks —that is, £100,000 down and £30,000 a year so long as his experiment succeeds— and we heartily hope he may. The country is sick to death of the avalanche of words, printed and spoken, which now precedes —and buries— every project for the benefit of the lowest poor. It is time that an actual experiment should be made, and the founder of the Salvation Army is the man to do it. We cannot like either the religious teaching or the religious ritual of his new Church, but that dislike does not blind us to the fact that Mr. Booth has a genius for organization, that he understands the English lower class as hardly any religious teacher does, and that though his method requires much preaching, he uses preaching as a means of reforming, and not as an end in itself.

But, again, it was in the pages of *The Times* —a *Times* growing increasingly distrustful of the Army's motives— that 'Darkest England' received its most thoroughgoing scrutiny and where public debate on its merits raged fiercest. In many respects, it was a continuation of the 'Outcast London' debate and very much followed its pattern: *The Times* itself pretending to stay aloof, allowed one person, Professor T.H. Huxley, to shoulder the critical burden of the debate and selected the most cogent (and sometimes sensational) letters to keep it in full heat.

At first, in keeping with the gracious ending of the preceding debate, there was an overwhelming chorus of congratulation extended to William Booth. *The Times* itself, in an October 20 editorial, merely damned with faint praise; but, for the subsequent two weeks or more, almost every issue contained a favourable report and/or congratulatory letters. From Cardinal Manning, Mr. Gladstone, the Bishop of Durham, the Bishop of Manchester, Archdeacon Farrar, the Prince of Wales, and even Queen Victoria, they came —a typical one being from the noted actor, S.B. Bancroft:

> Sir,— I know nothing of General Booth's scheme in detail, but it seems to me to be so noble in its object that something real, soon and surely, should be done to aid it.
>
> I read that the large sum of £100,000 will be necessary to insure an effectual trial, and, without the smallest pretence to hang on to even the skirts of philanthropy, I beg to say that, if 99 other men will do the same for the cause, I will give General Booth £1,000 towards it.
>
> I am, Sir, your faithful servant,
>
> S.B. Bancroft

Without exaggeration, the whole of England (and much of the English-speaking world) was talking about Booth's 'scheme.' At one end of the social spectrum, Archdeacon Farrar, preaching at Westminster Abbey, declared it was every Churchman's duty to "support it with all their influence and every effort." In a circular to all the clergy he urged that General Booth should have "a fair and adequate trial" and that the churches should provide every opportunity for their people to help him achieve his financial goal. At the other end, London's Dockers' Union recorded its vote of thanks to General Booth for instituting "such a practical scheme of social amelioration" and pledged its wholehearted support.

Of course it could not last. By the middle of November, at which time Booth had collected or been pledged as much as £50,000, letters of criticism began to appear in *The Times*, side-by-side with, and in equal numbers to, those supportive of Booth's efforts. Mainly from high-ranking clergymen, they focussed on three central concerns: (1) that the Army's appeal was diverting funds from the established Church charities; (2) that Booth himself was to be the sole trustee of the monies collected; (3) and that the whole thing was but "an ingenious design to raise the wind for the Salvation Army." The Reverend Eyton made it clear that he 'looked askance' at a scheme which "depended on the authority of one man or the grotesque performances of the Salvation Army." In Mr. Herbert Henson's opinion, to support Booth's scheme was to "declare confidence in the methods of the Salvation Army" and it was incumbent on any "who resent the fantastic impertinences which vulgarize the whole religious atmosphere of Salvationism" [i.e. all "churchmen, Christians and social economists"], to "think once, and twice, and thrice before they give their support to this 'large' and 'bold' device of the Salvation Army." And so it continued, with often as many as three full columns an issue devoted to the 'Darkest England Scheme.' It was a clearly focussed, fair-minded and non-personal debate until Professor Thomas Henry Huxley suddenly, and with great animosity, entered it on December 1, 1890.

What prompted Huxley, the famous evolutionist and Darwinist, to 'attack' The Salvation Army is open to speculation.[2] The reason he cited in his first letter was simply that he was responding in a public forum to a question, put by a friend, as to whether or not he should contribute to Booth's fund. "He had taken one look at the Salvation Army, another at Booth's *In Darkest England and the Way Out* — and suddenly realized with horror that he had discovered a grave national danger. Enthusiastic religion with 'corybantic' rites was bad. Religious fanaticism with military organization was infinitely worse."[3] But, perhaps it was more deeply-rooted than that: Huxley had, after all, coined the term 'agnostic' (coincidentally, in the same year the Army was founded) to describe his personal philosophy, and was certainly not a friend of organized religion; now, in his cantankerous old age, he was an out-spoken opponent of religious socialism of the 'band-aid' kind. He had just emerged, bloodied but unbowed, from a long public debate with Mr. Gladstone over the Biblical story of the Gadarene pigs. Now he was ready for another, and The Salvation Army happened to be in the news and available for close scrutiny.

Whatever the reason, once in, Huxley was not easily dismissed —"Attacking the Salvation Army [he wrote to his son] may look like the advance of a forlorn hope, but this old dog has never yet let go after fixing his teeth into anything or anybody, and he is not going to begin now." He carried the debate with great vigour through eight long letters between December 1 and December 30, the first two or three of which contained reasonable advice and legitimate concerns, but thereafter degenerated into what can only be called a personal vendetta. Even Huxley, the great scholar, teacher and thinker, could, as some historians suggest, let principle deteriorate into prejudice. "His campaign," states William Irvine, "was neither spectacular nor successful. The letters, swift and brisk at first with the excitement of denunciation and historical discovery, soon stagnated among the muddy technicalities of allegation and counter-allegation."[4]

What Huxley objected to was not so much the purpose of Booth's social scheme as the fact that it was promulgated by a group of religious fanatics, whose blind allegiance to their leader could, like that of the Jesuits, lead to "the corrupt use of the political and social influence which their organization and their wealth secure." People who contributed to the fund would be "setting up and endowing a sect in many ways analogous to the 'Ranters' and 'Revivalists' of undeniable notoriety in former times, but with this immensely important difference, that it possesses a strong, far-reaching, centralized organization, the disposal of the physical, moral, and financial strength of which rests with an irresponsible chief, who, according to his own account, is assured of the blind obedience of nearly 10,000 subordinates. I wish them to ask themselves, Ought prudent men and good citizens to aid in the establishment of an organization which, under sundry, by no means improbable contingencies, may easily become a worse and more dangerous nuisance than the mendicant Friars of the middle ages?"

Perhaps Huxley might have let the matter drop had he not, as he later stated, received such a "swarm of letters and pamphlets" in response to his accusations. Some of them, among the many published in *The Times*, were sympathetic to his views; more were in disagreement; and a few, not caring much about the issue, were simply aimed at ridiculing Huxley (no doubt in continuation of some previous argument). Lord Meath, for example, thought Huxley's views somewhat far-fetched: "I am not aware, for example, that 'General' Booth imposes any vows upon his officers except those of obedience during a service which they can quit when it pleases them to do so. And in days of unlimited and rapid intercourse between all civilized peoples, of general education, of free thought, and of a free Press, the prospect held out to us of the intellect of a nation being put down by organized fanaticism must have been evolved, surely, in the cave of some 'Giant Despair' rather than in the study of one of the most enlightened of our intellectual chiefs." Others, like Robert Buchanan, zeroed in on the truth:

> Am I wrong in suggesting that now, as always, the pragmatic temperament and the anti-theological bias have far more to do with Professor Huxley's attitude than any real conversion to the individualism he has hated so cordially and so long? I may be wronging a saint *in posse*, but I cannot help believing that Professor Huxley would be far less shocked by the Salvation Army if it used the shibboleth of science in lieu of that of Christianity; if it were beating its tom-toms in the name of David Hume instead of that of Jesus of Nazareth. Your scientist will endure a good deal of noise, a great deal of fussy organization, when the object is secular and not religious (Dec. 9, 1890).

Mistakenly perhaps, Huxley responded to his critics by veering off his original course and concentrating on 'Boothism' as a 'dynastic tyranny' rather than on Booth's social scheme. "Mr. Booth has captured and harnessed, with sharp bits and effectual blinkers, a multitude of ultra-Evangelical missionaries of the revivalist school who were wandering at large. It is this skilfully, if somewhat mercilessly, driven team which has dragged the 'General's' coach-load of projects into their present position." And, what weakened his arguments most was his rather unscientific evidence: quotations and so-called 'facts' from such dissident publications as J.J.R. Redstone's *An Ex-Captain's Experience of the Salvation Army*, Arthur Sumner's *The New Papacy: Behind the Scenes in the Salvation Army*, and S.H. Hodges's *General Booth, 'the Family,' and the Salvation Army*. The now-familiar charges of despotism, sectarianism, nepotism, and of 'starving the workers' to build an empire, were all trotted out and presented as coming from Huxley's own observations. It was, as many commentators pointed out, an argument in which egotism outweighed judgment. And, most surprising of all, *The Times* itself (i.e. its editor) fell into the trap, claiming that Huxley's deductions were "justified by facts"; that he had not confined himself to inference but had 'fortified' his arguments with the "testimony of men familiar with the internal economy of the Salvation Army" (Dec. 20, 1890). Even after it was proven that some of the 'testimony' was, if not false at least very suspect, *The Times* refused to retract or relent. It too had now become an implacable enemy of The Salvation Army.

By late December, 1890, the Huxley debate was becoming a rather tiresome affair, and very messy. It was, as one commentator said of an earlier debate, beginning to die of its own grotesqueness. Most writers now seemed more interested in discussing a "pre- versus a post-Darwinian sociology." When, in the midst of it all, the head of Booth's social wing, Commissioner Frank Smith suddenly resigned, the controversy took a new turn.[5] Sandwiched in between the Huxley commentaries were letters from and about Smith, sometimes relevant to the 'Darkest England' scheme and sometimes not. To most readers it must have been bewildering, and *The Times* was beginning to wonder how many of them were still genuinely interested in the debate. Was it a common opinion, as one journalist stated, that its pages were simply too full of 'Booth's Army'; and was it true, as Cardinal Manning suggested, that readers were simply by-passing the debate? "I have not the patience to read Professor Huxley's letters," wrote the Cardinal. "The existence of hunger, nakedness, misery, 'death from insufficient food,' even of starvation, is certain, and no agency as yet reaches it. How can any man hinder or discourage the giving of food or help?"

Sensing that the issue was no longer good copy, *The Times* decided to bring its coverage to an end by doing two things. It commissioned a 'special correspondent' to write three articles on "In Darkest England" and published them between December 27, 1890 and January 8, 1891. Not surprisingly, the writer's conclusions were quite negative: "Mr. Booth, surrounded by his family and his connexions, unable to retain the services of his most able supporters [a reference to the resignation of Frank Smith], and resolutely maintaining the position of an autocrat, has not completely established his claim to be the recipient of a vast sum of public money." It brought its letter debate to a conclusion —rather to an inconclusion— on January 2, 1891, by devoting a full page and a half to the 'Darkest England' scheme, adding nothing new to the public's awareness, but mainly re-hashing all the old criticisms. Thereafter *The Times* resumed its aloofness, according the Army normal journalistic courtesies —reports on major events and newsworthy activities— but refraining from a major coverage until 1929 when the 'Bramwell Booth affair' again brought The Salvation Army into its pages as conspicuously as had the 'Darkest England' scheme.

To sum up. Between 1878 and 1892 *The Times* of London, widely read and very influential among the upper-classes, did more to promote The Salvation Army, in an unintentional way, than any other newspaper —perhaps even more successfully than did William Booth's own flamboyant methods. For, as he often reflected (in amusement): think how much such publicity would have cost —at advertisement rates. In the early years, when its editors were disposed to treat the Army kindly in their editorials, the promotion was rather explicit and much appreciated by the Booths. In later years, when highly critical of the Army's methodology, the promotion was, ironically, even more to the Army's liking, especially when the Army's opponents allowed Professor Huxley to carry their banner. Though a highly-respected scholar, Huxley was not a popular person and his agnosticism and evolutionary theories were still not widely shared. Whom Huxley attacked, the public often supported. As Bramwell Booth later stated: "People wrote to us from all parts of the country saying. . . that they regarded it as a great proof of the rightness of what we were doing or proposing to do, that a man like Huxley should oppose us."[6] By January 30, 1891, just four months after the 'Darkest England' scheme was launched, the public had subscribed and promised £102,000, and Booth's social wing was firmly established.

But not exactly as he had planned it in his manifesto. For what *The Times* debate did, more than anything else, was to provide some very wise cautions and much practical advice which, though never explicitly acknowledged, resulted in a more practicable, less grandiose, social-reclamation policy. The 'panacea' —the universal remedy— that Booth envisaged, and pretty well outlined in his book, was not only an impossible dream but was too vast for one man, even with hundreds of dedicated followers, to undertake. Many of the poor, his critics insisted, would not wish to be helped; and still others could not be reformed. More realistic, they argued, were the particulars of the scheme —the rescue homes, the night shelters, the food depots, the labour yards. And, though Booth did venture into such social ventures as poor man's insurance, poor man's bank and poor man's legal services, it would be the more practical services for destitutes, rather than those for the poor, that would form the nucleus of his social wing. And, similarly, though his farm colony and emigration bureau became viable enterprises, they never amounted to the grand 'farm' and 'overseas' colonies that Booth had dreamt of.

From *The Times* debate William Booth no doubt learned a great deal about public relations, and especially about accountability of public funds. At first seemingly intent on merely collecting and controlling the funds himself, eventually, as a gesture of good faith, Booth allowed a public committee to undertake a scrutiny of both their intake and output. Through it all he gained invaluable experience in newspaper diplomacy, finding out just how valuable an ally a journalist could be but also just how fickle the newspaper's attentions. There would be many times in the future when such lessons would be worth remembering.

Ballington Booth's American Revolution: Bowing to Public Pressure

newspaper journalism

That the Fourth Estate has been, and still is, one of the most powerful influences in society is as much a truism as any. In most cases, of course, the exact nature and extent of the influence is problematic; just how much, and in what way, the T.H. Huxley letters in the London _Times_ affected William Booth's social program is a matter of some debate. In some instances, however, newspaper commentary proceeds in such a manner and coincides so neatly with an obvious political mood that one can say with certainty that the course of events was largely determined by the public debate. We saw, for example, with what determination the Toronto _News_ used Salvation Army troubles in the 1880s to promote its own nationalistic aims. And it was clear that the newspaper considerably influenced both the shape and outcome of the 'Philpott Affair.' Another such event, of wider significance in the overall history of The Salvation Army, was the 'Ballington Booth affair' in the United States in 1896. What might have been an organizational dispute was transformed by journalists, partly for political reasons, into a matter of national pride. And what might have resulted merely in a resignation (if even that) turned into an open rebellion and ultimately a schism within the Army's ranks.

In January of 1896, with his Salvation Army firmly established in England and making excellent progress overseas, William Booth once again, as he so often had before, turned his attention to 'appointments' —trying to infuse into his many territories new ideas and fresh vigour by circulating his most competent commanders. It was, to use the jargon, a means of 'keeping the pot boiling'; his commanders practised it in their territories —sometimes moving officers as often as every six months— and Booth himself applied the same principle on a more universal scale.

Except in one instance. In the United States, William Booth had allowed his second son, Ballington (and his wife, Maud), to stay in charge for nine years. In many ways, this had been a wise decision: the work had prospered and been consolidated under an able and uninterrupted leadership. In others, it had been a mistake: Ballington and Maud had, contrary to Army policy and the General's wishes, become thoroughly Americanized, even to the point of taking out American citizenship; they also had, as far as possible, 'Americanized' the Army and had made known their desire never to leave the United States.

It is, therefore, understandable that Ballington Booth should have been unwilling to relinquish command of the United States territory. And when one understands, with the hindsight of history, that Ballington was already becoming disenchanted with 'the system' which fostered nepotism and autocracy, one can fairly describe his resignation as 'inevitable.' As private letters attest, there were personal dissatisfactions, aggravated by an officious bureaucracy, which caused Ballington Booth grave concern. Some of these reasons, only slight at first, were exacerbated by General Booth's inflexibility (who felt that the American branch was slipping from his grasp) and the seeming officiousness of his Chief of Staff, his eldest son, Bramwell.

By the same token, one must also see William Booth's intransigence —his refusal to alter his 'marching orders'— as inevitable, for how could he make a concession in his son's favour when he had already sent the same orders to sixteen other commanders? "To have recognized the demands of nationalism in the case of the United States and Ballington Booth," writes Herbert Wisbey, "would have seriously weakened and perhaps destroyed the General's vision of a truly international organization.... with one faith, one aim, one flag, and one General."[1] That much seems certain.

What seems less inevitable, however, were the subsequent events: the major 'schism' in which hundreds of soldiers and officers (mainly

American) allied themselves with the Ballington Booths and, eventually, the formation of a new organization, called The Volunteers of America. Those actions were made to **look** inevitable because that was how the American public, represented by its newspapers and organized in mass meetings, wanted the various decisions to seem. And the public worked hard to ensure that these outcomes became 'inevitable.'

This hypothesis is not only supported by an analysis of the public's influence, as demonstrated in both newspaper reports and mass demonstrations, but by certain discerning commentators at the time. In *Scribner's Magazine*, for example, the influence of public agencies in the whole affair was clearly recognized:

Out of the many public absurdities and follies which the year 1896 has to answer for, there is none more gratuitous than the interference of —perhaps well-meaning— outsiders in the disagreements of the Booth family which led to a withdrawal of the American commanders. As a matter of fact, the details and merits of the disruption were purely the property of the Salvationists; but there was the most unblushing appropriation of a popular censorship, and the seceding elements were fairly egged on against their army superiors. The Salvation Army never suffered so vitally in its thirty years of rowdy assaults and universal jeering as from the meddlesome zeal which has exposed its unsightly trouble, with the usual distorting, to the people who were rapidly learning to reverence its work. It would have been a fine and inspiring accompaniment to that work, and a fitting climax to the record of self-sacrifice, if the dissenting American element had obeyed orders and humbly continued its work. Certainly General Booth's achievements have made it worth while to swallow incidental objections for the sake of decency and the future of the whole army. If the temptation to lose this great opportunity has proved too strong, it is largely due to the uncalled-for participation of people the majority of whom have given nothing to the Salvation Army except scorn and ridicule in its weaker days (May 1896: 657-58).

It is probably true that *Scribner's* was referring to the public meetings in support of the Ballington Booths, organized by some of New York's leading citizens; but it was also no doubt cognizant of the part played by the *New York Times* in the whole affair. A leading instigator of subsequent events, the *Times*, from the commencement of its coverage, on January 15, 1896, proceeded to sensationalize and falsify the impact of General Booth's 'farewell orders' and to typify them as an anti-American plot. The New York Headquarters, it reported, had experienced a "shock of a most unexpected and startling character" and "a panic has already set in. . . . The founder of the army, Gen. Booth, on his recent visit to this country, was not favorably impressed with American institutions, it is said, and this action on his part is looked upon as an indication of his determination to re-Anglicize the movement." It did not seem to impress the *Times* at all that Ballington Booth categorically denied the accuracy of that report, and stated emphatically that he was in no way responsible for the statements in its pages:

> They [Ballington and Maud Booth] have not seen a representative of the press, nor have they instigated any matter that has appeared in the press, nor are they inclined to see press representatives. They are sorry that any such sentiment as London's resolution to Anglicize the field should have appeared, and desire that officers will correct any such representation. . . . In the meantime it is the Commander and Mrs. Booth's fervent prayer that no officer of any rank, or soldier, or a recruit of any corps shall allow these tidings to interfere with the progress of their own advancement in the organization they have fought so long and so hard to upbuild and uphold. The Commander and Mrs. Booth will proceed with arrangements to farewell, as soon as they hear from London, but they will always regard their precious American troops with tenderness, affection, and undying interest (Jan. 16, 1896).

Such affirmations, however, did little to quell the revolutionary spirit of the New York *Times*. It continued to push for a revolt within the Army. Its editor expressed almost a childish disappointment that the Ballington Booths seemed to be submitting to the 'military discipline' of the Army and felt it would be a disappointment to all 'natural' men that "so fine an opportunity for an interesting and exciting rebellion has been allowed to go to waste. Here are all the makings of the prettiest quarrel that could be imagined, . . and nothing is to come from the situation except a job for the owners of moving vans!" (Jan. 21, 1896). And when prominent citizens of New York, perhaps taking their cue from the *Times*, decided to force the issue, they were applauded for upholding democracy against the incursion of military absolutism: "Secret and stealthy conspirators have been meeting in the study of Miss Grace H. Dodge, in this city, since the recall was issued, and have prepared for a great mass meeting, which is to be held the night of Feb. 3 at Carnegie Music Hall. . . . So there is to be a commotion about the departure of Ballington Booth, after all."

The extent to which the whole affair was becoming publicly controlled —leading towards a conclusion not initially anticipated by the Booths— was the fact that these meetings in their behalf were carried out without their sanction: "Commander and Mrs. Ballington Booth know nothing of this attempt to appeal to Gen. William Booth. So secret have been the preparations that only a few friends of the Booths were let into the plot, for fear that if the Commander learned of it he would issue an order forbidding the army from taking any part in it" (Jan. 25, 1896). Involved were many leading citizens —Dr. Lyman Abbott, Dr. Chauncey Depew, Mayor Strong, W.D. Howells, and Mrs. Grover Cleveland— aided by some officers at headquarters who were "working for it in secret" (though none would "appear officially at the meeting").

On the night of February 3, 1896, Carnegie Hall was crowded. Not a seat in the boxes or the gallery was empty. Praises of the Ballington Booths poured forth and, when reported by the press, they could not but assure the Commandant that it was he, and not The Salvation Army, who would be supported by the American public. The general sentiment of support was expressed succinctly by New York's Mayor Strong: "I believe that Commander and Mrs. Ballington Booth can do more good here in this country than in any other country on the face of the earth. I come here tonight with whatever dignity there is in the Mayor's office to protest against this recall." And the spirit of rebellion was voiced by the meeting's chair, Dr. Chauncey Depew, when he stated that "we have a habit of our expressing our own views, regardless of what London may think [and] the infant over here is large and alive and liable to kick."

And yet, even though public pressure was forcing a crisis, throughout January the Ballington Booths adamantly refused to be drawn into the quarrel; they would, they insisted, comply with the General's orders and be ready to leave by April 9. The *Times* quite naturally lamented their docility but acknowledged their loyalty: "Ballington Booth and his wife, by their submission to orders from headquarters, of whose unwisdom they must be convinced, are giving evidence that not in name alone, but in its discipline as well, is the military character of the Salvation Army illustrated. Of course, the matter is one to be settled by themselves, and if they have decided that the best use to which their right of private judgment can be put is not to exercise that judgment at all, there is nothing more to be said" (Jan. 21, 1896).

What the *Times* did not know, nor did the Ballington Booth's make public, was the fact that, though they would not cause a public rift in the Army's ranks and would return to England, they would not assume another appointment in the organization. This resolve had been conveyed to the General in a letter written by them on January 31. Their only request was that no member of the family should be sent to try and dissuade them. "It must not be said at any time that we left the Army because we were unwilling to leave America. This would be untrue as we have made no remonstrance, nor have we refused. . . . We have not taken advantage of the confidence of the troops and the public and retained this command, though, undoubtedly, many would have thought it the wisest for the country and the Army here."[2]

To the first wave of public pressure, then, the Ballington Booths, though no doubt heartened by the overwhelming support, seemed impervious. Had their London counterparts —particularly Bramwell Booth— remained as impervious, the whole affair might not have resulted in a major schism. But they did not. Responding as much to American criticism (and the fear of revolt) as to Ballington's letter, the ever-officious Bramwell Booth, then in charge while his father toured India, immediately dispatched Colonel Alex Nicol with an ultimatum —return to London immediately or face dismissal. Not confident of Nicol's effort, he shortly thereafter dispatched Ballington's younger sister, Evangeline, and finally his brother, Herbert. Such unwarranted interference not only exasperated the Ballington Booths but encouraged the American public, through its newspapers, to indulge in new rumours and speculative dramatics. Casting Herbert Booth as the villain and Ballington as the hero, the *New York Times* again sought to arouse the public to a sense of injustice:

'You know,' said Herbert Booth, 'that insubordination means dismissal.'

'I am aware of that fact,' said the Commander, 'and I accept the order as a notice of dismissal' (Feb. 22)

Ballington Booth was being removed, the *Times* declared, simply because he had "succeeded in almost completely Americanizing the Salvation Army in this country. His methods aroused the antagonism of a little English coterie, headed by Col. Eadie, the Chief Secretary, who came over from England one year ago. The General did not fancy that idea of the Army in America breaking away from the English precedents, and was finally prevailed upon to order the withdrawal of Ballington Booth." Nor was it, the *Times* continued, a secret that Herbert Booth had "for a long time coveted the position held by his younger brother, and it is not a surprise to Salvationists to know that he has practically succeeded his brother." There would be, the newspaper asserted (quoting what it claimed to be a Salvationist statement), "a declaration of independence. . . resulting in a reinstatement of the commander as the head of an independent American Salvation Army" (F 22).[3]

As yet, however, this did not seem to the Ballington Booths a preferred option; at least not if we can judge by their public resignation statement:

It is with inexpressible grief and heartfelt pain that we have to announce to our staff officers, field officers, troops, and friends throughout America the following important decision arrived at after protracted thought and careful deliberation. We beg that they will now and ever bear in remembrance that we feel there is no alternative left to our discretion.

First, we do not seek, nor shall we seek, to take any advantage of the strong feeling respecting our 'farewell,' existing in all parts of the country by attempting to sever the United States branch of the army from the parent organization as a separate or 'independent' movement.

Second— Despite our intense and undying love for America and our comrades here, we should have had no other thought or purpose than that of proceeding to England for another command, were we able to do so. But owing to conscientious feelings and private reasons well known to the General, we are unable to enter upon new duties and controversies in connection with a foreign command. . . . This does not mean that we will no longer be Salvationists, nor that we shall be any other than the warmest friends of our comrades throughout the world.

Third— We therefore proposed as wisely and as expeditiously as possible to relinquish and hand over our command, fully and absolutely to the incoming Commissioners when they arrived.

London Headquarters, however, sent over three separate representatives unannounced, (we grant at sacrifice and cost) who pressed us to an immediate decision, offering us proposals we could not accept. Yesterday, at midnight, with most positive and uncalled for precipitation, with the authority of International Headquarters, Commissioner Herbert Booth demanded that we hand over our keys and offices by 10 o'clock this morning. We had, therefore, no alternative but to accept our peremptory dismissal.

Fourth— None can fully comprehend what this step has cost us. The blade of disappointment has gone deep! The struggle and suffering have been long. We have sought not to be hasty in this matter, but the International Headquarters have pressed us hourly to a definite decision. In relinquishing our command, we are giving up all, nor have we any plans or prospects for this emergency.

Fifth— Finally, we know full well that by some persons, untrue and unjust motives will be attached to our action, but we feel consoled in the fact that those who have witnessed our lives, together with our toil and effort during the past nine years, at least, will give us credit for acting conscientiously and disinterestedly, and for doing right before the Lord of our hearts.

We have repeatedly called upon all our troops to stand by the army, its General, and its principles. We do so again. May God's blessing rest upon our country, the army, and all (*Times*, Feb. 22).

The whole affair had reached a point, however, where private resolve was becoming powerless in the face of public pressure. That pressure was already being responded to by officers in the ranks who were translating it into action among the soldiers. Rifts were beginning to show, some Corps were on the verge of seceding, and the *New York Times* was not slow to encourage them.

In fact, when it came to reporting Ballington Booth's second-last visit to his headquarters, on February 23, the *Times* infused as much melodrama as possible into the affair. Read today, its tone is one of high comedy, but to contemporary readers (especially to weakened Salvationists) it must have been a moment of high drama, one which made their popular leader look like a deposed monarch trying to hold on to power. On the evening in question, while a Sunday meeting was in progress at the Army's headquarters on West Fourteenth Street, Ballington Booth arrived quite unexpectedly, called together his staunchest supporters, and declared (according to the *Times*) that he

would not "relinquish command of the army in the United States."
The *Times*, rejoicing to think that this, at last, was Ballington Booth's
decision to "reorganize the army in this country on an independent
basis," went on to describe the purported *coup* in this fashion:

Commander Booth's arrival at headquarters was entirely unexpected,
and took the opposition by surprise. The regular Sunday evening
meeting was in progress, and the large hall was well crowded. Early in
the evening a spirit of insubordination was manifested by several
members of the corps, who refused to don their uniforms and join the
corps inside. They retained their citizen's dress, and stood on the
sidewalk in front of the building. One of these was Major Glenn, who
is Commander Booth's most intimate lieutenant.

Major Glenn stood near the curb, watching the horse cars. A few
moments past nine o'clock a tall, slender man, with a prominent nose
and long hair, and enveloped in a long army overcoat, sprang from a
blue-line car going westward. He was instantly recognized as
Commander Booth, and in a moment a cheering crowd surrounded him.
With him was his lawyer, Mr. Alexander. Followed by Major Glenn,
they hurried into the building and rushed into the elevator, which
carried them up to the fourth floor, where the Commander's private
office is situated. As quickly as possible they entered the office, and the
door was locked and barred against intruders.

Commander Booth looked excited as he hurried inside. He held an
open manuscript which he seemed anxious to read to his friends.
Messengers were dispatched to various officers scattered through the
building, and in a short time about thirty were closeted with the
Commander. Among them were Brigadier Evans and Fielding of
Chicago, Major Stilwell of Michigan, Major Glenn, Staff-Captain
Crafts, Major Marshall, and Ensign Taylor. When all were seated,
Commander Booth rose and addressed them.

He had spoken but a moment when he was interrupted with a burst of
applause, and similar demonstrations were repeated during his speech.
Members of the staff then expressed their views, and messengers were
sent for Cols. Nicol and Eadie. They responded, but did not relish the
idea of meeting Commander Booth just then, and they did not remain
in the room long. It was shortly after they retired from the Commander's
presence that the message announcing the appointment of Ballington
Booth's successor [Commander and Mrs. F. de la Tour Booth-Tucker]
was received. It was handed to Col. Eadie, who immediately regained
his spirits, rushed to the council chamber, and delivered it. It was

received in silence, and he left the room, smiling. Then Commander Booth told his hearers that he did not believe the message was authentic, and he would not consider it of any account until it was verified. This aroused enthusiasm, and he was cheered again and again....

Commander Booth remained with his officers until 11 o'clock. The elevator was ordered to the floor, and when it was in readiness the room door was opened and Commander Booth and his friends made a rush for it. They were hurried to the ground floor, where another rush was made for the street. A carriage was waiting for the Commander and he sprang into it.

A great crowd was gathered to see him leave the building, and it followed him, shouting and cheering, as he was driven away. At Sixth Avenue the carriage was driven to the sidewalk. Commander Booth leaped from it and ran up the steps to the elevated railway station. A policeman, seeing the crowd pursuing him and shouting, thought he was someone trying to escape capture, and followed him up the steps. Commander Booth jumped on a train that was pulling out just as the policeman got to the ticket box, and so failed to catch the Commander.

The gospel meeting was cut short because of the arrival of Commander Booth at headquarters and the fear that if the audience learned that he was in the building a demonstration would be made. Col. Nicol was to have led the exercises, but while passing through the corridors he was hissed by a number of outsiders, and he had reason to believe that he would be received on the platform with manifestations of hostility. So his chair on the platform remained vacant.

Several messages were sent to officers of the army on the platform during the meeting, and the audience could see that something unusual was going on, but it was not told that Commander Booth was in the headquarters. Shortly after his arrival the meeting was brought to a close and the lights were turned out.

On the following day, Monday, February 24, a similar scene was enacted at the New York headquarters, with a similar expectation that Ballington Booth would "lead a revolt if he were assured of sufficient support."

This hope inspired his friends among the staff officers to call a meeting for 10 o'clock yesterday to consider the situation. Commander Booth and Mrs. Booth arrived about 9 o'clock, and the Commander summoned Brigadier Perry, who has charge of the Land Department, to deliver to him all the deeds of property in his possession. Brigadier Perry refused to receive them, and Commander Booth sent for his lawyer, Robert C. Alexander, who soon persuaded the Brigadier to obey orders. Commander Booth next ordered the destruction of a great number of type-written circulars attacking him. These circulars Col. Nicol and Col. Eadie had prepared the night before.

Commander and Mrs. Booth then attended the meeting of division officers and others, which was held in their private office. Some of those present were Brigadiers Richard Evans of the Central Division, William Evans of the Atlantic Coast, Fielding of the Northwestern District, Brewer of the New-England District, and Holz of New York State. Brigadiers Keppel of the Pacific coast, Sully of the Southwestern, and French of the Midland Divisions, were absent. While they were discussing affairs, Cols. Nicol and Eadie, who had not been invited to the meeting, asked for admittance, and explained that Commissioner Eva Booth desired to make a statement. Permission was given for her to appear, and Col. Nicol went down stairs and escorted her into the room.

Miss Booth was weeping and seemed greatly agitated. She was informed that she could speak fifteen minutes, and at the expiration of her time she was told that she would have the opportunity to finish her remarks in the small meeting room on the ground floor, to which place the officers would adjourn. Commander and Mrs. Booth then resumed their conference with their officers.

It was past noon when the meeting broke up, and many then went below to the hall, which was well filled. Brigadier William Evans presided over the meeting, and said that, as the American Salvation Army was bound sooner or later to be independent of the English organization, he moved that the Field Staff offer the Generalship to Commander and Mrs. Ballington Booth, whose work had built up the army in the United States.

The motion was greeted with applause, and Brigadier Fielding seconded it. Brigadier Bown also seconded it, and said she would stick to the Army, whether it became independent or remained a branch organization.

Commander Eva Booth advanced to the front of the platform and made a plea for the Army to remain loyal to Gen. Booth.

'You have all met my father, our dear General,' she said, with emotion.

'Yes,' interrupted Adjutant Caygill, who sat in a front seat, 'unfortunately, we have met him.'

Eva Booth was too shocked to reply. She took up the argument in another direction.

Brigadier William Evans went out, and in a few moments returned with Commissioner and Mrs. Booth. As soon as they were seen inside the door nearly everybody in the room rose and cheered enthusiastically, waving hats and handkerchiefs. Miss Booth stopped speaking, and Commander Booth took the floor and made a vigorous address. He said his younger brother, Commandant Herbert Booth, was the cause of the whole trouble. Commander and Mrs. Booth retired to their offices, and the meeting was soon adjourned, the officers going up stairs. There Commander and Mrs. Booth notified them that they would not question the authority of their dismissal, but would quietly withdraw.

At this juncture, however, 'quiet withdrawal' was impossible. Ministers of other denominations were now preaching on the topic, trying to persuade Ballington Booth to start a new organization. As the Reverend Dr. Scudder, pastor of the Congregational Tabernacle suggested: "[The Booths] are too useful to be idle. They understand our people, and have their confidence, affection, and support. Why, then, we ask, do they not organize a new and distinctly American army? Why should not Commander Ballington Booth become Gen. Booth from this time on? Hundreds of thousands would like to see him occupy that position, for he is a naturalized citizen, has demonstrated his ability as a leader, and will certainly be upheld by the American people."

More significantly, the public agitation was beginning to infect the Army's rank and file: tempers were becoming frayed (as the case of Adjutant Caygill demonstrates), rumours of secession were flying, many soldiers were wearing a new badge with the portraits of Commanders Maud and Ballington Booth as both a show of loyalty and of defiance, and some were talking openly of revolt:

A Staff-Captain talked freely with a reporter for The Times. He followed the reporter out of the headquarters building and walked up Sixth Avenue. Then, not without sundry backward glances of apprehension, he tried to throw some light on the situation. . . . 'Every man, woman, boy, and girl in the army loves Commander Booth and Mrs. Booth. They are honest and true, and we are devoted to them. If they should decide to organize the army independently of the home organization, we would all stand by them. I don't know of anyone who would desert them. No man or woman can take their place at the head of the army in the United States and hold it together as they have done. Not only is the army behind them at this time, but thousands of influential men and women throughout the country are too. If they would but give the signal the entire army would declare its independence of the home organization in England and follow Commander and Mrs. Booth.

An exaggerated claim, perhaps. But no one, not even Ballington Booth, could deny the tidal wave of support which was dictating only one decision: the formation of a new evangelical organization, perhaps modelled on The Salvation Army and thereby attracting many of its disaffected members. On March 1, therefore, Ballington Booth acceded to the wishes of an importunate public:

> Mrs. Booth and myself have received hundreds of telegrams and letters from responsible men and women, asking us to assume the leadership of an independent evangelical movement. They offer us all the money necessary for expenses, and leave to us the plan of operation, the scope of organization, and the methods of work.
> We shall not start an independent Salvation Army, but will devote our lives to the work of evangelizing America. I am not prepared to give any idea of our plans, but they will be on the grand lines, in concurrence and in sympathy with American principles, and in sympathy with the citizens of this great Republic.

It would be some time before the Volunteers of America was officially launched, but the decision had been firmly made and already the internecine fighting had begun. Commander Booth, the *Times* suggested, had only to "give signal and a large portion of the army will leave its ranks and support him in a new movement." And, for the next few weeks, the newspaper took delight in announcing the resignation of officers, the defection of some soldiers at the Bowery Corps, the 'open revolt' of the corps at Seacliff, Long Island, the slanders being spread by both sides, and the resignation of members of the Auxiliary League: "Frank Harris, Secretary of the Orange, N.J., Auxiliary League, sent his resignation to Staff Captain Edith Marshall yesterday. He wrote that he would never contribute another cent to the Salvation Army. His letter did not brighten the outlook for the army, for similar decisions have been announced by other members of the Auxiliary League." It all seemed, in fact, very much like a mock-serious comedy, as *The Catholic Mirror* of Baltimore thought it might be:

> The wrangling in the Salvation Army among the 'Generals' and 'Colonels,' male and female, and the various 'orders' and 'manifestoes' from different persons in authority, who appear to have no authority, have excited a good deal of amusement during the past week, and remind one of broad stage burlesque. The whole thing, in fact, with some comic lines and a topical song or two, and a little marching and dancing, would make a capital subject for a piece at one of the minor theatres, and in this spirit the incident has been received by the readers of newspapers. The editors, who like something to enliven their columns in the present universal dulness of politics, have given a good deal of space to the Salvationists, and the public has been let into a knowledge of the workings of the 'Army' more definite than it would, perhaps, have had at a period when there were more serious matters to claim attention.[4]

True or not, the *New York Times* continued its melodramatic coverage almost daily, following not only the movements of the Ballington Booths but of their sister Evangeline who was valiantly striving to secure the allegiance of those who had not yet defected. Temporarily in charge until the new leaders, Commanders Frederick and Emma Booth-Tucker, arrived, she spoke to large audiences at Cooper Union, New York, and Newark, New Jersey:

> Amid a storm of hisses, partially counteracted by cheers from several hundred Salvation Army soldiers, and the playing of the 'Star-Spangled Banner' by a brass band, Miss Eva Booth, the temporary commander, made her first appearance before a New York audience in Cooper Union last evening. The hisses were repeated again and again, and each time the band played the Salvationists cheered and Miss Booth, standing in the middle of the platform, smiled while those about her whispered to her to keep up her courage.
>
> It was trying ordeal. The audience seemed, after a while, to appreciate the pluck of the frail young woman and desisted from hostile demonstrations, but not once during the evening did it manifest any evidence of friendship for her.
>
> The great hall never held a larger audience. When the doors were opened at 7:35 o'clock the streets around the building were blocked with crowds that clamored for admission. Fifteen minutes later every

seat in the auditorium was taken. Rear spaces around the hall were packed, and the police were compelled to refuse to let anyone else inside the entrances. Many hundreds were turned away....

When Miss Booth was recognized a tempest of hisses swept across the hall. The musicians seemed astonished and stopped playing, and the hisses became stronger.

'Play! Play!' shouted Ensign March to the band, and again 'The Star-Spangled Banner' was given. The audience hissed, the soldiers cheered, and the tambourines kept time with the band.

Miss Booth looked appealingly to her friends and her chin quavered. Col. Nichol whispered to her, and she faced the hissing audience, and bowing to the right and left smiled, as bravely as she could. Still the crowd hissed, and again the soldiers cheered and fluttered their handkerchiefs (March 2).

In Newark, New Jersey, the reception for the 'establishment' was very similar. The two thousand people who crowded into the Washington Street citadel were again divided in their allegiance as evidenced by the "mingling of cheers and hisses."

As Miss Booth rose there was a scene of great confusion. Hisses greeted her from every section of the big citadel. Some of her followers seated on the platform rose and waved their hands to the audience.

A pleading looked posed on the face of Miss Booth as she lifted the Bible which she carried in one hand and gently swayed an American flag in the other hand.

'Don't disgrace the American flag!' she shouted, as the noise became deafening.

This appeal to the patriotism of the assemblage had a good effect. A portion of the audience waved their handkerchiefs and cheered loudly, completely drowning the hisses (March 2)..

And, like those audiences, the American press seemed also divided in its assessment of the situation, though sympathy for the Ballington Booths (or at least anger against the autocratic control of William Booth) seemed to dominate the commentaries.

The Outlook: Loyalty doubtless required that all the members of the Salvation Army should accept with unquestioning obedience the orders of their Commander-in-Chief, but it does not require that the general public should do so, and it must be frankly said that this recall has administered a severe blow to the public confidence which Commander and Mrs. Booth had won for the Salvation Army by their consecrated zeal and practical wisdom.

The Mid-Continent (Philadelphia): One-man powers always have serious weaknesses. It is in the very Booth monarchy that we have for years foreseen possible future danger in this band of Christian workers, which in spite of crudities and some serious faults in their attitudes toward the sacred ceremonies of the Lord's Supper and baptism, have become a sturdy army in the cause of Christ.

The Episcopal Recorder: Without attempting to judge of the merits of the case, and while admitting that Mr. and Mrs. Booth have felt wounded and hurt, we yet deplore their hasty action. A resignation should never be tendered hastily or under trial. Self-respect, personal dignity, consistency, and, above all, the well-being of the cause of Christ they have at heart, should absolutely prohibit persistence in action now.

The Christian Observer: Ballington Booth has many friends here [Louisville], and may have a large following. Of course we all recognize the original error in introducing a monarchial and despotic element into the government of this branch of the church. Out of this grows rupture.

The Commercial (Buffalo): Ballington Booth has become an American citizen. He wants to live here and bring up his children as Americans. He and his wife have won universal respect and popularity here. Naturally they shrink from tearing up all these associations by the roots and moving at what some of our exchanges call the 'tyrannical and arbitrary whim' of the general, who is said to be jealous of his son's success and authority. All this is intelligible, but it does not justify Ballington Booth's refusal to obey his orders. If without question he can not do that, he does well to resign. If he and his wife are the unselfish and devoted persons they have been supposed to be they will not listen to the voice of the tempter that comes to them in the form mainly of newspaper suggestions that they start a rival and warring American Salvation Army.

The Chronicle (Chicago): Organization involves obedience, for without obedience organization is impossible. Into the thoroughly efficient but unfortunately non-permanent organization known as the Salvation Army, insubordination has entered, and we may look for the beginning of the end. The Commander of the Army in this country indulged himself, defied authority, thought more of the things of this world than of the reward which he had pictured to himself in another, and, refusing obedience to the central authority, leaves an organization which his conduct will decidedly demoralize.

The Transcript (Boston): The Salvation Army during the last half-dozen years has won the respect and approval of the American people and press by its untiring efforts and its amazing results. If it is to now advance it must be by the efforts of those Americans who have established and directed it, and as an American, elective, self-governing body. There should forthwith be 'a free and independent' American Salvation Army.

Some Army historians —Herbert Wisbey, for example— have suggested that the reaction of the press to the Ballington Booth affair stemmed largely from a widespread animosity towards Britain and things British:

Anti-English feeling in the United States in 1895 and 1896 was at a height over the Venezuela boundary dispute. The dispute itself was one of long standing between Venezuela and British Guiana. England refused to arbitrate the matter. When Secretary of State Olney sent a strong request for arbitration of the dispute, which he said concerned the Monroe Doctrine, the British Government replied, after a delay of four months, that it could not accept this interpretation of the Monroe Doctrine. Again it refused to arbitrate. President Cleveland was 'mad clear through.' On December 17, 1895, he sent a message to Congress that in effect asked the United States to run the boundary line itself and if necessary fight to maintain it. Congress responded by voting the appropriation for a commission promptly and with great enthusiasm. A wave of jingoistic patriotism swept the country, and talk of war became common. With diplomatic relations between the United States and England thus strained almost to the breaking point, the news was made public that the English General of the Salvation Army proposed to remove the naturalized American Commander of the Salvation Army in the United States.[5]

Support for such a claim, however, is scanty at best. While one can sense, in some of the journalistic comments, a rancour which manifested itself in such phrases as 'the English General,' the overall tone seemed to be one of confidence in the abilities of Americans to run their own organization —a definite national pride which saw that as a right not a privilege. But, most of all, as we see in the preceding quotes, the criticism of the Army and the support for Ballington Booth (though both may have stemmed from personal biases) were based on the perceived evils of 'autocracy,' 'nepotism' and 'Boothism.' Whether these were now genuine concerns, or just convenient whipping-boys, is difficult to say.

Equally problematic is the contention, voiced again by Army historians, that The Salvation Army in America —in spite of the mass defections and the competition for public support provided by Ballington's 'Volunteers'— actually benefitted from the affair. Certainly, it seems to have recovered remarkably well under the new leadership of Frederick and Emma Booth-Tucker, but how well it might have done without the bad publicity, and how changed it became because of it, are matters yet to be addressed by historians. What seems clear is that the controversy did teach William Booth several things: not to upset Americans again by forcibly removing a beloved Commander (Booth-Tucker served until the 1904 death of his wife made him request a change; Eva Booth then served from 1904 to 1934 when she became General), to allow the American branch to assume an American personality, and, finally, to begin accepting other territories as equal partners in the salvation war. Perhaps the *New York Times* was satisfied with that small achievement.

The Salvation Army and a Literary Public: or, Sally Ann Among the Literati

If imitation is, as many people aver, the sincerest form of flattery, then The Salvation Army has been sincerely flattered many times —the establishment of the Church Army, evangelical wing of the Church of England, is a case in point. But there is another form of flattery which, if not always as sincere, is certainly no less indicative of just how firmly the Army has implanted itself in the public's imagination. This flattery exists in an *imitatio* of a literary kind. When poets, novelists, short story writers and dramatists began to fictionalize Salvationism, either as an incidental motif or a central metaphor, we can be sure that it had become as recognizable and popular as royalty or Sunlight Soap.

What is most remarkable is just how early the 'banners and bonnets' were given literary life. The first published 'Army' story, Charles Edwardes' "Colonel Eva," appeared in the prestigious London society magazine *Belgravia* in 1892; and before the century was out a whole spate of poems and short stories, featuring Salvationist themes or Salvationists as central characters, were published in magazines on both sides of the Atlantic. Many of these, such as Frances Green's "Captain Nancy: A Pit-Brow Romance" in the *Sunday Magazine* (1899), were, though ostensibly uplifting, of a very sentimental nature; while others, such as John Buchan's "A Captain of

Salvation" (*Yellow Book,* 1896) were in the vanguard of the realistic tradition. After the turn of the century, the preoccupation with Army motifs increased and engaged the talents of some of the world's leading writers and dramatists: James Norman Hall, Henry Lawson, Vachel Lindsay, Damon Runyon, Sara Jeannette Duncan, Bertolt Brecht and George Bernard Shaw. The Salvation Army —unorthodox, unusual and downright interesting— had become both a 'fit' and 'profitable' subject for fictional or poetic depiction.

Before we look more closely at the mainstream literature, it is worth noting that there is an incidental Army motif that appears in a great many novels, poems and plays whose overall subjects have nothing to do with Salvationism. Many of us have, in fact, often been startled or amused in the course of our reading to find, with no contextual significance, a fleeting reference to some Salvation Army activity. It might be Margaret Atwood's *The Edible Woman* in which a character states: "There are some dresses hanging in the closet I don't wear any more. I'll give them to the Salvation Army." Or perhaps a stanza in Leonard Cohen's poem "Suzanne" with its mesmerizing rhythm:

> Suzanne takes your hand
> and she leads you to the river
> She is wearing rags and feathers
> From Salvation Army counters.

Or it might be that fleeting image, so poignant for both the character and the reader, that one comes across in Morley Callaghan's *Strange Fugitive*:

> On Sunday night the city was quiet but many loud voices cried out on Albert Street. He stood on the corner, his hands in his pockets, his straw hat tilted back on his head. . . . He stood there, feeling important but not thinking of anything, though listening to the Salvation Army man making a speech to the meeting on the corner. He was looking directly at the speaker but wasn't hearing a word.

Occasionally, though still incidental to the main theme, the 'Salvation Army' allusion is meant to provoke amusement or indicate irony by its juxtaposition with the dominant image. In his incomparable *Sunshine Sketches*, for example, Stephen Leacock offers a characteristic piece of bathos:

> So it came about that, little by little, the antagonism [to the fact that Smith served liquor] died down. Smith's hotel became an accepted institution in Mariposa. Even the temperance people were proud of Mr. Smith as a sort of character who added distinction to the town. There were moments, in the earlier quiet of the morning when Dean Drone would go so far as to step in to the 'rotunda' and collect a subscription. As for the Salvation Army, they ran in and out all the time unreproved.

And, in his popular thriller *Call for the Dead*, John Le Carré pokes fun at the assumed gentility of one his characters in a similar vein:

> The Fountain Cafe (proprietor Miss Gloria Adam) was all tudor and horse brasses and local honey at sixpence more than anywhere else. Miss Adam herself dispensed the nastiest coffee south of Manchester and spoke of her customers as 'My Friends.' Miss Adam did not do business with friends, but simply robbed them, which somehow added to the illusion of genteel amateurism which Miss Adam was so anxious to preserve. Her origin was obscure, but she often spoke of her father as 'The Colonel.' It was rumoured among those of Miss Adam's friends who had paid particularly dearly for their friendship that the colonelcy in question had been granted by the Salvation Army.

One could continue to cite such references, from Eugene O'Neill's *The Hairy Ape* to Dorothy Livesay's "In Green Solariums," and the total count would be impressive. But what is more impressive is that these writers should have been convinced that even a passing reference to The Salvation Army would be immediately recognized by a majority of their readers. And, even though the allusions are most frequently to the Army's social work or to its open-air ministry, one must acknowledge that they imply a public awareness not generally enjoyed by many small religious institutions. It might be argued, in fact, that the 'incidental' references are perhaps better indicators of public recognition than are full-length literary works. For, unlike the latter which will give the reader some idea of what the Army is all about, the former, by merely alluding to 'The Salvation Army,' assumes that the very words themselves are enough to conjure up brass bands on street corners, *War Crys* in pubs, downtown shelters or second-hand furniture stores.

This sort of public recognition is analogous to that experienced by the Army in the many hundreds of cartoons that have featured its activities from its early days to the present. When the subject of the cartoon was the Army itself, the cartoonist was obviously relying on a current newsworthy event to provide a contextual meaning. For example, when William Booth launched his 'Darkest England' scheme in 1890, there were dozens of cartoons which depicted him as benefitting personally from the money donated. When, however, the subject of the cartoon was another public figure —say, Prime Minister Gladstone— caricatured as a Salvationist (perhaps trying to convert the House of Commons), the cartoonist is obviously implying that the Army is an immediately-recognized public institution. Army bonnets on well-known actresses, a noted Parliamentarian banging a tambourine, a caption which states 'Boothism in Parliament' —all such incidental references, like those in novels and plays, bespeak an almost instantaneous and universal familiarity with at least the outward trappings of Salvationism.

When we turn to the so-called 'Army literature' itself, we are presented, either as settings or conflicts, with those features of the Army which were not merely the most attractive to writers but which were *perceived* as being its distinguishing trademarks. The Army was, as we have seen in earlier essays, insistent on 'getting to the people' —holding their open-air meetings outside the pubs— and could be seen on the street-corners of most cities or even in such remote towns as Bourke, Australia, where that country's poet laureate, Henry Lawson, spent some time. In a town with little entertainment, writes Lawson's biographer, "one of the main evening occupations —almost as interesting as a dog-fight— was to watch the efforts of the local

Salvation Army. The Salvationists regarded Watty's pub as the main menace to the morality of Bourke, and they performed longer and more often outside his premises than anywhere else. Lawson spent hours watching Watty's reaction to them."[1] And he wrote an amusing poem about it called "When the Army Prays for Watty":

When the kindly hours of darkness, save for light of moon and star,
Hide the picture on the signboard over Doughty's Horse Bazaar;
When the last rose-tint is fading on the distant mulga scrub,
Then the Army prays for Watty at the entrance of his pub.

Watty lounges in his arm-chair, in his old accustomed place,
With a fatherly expression on his round and passive face;
And his arms are clasped before him in a calm, contented way,
And he nods his head and dozes when he hears the Army pray.

And I wonder if he ponders on the distant years and dim,
Or his chances Over Yonder, when the Army prays for him,
Has he not a fear connected with the warm place down below,
Where, according to good Christians, all the publicans should go?

But his features give no token of a feeling in his breast,
Save of peace that is unbroken and a conscience well at rest;
And we guzzle as we guzzled long before the Army came,
And the loafers wait for 'shouters,' and they get there just the same.

It would take a lot of praying, lots of thumping on the drum,
To prepare our sinful, straying, erring souls for Kingdom Come;
But I love my fellow-sinners, and I hope, upon the whole,
That the Army gets a hearing when it prays for Watty's soul.[2]

The Army not only ministered to what were usually referred to as the 'down-and-outs' but drew, as most writers were quick to vivify, many of its members from the lower-classes. Like Robert Buchanan's "Hallelujah Jane," a woman from London's slums, they were 'converted' to the Army's cause by its demonstrations of joy. Here is how Jane describes her conversion:

But one mornin' when The Army was a-gatherin', I stood by,
And they 'ollered, 'Glory, glory, to our Father in the sky!'
And I thought the tune was jolly, and I sang out loud and gay
And the minute I began it, 'arf my trouble pass'd away,
And the louder as I sung it, that great lump I felt inside
Grew a-lighter and a-lighter, while I lep' and sung and cried!
And he sez, 'That voice of yourn, Jane, is as good as any three!
Why, you're like a op'ry singer' he sez, larfin... 'Never mind,'
He sez (for I look'd sulky, and his heart was allays kind!),
'Never mind —there's many among us of such singin' would be
proud—
He's a long way off, is Jesus, so we've got to make it loud!'
Then they marched, and I went marchin', for I seem'd gone mad that
    day,
And my 'eart inside wass dancin' every footstep of the way.
Yes, and that there singin' saved me! For the louder as I sung,
Why, the more my load was lighten'd, and it seem'd as how I
    sprung
From the ground right up to Jesus, and I 'eard Him 'oller clear,
'Keep a-marchin' and a-singin', for you've got to get up 'ere!'[3]

Though changed (and often made attractive) in outward appearance
by the uniform and their elevating mission, many of the fictional
converts could still be revealed, in moments of crisis, as persons of
lower-class distinction. If, as sometimes happened, a person of
'quality' joined the Army, the conflict (in the minds of writers) was
intensified. The tension then manifested itself in a conflict between the
character's social upbringing (like that of Shaw's Barbara Undershaft)
and a sympathy with the Army's social mission or with such clients as
Snobby Price and Rummy Mitchens.

For example, in Elliven Earle's "A Salvation Lass" (*Belgravia*,
1894) the heroine is the daughter of an upper-class family, "well
educated and trained for a nurse," who has somehow gotten "mixed
up with the Salvation Army." Not unexpectedly, when she falls in love
with Phillip Sinclaire, a man from her own social stratum —"university
man and cultured skeptic"— she is forced into choosing between her
lover and the Army. After some to-and-froing, Earle brings about a

resolution of the conflict in a very melodramatic and most implausible dénouement: her heroine gives her life for her lover, pushing him out of the path of an oncoming train, living only long enough to whisper: "There was no time for anything, and I knew you were not ready to die." The story is, all said, a poor one, and is not intimate with Salvationism, but it does typify a common perception of its membership.

A similar kind of conflict, but one which brings its reader a little closer to the reality of Army life, provided the thematic structure for John Buchan's "The Captain of Salvation" (*Yellow Book*, 1896). Buchan, just twenty years old when he wrote the story, presents a conflict between his Captain's sworn duty to the Army and the allurement of the outside world; but, unlike Earle who depicts that conflict solely through external pressures, Buchan is interested in the psychology of the struggle. Thus, though the plot is conventional, the juxtaposition of external images with internal doubts lends the story a psychological reality that makes it both convincing and poignant. The Captain is a well-to-do man, a "gentleman born, a scholar after a fashion, with a full experience of the better side of civilization," who had fallen into difficulties, been 'converted' in the Army and become an officer in its ranks. But the past is always present; as he marches in the streets he sees the fancy restaurants in which he once dined and is drawn, against his will, into sinful reveries.

> He had seen crowds of well-dressed men and women, some of whom he dimly recognized, who had no time even to glance at the insignificant wayfarer. Old ungodly longings after luxury had come to disturb him. . . . When he came to the stuffy upper-room where the meeting was held, his state of mind was far from the meek resignation which he sought to cultivate. . . . The meeting did not tend to soothe him. Brother followed sister in aimless remarks, seething with false sentiment and sickly enthusiasm, till the strong man was near to disgust.

Torn between what Buchan characterizes as the "hateful right and the delicious wrong," the Captain of Salvation agonizes for some pages over his commitment until finally, in Army parlance, he "gets the victory" and fulfils the title's promise:

> A spasm of convulsive pain, of exquisite agony, of heart-breaking
> struggle came over the Captain's face, stayed a moment, and passed. He
> turned to his followers. "Sing louder, lads," he cried, "we're fighting a
> good fight." And then his voice broke down, and he stumbled on, still
> bravely clutching the flag.

Another public perception of the Army —one quite justified by the
facts— was that its evangelical and social work was undertaken and
made successful primarily by young women. 'Hallelujah Lasses' were
a favourite not only with unsaved young men but with cartoonists,
illustrators and writers. Even their titles alone —"Captain Kitty,"
"Captain Nancy: A Pit-Brow Romance," "Colonel Eva," "Salvation
Nell," "Jane Hubbs's Salvation," "The Slum Angels" and "Major
Barbara"— are indicative of just how fascinated writers were by the
idea of pure and pretty females refining male corruption. In blue
uniforms and poke-bonnets, Salvationist Joans of Arc waged their war
against sin and poverty in numerous novels, plays, short stories and
poems, one typical example being John William Bengough's "The War
Cry":

> In the elegant rotunda of a fine up-town hotel
> (A favourite lounge of tourist, commercial man and swell),
> In little knots and circles, in coteries and sets,
> The idlers chatted gaily and enjoyed their cigarettes.
>
> A drummer from Kentucky (in the wine and liquor trade)
> His stock of brand new stories to a genial group displayed,
> And bursts of merry laughter acclaimed each happy hit,
> Like thunder-peals responding to his lightning flash of wit.
>
> Within the vaulted entry and across the polished tiles
> To'rds the group of flippant gossips, under fire of rakish smiles,
> Came a pair of mild-faced maidens, clad in modest navy blue,
> With scoop-bonnets of the Army and the badge of crimson hue;

And with gentle step approaching, as the loungers stood at ease,
Spake in accents low and winning: "Will you buy a *War Cry*, please?"
Offering a sample paper from the bundle that each bore,
"Will you please to buy a copy? —it will tell you of the war."

"Bless my soul!" exclaimed the drummer, with an air of mock alarm,
Putting on his gold-rimmed *pince nez*— "A *War Cry*, little marm?
Why, I thought the war was over and ended long ere this—
Been another Indian slaughter? or what's the matter, miss?"

A smile went round the circle at this clever, ready jest,
And the hand that held the paper trembled as it fell to rest;
But upon the jester's features the lass's eyes were set,
The sweetest yet the saddest eyes his glance had ever met.

"No," she said, in earnest, quav'ring tones, and tears were in her voice,
"The war is not yet over, nor the time come to rejoice;
With dead and dying comrades the trenches yet are filled,
And the field is strewn with victims —but not by Indians killed.

"'Tis sinful human passion, the lust and greed of gold,
That slaughters these our brothers today in hosts untold—
That slays them, not with bullets, but with ardent spirits fell,
With wine, and beer, and whiskey, the artillery of hell.

"Oh, sir, are **you** a helper in this awful work of woe?
Do eyes of murdered babies glare icily at **you**?
Do ghosts of famished mothers and wraiths of ruined sons
Cry from the tombs for vengeance on you, who man the guns?

"May God forbid! but, oh, sir! this long and weary fight
Is raging all about us —nor ceases day nor night—
And you, who praise the soldier who faces shot and shell,
Have you no manly honor for us who fight as well?"

"Think you 'tis any pleasure that we, two puny girls,
Should go where laughter greets us or the lip of scorner curls?
Nay; but our Master's colors we dare to hold aloft,
And bear, as once He bore for us the taunts of those who scoffed.

>"'Tis for your souls we labor; we do not prize your gold;
>But oh, don't slight our Master; His love can ne'er be told.
>You do not mean to be unkind, your hearts are not all bad,
>But your thoughtless mirth makes sadder our hearts already sad!"
>
>No man in all that circle now bore a leering smile,
>But moistened eyes were fixed upon that face so free of guile;
>And the jester whispered softly, his manner ill at ease,
>Said huskily, "God bless you! Sell me a *War Cry*, please."

It is little wonder, then, that men 'fell in love' with the ideal and sometimes with the Lasses themselves. In Sara Jeannette Duncan's 1899 novel, *The Path of a Star*, Mr. Duff Lindsay, a young, rich and handsome British socialite living in Calcutta, is enraptured by the vision of Captain Laura Filbert dressed in native costume (a practice adopted by English officers in India):

>Just where the sun slanted into the room and made leaf-patterns on the floor she turned and stood for an instant in the full tide of it; and it set all the loose tendrils of her pale yellow hair in a little flame, and gave the folds of the flesh-coloured *sari* that fell over her shoulders the texture of draperies so often depicted as celestial. The sun sought into her face, revealing nothing but great purity of line and a clear pallor, except where below the wide light blue eyes two ethereal shadows brushed themselves. Under the intentness of their gaze she made as if she would pass without speaking; and the tender curves of her limbs, as she wavered, could not have been matched out of medieval stained glass.

It is a vision he must cherish and to do so Lindsay seeks out the Army barracks, reluctantly sits through what he thinks are distasteful meetings, gives generously enough to keep the Ensign happy, and feasts his eyes and his ears on Laura, for even her "hallelujah!" is like "clear music above a sordid din."

But it is, after all, the vision that he desires. When, after much persuading, Laura finally agrees to be his wife, and is divested of her *sari*, she stands revealed as a rather common English girl:

In the course of a few days one of the costumes was completed, and when he came she had it on, appearing before him for the first time in secular dress. The stays insisted a little cruelly on the lines of her figure, and the tight bodice betrayed her narrow-chested. Above its frills her throat protruded unusually, with a curve outward like that of some wading bird's, and her arms, in their unaccustomed sleeves, hung straight at her sides. She had put on the hat that matched; it was the kind of pretty disorderly hat with waving flowers that demands the shadow of short hair along the forehead, and she had not thought of that way of making it becoming. Among these accessories the significance of her face retreated to a point vague and distant, its lightly-pencilled lines seemed half erased.

Duff Lindsay —part idealist, part cad— is mightily relieved when Laura, perhaps sensing his disappointment, changes her mind and renews her commitment to the Army. She then, quite precipitously, marries a Salvation Army Colonel. It was just as Ensign Sand had stated: "Society people ain't fond of the Army, and never will be."

There can be no doubt that these fictional representations of Salvationism, few of which were unsympathetic, helped entrench the Army's public image and probably helped fill its proffered tambourines in pubs and at open-air meetings. Established writers, unlike those who merely wrote parodies and lampoons, were doing the Army a distinct favour. Their audience was certainly a large one and, though one might wince at the inclusion of an Army story in the notorious *Yellow Book*, one could only be pleased that such popular magazines as *Pall Mall*, *Belgravia*, *Everybody's*, *Our Day*, *Harper's*, and *Literary Digest* were helping promote, however unintentionally, the Army's good work.

It was the theatre, however, which gave the Army its greatest public exposure, for plays were as much public spectacles as were Army open-air meetings; they not only offered the public a 'view' of Salvationism but allowed, as magazines could not, the Army opportunities to take advantage of the publicity incurred by the plays themselves —something the Army was pretty adept at doing. Two cases in point are George Bernard Shaw's *Major Barbara* and Edward

Sheldon's *Salvation Nell.*

When *Major Barbara* opened at the Court Theatre in London, on November 28, 1905, some critics thought it was an indictment of the Army. Shaw, who had no such intention, and was confident that Salvationists, of whom he was very fond, understood that the Army motif (and the Undershaft bribery) was a metaphor for a larger social and spiritual issue. For, though he abhorred certain Army practices (and 'salvation' itself), Shaw had a great liking for the Army, and especially its music. When a London journalist compared some detestable noise to "a Salvation Army band," Shaw, a noted music critic, wrote to the paper, deploring the libel and praising the musical accomplishments of Army bands. William Booth thereupon invited him to a festival of massed bands at Clapton Congress Hall; Shaw accepted, and "when the band played 'When the roll is called up yonder'," he wrote, "I stood in the middle of the centre grand tier box, in the front row, and sang it as it has never been sung before." If the *Times* got hold of it, he facetiously suggested, it would announce his conversion in its next issue. Shaw, in fact, wrote a technical critique of the performance for Booth and even offered to write plays for Salvationists to perform, an offer which Mrs Booth flatly declined, for the theatre was, she felt, the 'gate of hell' to Salvationists.

Knowing this, it must have come as something of a surprise to Shaw to see at the premiere performance of *Major Barbara*, among all the intelligentsia of London, a number of high-ranking Salvation Army officers in full uniform (though the Booths were not among them). Such an unprecedented indulgence in 'sinful pleasure' could only have occurred if someone in authority had read the play and approved of it; for not even the friendship of Shaw would entice the Army hierarchy into a situation of which they were ignorant and which would not be, as they expressed it to the censorship committee, an 'excellent advertisement' for the organization. The critics clearly had it wrong: in Shaw's opinion the Salvationists were "more accessible to the religious character of the drama than the playgoers to the gay energy and artistic fertility of religion."[4]

If it seemed strange to some people that Salvationists should show an open support of *Major Barbara*, written by a man who made it known that he loathed the Cross (as he loathed all gibbets), and in which some uncomplimentary things are said about them, it did not seem at all strange to the Salvationists themselves. And the reason had little to do with the fact that the Army had grown more tolerant of 'worldly pleasures' —less antagonistic towards French novels and the theatre. Rather, it was what the Army had always insisted on: they would consort with the Devil himself if they thought they could turn the occasion to some good. And, without question, such an event as the premiere of *Major Barbara* was good publicity and a lot more enjoyable than confronting publicans in their dens. They most likely realized, as some reviewers did not, that what the public would most enjoy in the play was not its half-baked socialism or the parlour wit, but the scene in the West Ham Shelter which occupies the whole of Act II and which, though slightly accusative, vivifies with appropriate dramatic tension the dedication of Salvation lasses.

Unlike Shaw's intellectual treatment, Edward Sheldon's *Salvation Nell* is a socio-realistic play set always in the slums of New York, and, as such, it was more sympathetic to the Army's work and its religious aims. Its two chief protagonists are Nell Sanders and Jim Platt, both denizens of the New York Bowery. When Jim stabs an adversary and is sent to jail, Nell, having nowhere to live, is sheltered and 'rescued' by the Army. This is Act I. In Act II Jim returns from jail and the remainder of the play dramatizes his attempt to reclaim Nell from the Army and in the eventual triumph of Nell's new faith.

When the play opened at the Hackett Theatre in New York on November 17, 1908, The Salvation Army —the Americans perhaps being more audacious than the British— actually "placed young women at the doors of the theatre, and between the acts had them go throughout the audience soliciting contributions." Alexander Woolcott recalled that one of his friends, Alicia Rudd, was so greatly affected by the play that between acts she tore a corsage from her dress and 'thrust' it into the tambourine of a Salvation Army lassie standing in the lobby."[5]   1908

Featuring the famous Mrs. Fiske as Nell, the play ran for sixty-five nights before moving on to other cities; and one of the curious measures of its success, according to a theatre director, was the renewed public awareness of The Salvation Army: "It seems to me a fine, sincere piece of work with a precious accent of life throughout! The silence of the audience that left the theatre and the dollar bills in the tambourines of the Salvation Army lassies at the door were eloquent proofs of the impression created by the play."[6]

It goes without saying that hardly any of these writers intended to 'promote' The Salvation Army. They were, for better or worse, mainly concerned with their craft, and sometimes through that craft to make statements about the human condition. One exception, perhaps, was Vachel Lindsay, the well-known American poet who, though certainly a conscientious craftsman, wrote "General William Booth Enters Into Heaven" (1912) as a memorial to Booth and a sincere tribute to the Army. The poet's attitude, his respect for the Army's evangelistic and social work, is clearly evident throughout the poem and pointedly so in the final stanza:

> And when Booth halted by the curb for prayer
> He saw his Master thro' the flag-filled air.
> Christ came gently with a robe and crown
> For Booth the soldier, while the throng knelt down.
> He saw King Jesus. They were face to face,
> And he knelt a-weeping in that holy place.
> *Are you washed in the Blood of the Lamb?*

In the final analysis, of course, authorial intention is of little matter. Equally unimportant is whether the Army itself was, intentionally or not, 'promoted' by such literature. The essential point being made here is that the authors of these works were acknowledging, by their conscious choice of subject, that The Salvation Army had entered the mythology of popular culture. To be written about is to be immortalized.

Essay Nine

Public Elegies to a Dead General: The Funeral of William Booth

When great men die, nations mourn. The pictures of London's streets, packed twenty deep on either side for miles, as the funeral cortege slowly wound its way to Abney Park Cemetery; newspapers full of tributes and life-sketches, some being 'special issues' devoted solely to the life and death of William Booth; many thousands of letters and telegrams from heads-of-state —kings and queens, presidents and prime ministers— around the world; a three-day queue of mourners, from pot-boys to politicians, viewing the body of General Booth as it 'lay in state' at Clapton Congress Hall. Even today, the outpouring of respect, honour, and love seems quite remarkable. That this poor son of a Nottingham pawnbroker, who left but £487 to his children, should have been accorded funeral courtesies as impressive as those of any royal person; that someone so vilified in 1892 should have been so universally applauded in 1912 is fascinating to witness, even though one knows that The Salvation Army had finally become a respected and cherished British institution.

Though it might seem ungracious, it is fair to say that the funeral obsequies for William Booth, who died at 10:20 pm on August 20, 1912, provided the British public with an ideal opportunity to extol the virtues of The Salvation Army —to retract past criticisms and apologize for past assaults— and acknowledge the genius of its founder. "Thirty years ago," commented *The Nation*, "representatives of every religious organization in England were rivalling one another in sneering condemnation of the methods of the self-styled 'General' and his Salvation Army, with its trumpets and tambourines, its mock uniforms, its threatenings of hellfire, and its blasphemous familiarity with the Deity. Now, when the man whose restless energy called this vast organization into being enjoys respite from his labours, there will scarcely be found a religious body to withhold tribute of praise to the memory of a great man who dedicated his life to the service of Christianity" (Aug. 29, 1912).

Nor was there one. Gone were the inverted commas: no longer 'General,' in tones of derision, but **GENERAL** in bold caps. William Booth was now "The Greatest Apostle of the Age," "The Greatest Revivalist of His Day," "The One Supremely Great Religious Leader of the Nineteenth Century," "One of the Most Remarkable Figures in the Religious History of the Modern World"; and his Salvation Army had reached the apogee of public acclaim.

In describing Booth's funeral ceremonies, the overall tone of the commentaries was one of wonderment: at the overwhelming public expression of sympathy and gratefulness; at the sheer numbers of Salvationists; and at the unusual nature of Army funeral 'celebrations.' More than one hundred thousand people paid their last respects, queuing for three days at the Clapton Congress Hall, rich and poor mingling to view at close range the face which, though familiar, few had ever had a chance to study. "I watched part of the endless procession of men and women," wrote Philip Gibbs in *The Graphic*, "and the memory of it will linger with me."

Illustrious persons had sent wreaths and tributes, and now and again a carriage stood outside the hall, but for the most part those who came to get one moment's glimpse of the old General's face were the children of poverty. Here were working-men in their working clothes, and the women of humble life —those people who live always on a thin crust above the abyss, and who need great courage, great strength, great luck to prevent themselves falling through. There were poor clerks, and down-at-heel fellows of shabby gentility, and out-of-works who have been into many an Army 'shelter' on a winter's night, and poor devils who still look to the Army for something hot to drink, and something to ease the hunger pains. The instinct of loyalty, a genuine love for 'the old man,' a remembrance, perhaps, of some moment of rare emotion when their horny hands clutched up to God, had brought them, perhaps at the risk of losing a day's job, to his bier. There was no unrestrained emotionalism. Only by the quiver of a lip, by a moist eye, by a queer scared look on a rugged face, did one see that these people were moved profoundly. But it was a great and solemn sight, and men like myself, the lookers-on of life, the critics, the reporters, who have not been followers of the General's flag, who follow perhaps other flags, or none at all, saw here the testimony to General Booth's greatness and the victory of his life (Aug. 31, 1912).

On the day of the funeral an estimated *two million* people, taking advantage of a very rare 'declared' half-holiday, lined the procession route —five miles from the Victoria Embankment through the heart of the City to Abney Park— massed twenty deep at choice viewing locations. The mile-long procession itself included a larger number of brass bands than anyone could ever remember seeing or hearing in one event —more than forty interspersed throughout the fifty-one Salvation Army corps contingents from all over Great Britain. It was a spectacle both dignified and impressive:

From beginning to end it was a triumphal procession for the Army and its dead chief. . . . At [its] head was a group of bright banners, representing in many colours, the numerous countries in which the Salvation Army conducts its work. All down the great line the familiar banners of the Army waved like oriflammes of war, and at intervals there were flags with inscriptions, showing that the Army had sent its representatives from all parts of the Kingdom and from all countries within reach of London.

Of the many impressive incidents of the day, the first and most touching was witnessed outside the International Headquarters in Queen Victoria-street. There the hearse stood with officers on guard round it, and, as each brigade approached, the colours carried by the senior officer were slowly drooped, and every officer and soldier turned reverently towards the coffin and gravely saluted the dead leader. It was at this point that General and Mrs. Bramwell Booth joined the funeral procession, and positions immediately behind them were taken by the commissioners, colonels, and lieutenant-colonels, with their wives.

It was 11:30 when the first of the 51 brigades set out from the Embankment; and at least an hour later, after the 47th brigade, consisting of the International Headquarters Staff and two bands, under the command of Colonel George Mitchell, had passed, that the funeral carriage took its place in the long line.

City thoroughfares were packed from end to end, and every high window was occupied by spectators. Business men had deserted their desks, and clerks had forsaken their stools. All business seemed to be suspended, and on every side were signs of respect and reverence for this religious leader. Flags were flown at half-mast, and on the balcony of the Mansion House the Lord Mayor's deputy (the Lord Mayor being out of town) stood in his robes and chain of office, surrounded by members of the City Corporation and officials, and saluted as the hearse passed. On the roof of the Bank of England, on the steps of the Royal Exchange and of the Baltic in St. Mary-axe business men watched the great pageant go by (*Daily Chronicle*, Aug. 29).

It was a strange funeral indeed: viewing the procession, one was certain it celebrated the "triumph of some great hero"; looking at the crowds, "factory-girls, labourers, hawkers, navvies," showing so many signs of easy familiarity in their farewell gestures, one was convinced that it marked the end of a personal relationship. "To be all things to all men —was not that the secret of it? To be vulgar to the vulgar? Perhaps! But, then, vulgarity —that was a weapon on the way. The real force all through in him was a never vulgar instinct we call *love*. Love alone, let us believe, prompted him to his work, made him a missionary amongst them. Love, too, came back to him many thousand-fold in those multitudes gathered to take leave. For the sake of the love in him, even the careful and fastidious will forget the vulgarity they seemed to find. For the sight of the thousands, they will forgive Olympia, the flashing lights, the noise of brass and drums" (*Daily Mirror*, Aug. 30, 1912).

The last statement, the only jarring note in all the commentaries, was a reference to the Army's own 'memorial' service held at the London Olympia on August 28 at which some 25,000 Salvationists re-dedicated themselves to the dead General's mission. Though it was, by all accounts, somewhat unusual in its spectacle of brass bands, many flags, white ribbons, joyful singing and promises of allegiance, the affair was marvelled at by nearly all commentators as a 'wonderful manifestation' of the positive effect of Booth's Salvationism on so many people. And it was, as William Booth would have wanted, a declaration of faith and renewed determination. "Some of us there," wrote a reporter for the *Daily Chronicle*, "the lookers-on —the reporters of life— had seen the funerals of kings and princes; had watched many strange scenes of history, but never before had any of us seen such a burial as this, or such a drama of reality."

It was a mingling of triumph and gladness with personal and poignant grief. It was a passionate tribute to the glory of a great man, and a humble assertion of faith before God. It was a proclamation to the

NOW, MR. BOOTH, LET US KNOW WHAT YOU ARE GOING TO DO WITH ALL THIS MONEY!

Two views of William Booth: early, as a money-grubbing charlatan and, later, as the much-admired evangelist.

Daily Mirror photo indicating the vast crowds that witnessed the William Booth funeral cortege.

world of a work born of the genius of this man whose dust lay coffined there, but also the outpouring of sorrow by a family bereft of its chief. It was the homage of an Army joyous in the thought of victories won by their departed General, but stricken with an intimate and individual emotion at the thought that never again would they see their inspiration, their prophet, their great captain, their friend.

So was the scene set for the last coming of the old General among his troops. At 7:30 the bands rose, there was a glitter of brass, a baton waved to them, and suddenly out of the a great silence there rose the tremendous sound of a Salvation Army hymn played by the bands and sung by thousands of voices. It was one of those hymns which Salvationists love, not sad and dreary, but triumphant with a kind of lilting joy, as men may sing on a march to victory or death.

There is a better world they say, oh so bright!

Where sin and woe are done away, oh so bright!

... What followed was certainly one of the greatest victories of simple faith and of religious organization which the modern world has seen. The spirit of the Salvation Army —with its discipline, its ordered emotion, its training in devotion, in prayer, in choral singing— was seen at its very best. . . . Those people did not sing from their throats alone, but from their hearts. There was in this thrill of the voice, in this ardour of sound, the spirit of men and women who have sung such songs in haunts of misery, in the quarters of despair, on the battlefields of vice and crime. When they sang the general's own hymn—

O boundless salvation, deep ocean of love—

they seemed as though once more they saw the figure of the old General himself, beating time, raising his arms, singing in his hoarse whisper, with the melody in his eyes and the joy of the words illumining his face (Aug. 29, 1912).

Not only was the Olympia congregation "impressive in its immensity," but moreso in its display of Salvationism. "It had no thought for the ritual of sorrow. It sang lustily with a cheerful voice in the presence of its dead leader; and throughout the service the dominating note was one of sturdy confidence and happy resolution rather than one of regret or lamentation. Then a few simple sentences came out from Commissioner Lawley's prayer, and we began to understand. He prayed in a voice of extraordinary volume, and he delivered up thanks to the Creator for 'triumph in the battle, for faith in the darkness.' And then, as the bearded Commissioner cried out, 'We praise Thee for victory in death,' those who were strangers looked up and realized that here was a victorious army celebrating the greatest of triumphs, and not a retinue of sad-eyed mourners weeping for the dead" (*Daily Graphic*, Aug. 29).

When it came time to assess William Booth's career, most commentators were unanimous in ranking him, in the words of the Chicago *Continent*, as one of the "greatest servants of Christ and benefactors of men whom all the centuries have produced." The natural comparison, which sprang to almost everyone's mind, was John Wesley. "It is impossible," wrote the editor of *The Methodist Times* "to refrain from comparing and contrasting the career of General Booth with that of John Wesley."

The same unquenchable evangelism and marvellous vitality marked the lives of each. Both were unresting travellers, scouring the British isles for converts. Open-air preaching played a prominent part in their religious work, and each had occasion to break away from the established religious conventions of his day. Both reached and passed their fourscore years without any abatement of their natural powers or their strenuous labours; and both founded great religious organizations which during their lifetime they ruled with autocratic powers. There the comparison ends, and the contrast begins. Wesley was a scholar, an Oxford don, with a temperamental love of order and restraint. William Booth had little education and an immense contempt for orderliness and usage in matters ecclesiastical. Wesley traversed slowly and often painfully his 4000 miles a year in Great Britain and Ireland on horseback, riding with slack rein and reading as he went. Booth sped swiftly from one end of the world to the other by motor-car, fast train, and steamer. Wesley suffered much from his matrimonial experience; General Booth owed more to his wife, the saintly Catherine Booth, than to any living person. Wesley provided for the continuation of his work by means of a form of government which was representative, though in a limited degree; General Booth has deputed his autocratic powers to a successor (it is understood that he is Mr. Bramwell Booth) who in turn is to hand them down unimpaired to his successor in due course. The contrast might be carried further, but enough has been said to show that while General Booth shared many of the great qualities which distinguished the founder of Methodism, he lacked others which secured the permanence of the religious organization which he left behind him (Aug. 22).

Unlike the Methodist journals, which were reluctant to give Booth precedence, crediting him with "the happiest blend of spiritual fervour and social enthusiasm known to the world *since* the days of John Wesley," most others were willing to accord him an influence equal to that of St. Paul, Loyola, Augustine, George Fox, John Wesley and Dwight L. Moody. He was, stated the Boston *Congregationalist*, "on a plane with the greatest philanthropists and Christians of all times." A few, however —perhaps sensibly— suggested that, while the future might reveal a suitable comparison, for now one must simply acknowledge the 'uniqueness' of the man. "His career," stated the London *Daily News*, "has that quality of independence and isolation which is the hall-mark of great creative minds. It owed nothing to others; it was indifferent to conventions and traditions and schools; it flashed across the sky on an orbit of its own that nothing could deflect. He began his amazing crusade amidst the brick-bats and ribaldry of the East-End, he ended it amidst the sanction of the whole world; but throughout he remained careless of the verdict of men. He was alone with an idea that burned at a white heat and consumed all that lay in its path" (Aug. 21). It was no use, then, trying to classify William Booth: he was "an individualist of the deepest dye —an egotist," and only inasmuch as other great religious leaders were the same could they be compared.

It was this kind of commentary —an attempt to discover the secret of Booth's remarkable success— that began to divide public opinion. The weight of argument seemed to be in favour of his "genius for organization," the *Congregationalist* suggesting that "the greatest captain of industry, the most expert professor of the modern gospel of business efficiency might profitably have sat at the feet of this plain and consecrated Christian man." His autocratic method —his ability to keep "an iron grip" on every Army activity without causing undue discord— was itself a mark of organizational brilliance. The Episcopalian *Churchman* (of New York) summed it up this way: "William Booth in his autocracy was intellectually at one with Rome in her autocracy. He did not want to bother others or to be himself bothered with questions of intellect. Some one once asked how he squared the idea of eternal punishment with his belief in God's eternal love. 'What's the use,' he answered impatiently, striking his hand upon the table, 'what's the use of wanting to explain things and worrying about interpretations? That's how work is stopped'."

Those who seemed to know The General best, however, felt that it was his charisma, his dominant personality, his imaginative impulse and his singleminded devotion to his dream which marked him as a 'man above other men.' "Many may have thought," remarked the *Methodist Times*, "they discovered his secret in a genius for organization. It is quite likely that they were mistaken." And even if it were so, the writer argued, the explanation would be insufficient. "The mere organizer is not a creator. He must have something given to him to organize. That something must consist in truth and life called into new activity by an outstanding personality. And general Booth was that. Conditions of all kinds were against him. His drawbacks and deficiencies were obvious. Yet he had the one supreme gift, and before it all else became but as chaff before the wind. General Booth believed, above all things, in his God, in himself, and in his commission. He believed, so unquestionably and so fearlessly that he knew nothing of half-measures, was heedless of ridicule, and turned all kinds of opposition into fresh instruments of his own over-mastering and victorious purpose" (Aug. 29).

The *Daily Express* probably summed up this viewpoint most succinctly. Booth had, it stated, in a very full degree, "that strange, magnetic attractiveness inseparable from the born leader of men, allied with an entire absence of self-consciousness, and an almost childlike simplicity, which made willing followers of the most unlikely subjects" (Aug. 22). According to this view, The Salvation Army was an expression of and gave expression to Booth's personality. "He had his message and he gave it. Its truth shone out upon him with self-evidencing splendour. He felt no need of either arguments to justify it, or of reason to find its coherence with the nature and history of the universe. . . . Thus a harmonious institution and a consistent plan fulfilled and served the great personality that created them both. The work is the self-expression of the man, and proclaims his power to command conditions and to control circumstances" (*Methodist Times*, Aug. 29).

It was this conviction —that The Salvation Army had been brought into existence and sustained by the force of William Booth's imagination and personality— which gave commentators the greatest pause. Could the Army survive without that power? The arguments, using almost the same rationales, swung between two poles. If, as knowledgeable people such Harold Begbie suggested, William's son, Bramwell, was the organizational 'mastermind' directing all the Army's international activities (his father being the 'heart and soul'), then the Army could survive because it had been set on its course and the dead General's fire would continue to burn in the hearts of his converts. The troops had been inspired by his "devotion to the popular welfare," fired with an enthusiasm that "stopped at no obstacle and feared no sacrifice," and would continue to work as zealously as ever. The organizational skills of his son were therefore ideally suited to ensure the continuation of the father's dream.

By the same token, however, it was suggested in several quarters that, because the son did not possess the fiery zeal, the platform charisma, the 'simple touch,' but was primarily a religious businessman, the Army would also soon lose its distinctive personality. The greatest fear (or, at least, expression of uncertainty) was that while the autocratic system seemed well-suited to William Booth's system of 'control by enthusiasm,' it would not be so for a leader without the same magnetic personality. Allied to it was a concern that Bramwell Booth was more interested in pushing the social work than was his father. Already, it was noted, the Army had changed considerably —more dedicated to social reclamation than to evangelization— a change brought about largely through the influence of Bramwell Booth and likely to be emphasized under his leadership. *The Lutheran* expressed a common view, to the effect that if this trend towards 'humanitarianism' continued, the movement would, sooner or later, lose its evangelical zeal and "become a charity organization chiefly."

In all the vast commentary on Booth's funeral, however, the question 'What will his successor make of The Salvation Army?' was an insignificant one; not merely because the moment, being sacred, demanded politeness, but because most firmly believed that the record of Booth's life, his splendid achievements, spoke for themselves. Thus, the eulogies predominated, the life was celebrated, and, as this final tribute by the noted author, Philip Gibbs, attests, William Booth's death was indeed 'swallowed up in victory':

The death of the General was the last victory in his long campaign. For when the world knew that the flame which has burnt in that frail old figure had flickered out, when they learnt that this old warrior —the chief of a great Army which has flung its outposts to the farthest corners of the world— had surrendered his sword to death, all his critics, all his scoffers, were silenced, and we little men of life knew that a great one had passed away from us.

I saw him many times when his spirit was bright and burning. I watched him when he put his spell upon great multitudes of vulgar men and women, out of whose vulgarity he drew heroic and ideal qualities of courage and compassion and chivalry. I have seen that tall old man, whose eyes, even when they were almost sightless, burnt with great spiritual fires of love and hate —a simple love for God and man, a simple hate for the devil and evil things— touch these people with the divinity of tears and laughter, and, by some magic, uplift them to great heights of enthusiasm and faith.

The mere sight of him, standing above them on a platform in some great hall, his white beard flowing over his General's coat, his eagle face peering down at them, his body swaying as the noise of their applause came up to him in gusts, was enough to stir his soldiers with an emotion which seemed to tear at their heart-strings. The sound of his voice, that hoarse whisper which used to reach one's ears from a far distance, seemed to strip off the rags and bindings and mummy-clothes of the human soul and leave it naked and quivering before him. Brutal men, foul women, the dregs of life were caught by the throat, in the grip of his passion, so that in a little while he had them groaning and wailing at their beastliness and crying like children for 'salvation.'

He used every art and trick of oratory, every crude and vulgar method to 'win souls to God.' He would gibe and jest at them with a biting humour. He would use the slang of the slum, and the cant of the thieves' alley. He would sing to them and dance to them, in a kind of religious ribaldry. He would make himself a buffoon for the love of God, and by these methods, he would drag people up from the depth of misery, drag them by the scruff of the neck from the mire to cleanliness, give them back their manhood and womanhood, and fan into a flaming torch the little spark of divinity which never goes out in the human heart, however deep it is in the abyss of degradation (*Graphic*, Aug. 31, 1912).

Harold Begbie, his biographer, neatly (if somewhat melodramatically) summed up the universal approbation of the moment. "The world recognized that with the death of this man one of its great fighters had passed away; and not to England alone, not to the British Empire alone, but to the whole world of humanity —the men, women, and children of every nation under Heaven— did this recognition come. No man ever finished his earth's battle with so universal a triumph. Grief, and grief of a most close and personal a character, burst from the heart of the human race. But it was not merely that every newspaper of any consequence throughout the whole civilized world paid its tribute of admiration and respect to the dead warrior; it was not that messages of sympathy from the great people of the earth rained in from every quarter of the globe; these things spoke for much; these things witnessed to the respectability for one who had been in his middle life the most assailed, ridiculed, and persecuted of men; but what attested more than anything else to the triumph of his life was the individual sorrow of the poorest and lowliest in every country throughout the world."[1]

An End to Autocracy?
The 'Bramwell Booth Affair'

That the public, of whatever country, should consider it has the right to question Salvation Army policy and have opinions about its internal disputes is largely attributable to the financial demands the organization has always made on that public. It is probably true that more non-Salvationists have supported the Army's work than have the non-members of any other religious group. The Salvation Army is, in essence, a public corporation —responsible to the public which supports it. Its troubles, therefore, have always been very much public property.

Up to 1929 most of the Army's internal disputes were local ones; of concern mainly to a narrow public represented by either municipal or national newspapers. The British, for example, were not very much interested in the Philpott affair in Canada or the Ballington Booth resignation in the United States. Nor were the Canadians or Americans much interested in the defection of Commissioner Frank Smith. That is, though all these events were known around the world, being reported in the 'foreign news' sections of most major papers, they were not cause for much editorial comment.

In the early months of 1929, however, almost every newspaper in the world, and most major magazines, were expostulating on the future of the Army. Incredibly, Bramwell Booth, the second General, had been deposed. The world was shocked, and public reaction ranged from anger to satisfaction. The anger stemmed from a feeling that the Booth family had been usurped; that an ailing man had been treated in an unChristian manner; that upstarts had taken advantage of personal tragedy. The satisfaction derived from the conviction that The

Salvation Army would cease to be governed —as so many public persons had been suggesting for so long— by an autocrat and become both more democratic, decentralized and, hopefully, less British in its control.

The precise mechanism for the deposition of Bramwell Booth had been established some years earlier by his father. Its conception was consolidated, say historians, as early as Christmas of 1896 when William Booth was accorded a formal *tête-a-tête* with Britain's senior statesman, the eighty-seven year-old ex-Prime Minister William Gladstone. After a wide-ranging conversation, Gladstone expressed curiosity about how the General maintained his power and, most specifically, how he intended to ensure his successor. William Booth explained how, under the Trust Deed of 1878, each General had the sole authority to appoint his successor. Shortly after accepting office, that General would deliver to the Army's solicitors a sealed envelope naming the person he or she had chosen. This envelope would be opened and the successor named immediately after the General's death.

Describing that interview, William Booth wrote that Gladstone "appeared to sympathize with me closely when I described the anxiety with which I had regarded the question, and how, for years it had been considered steadily; and he was still further interested when I mentioned a scheme, now being completed, for providing against the possible contingency of a General passing away who had neglected the appointment of his successor, or who, for some calamitous reason, had been proved incapable for, or unworthy of, his position, and for selecting a new general in an assembly of all our Commissioners throughout the world. I named one or two possibilities that might occur, and he added, 'Yes, and the possibility of heresy would come under this category'."[1]

For several years thereafter, William Booth and his son Bramwell discussed with other high-ranking officers and solicitors the possibility of a High Council —a body of senior Commissioners— which could be convened to nominate a General should the present incumbent prove unfit. And in 1904 Booth submitted to Parliament an amendment to the Constitution of the Salvation Army, known afterwards as the Deed Poll of 1904, which provided that the Chief of

Staff and four Commissioners, or seven Commissioners without the Chief of Staff, could summon a High Council to adjudicate on the matter of the General's fitness and, if necessary, elect his successor. Such a Council, to be composed of the Chief of Staff, the Secretary for Foreign Affairs, and all Commissioners and Territorial Leaders, was to be dissolved immediately following such a decision.

There were three reasons for which a General might be declared unfit for office:

1. permanent incapacity by cause of lunacy or mental or physical infirmity;

2. bankruptcy, insolvency, dereliction of duty, notorious misconduct, or other circumstances making him unfit for office;

3. unfitness (undefined).

To remove the General from office there must be a four-fifths majority vote in the High Council on the first clause; a nine-tenths majority on the second; and a three-fourths majority on the third. When Bramwell Booth accepted office as General of The Salvation Army on August 21, 1912, he accepted the conditions set forth in the Trust Deeds of 1878 and 1904. In the latter was contained what William Booth had described as "The single safeguard against the evils of an autocracy which might become despotism, which in turn might become tyranny."

On paper, the causes seemed clear and the procedure straight-forward. In reality, they were complicated, legalistic and painful. For when it became necessary to invoke the Deed Poll's provisions, there was much more than a Generalship at stake; there was the larger, more problematic, issue of autocracy —an autocracy growing into tyranny. Any High Council action would be, as many Salvationists and the public saw it, an ultimate confrontation with what had been called 'Boothism' in the Army. And it could not be anything but a painful experience.

Under William Booth's generalship, the dictatorship had been benevolent. The Founder had so inspired his troops that disobedience was rare. It was generally conceded that Bramwell, though a superb administrator, was not a born leader; he knew only how to 'order' his troops. Born into the Army, his father's right-hand man since the age of sixteen, having practically run the organization for half a century, it was natural that he should think the Army belonged to him. "As the years went on," one observer wrote, "this view became almost an obsession. . . . He grew into the way of regarding his subordinates as his 'servants' and of saying so. 'He is my servant; I can order him to do what I like,' was a phrase he used more than once." He developed, as a later General, George Carpenter, attests, into an imperious autocrat. To many of his associates, his International Headquarters staff, all colonels and commissioners, he became a task-master, full of whims and moods, and subject to wrathful decisions. Here is how the well-known journalist, F.A. McKenzie, described Bramwell Booth's last years as General:

> Men who had not intended to offend found themselves suddenly in disgrace. A high official in London would, because of something he had said that the General did not like, find himself sent to a minor post at the ends of the earth. The leader of a section of the Army would be contemptuously rebuked in front of his subordinates. A system of retirement, initiated with the best of intentions, was used as a weapon of punishment. High officials were retired or exiled, and some of the old General's chief supporters found themselves deprived of office.
>   The thing reached a point where it became known by a nick-name, 'The Freezer'. 'He is sent to "The Freezer"' was a byword among the staff officers. Be it noted that this administrative harshness affected the staff organizers, not the field officers or the rank and file. And the very organizers who suffered most from it did their best, out of a sense of loyalty, to keep what was happening from the public, and from the lowest ranks of the Army.

Though Mackenzie's picture is perhaps an exaggerated one, there is enough evidence to suggest that the kind of absolute despotism decried by many outsiders in the early days of the Army, which they predicted would bring about its downfall, was being practised by Bramwell Booth in its worst form. It reached such proportions that in 1925 an anonymous manifesto, addressed "To Staff Officers Only," was being secretly circulated among high-ranking officers. In it, the writer attacked the General's autocratic behaviour which, if unchecked, would bring disaster on the Army. "Political despotism," he argued, "if truly paternal, may be bearable, but when its decrees are wrong and enforced by a power that holds its subjects in humiliating servitude, it becomes insufferable. Such despotism never has and never can survive. It topples of its own pride or is overwhelmed by popular revolution." The writer's major cause of complaint was the "perpetuation of power in one man" and the lack of any means by which opposing views could get a fair hearing. "If there has been no open manifestation of the prevailing dissatisfaction, it is because such an expression would inevitably result in immediate expulsion from the Army or in a humiliating reduction in rank." The writer objected strongly to the method of appointing the general's successor, and suggested that such appointments, along with the oversight of finances, should be handled by a governing council.

One unfortunate consequence of the manifesto, whose authorship has never been established, was proof of what it maintained. Colonel George Carpenter, then assistant-secretary to the General, regarded by his associates as the gentlest of all men, bore the brunt of Bramwell Booth's displeasure when he endeavoured to persuade the General that the discontent was not unique or without grounds —and that changes should be made. Colonel Carpenter was immediately sent (some would say 'exiled') to Australia, to a lesser appointment than he had held twenty-two years before. (He was eventually vindicated by his peers when elected to the generalship in 1940.)

What made the 'Bramwell Booth affair' so complicated —and perhaps so fascinating to the public— was the self-appointment of Evangeline Booth, then Commander of the United States, as leader of those seeking reform within the organization. Very much like her sister Catherine, whose magnetic personality had captivated France and Switzerland, she was a born spiritual campaigner —attractive, dramatic, and eloquent; but, like her father as well, she had great leadership qualities. She had brought the Canadian territory through tough times between 1896 and 1904; and for more than twenty years since then she had been in charge of the Army in the United States. Through her perseverance and personality she won back many of the supporters who had shunned the Army since Ballington's resignation; and she brought it to national prominence when she sent her 'Doughnut Girls' to the very front during WWI. When the American troops returned home, they expressed their gratitude by supporting her Home Services Campaign in 1919 which raised $16,000,000. It was, as one writer put it, America's open-hearted way of showing her gratitude for what the Salvation Army had done during the war.

Without any doubt, by the late 1920s Evangeline Booth was the most popular Salvationist, not only in America but throughout the world —popular partly because she did not share or approve of her brother's mode of leadership, and openly declared for an elected successor. Already, in open confrontations, she had shown just how tactful but firm she could be; and already the public was sensing that Evangeline was the natural superior. As early as 1922 she had emerged victorious from a test of wills when Bramwell, almost precipitating another 1896 schism, tried to remove her from her command. American protest made him back down and, as her official biographer states, "The prestige of General Bramwell Booth was shaken." More than this, however, "the power of Evangeline Booth was shown and the long-smoldering disagreement between brother and sister was brought to a head."[2]

There was little doubt, then, who should be the vocal advocate of reform; the family name, the iron will, and (not least) an immunity to punishment being reasons in her favour. With no self-interest but merely the good of the Army in mind, she began her task in earnest in 1927. Stopping over in London, on her way back from Paris, she arranged a meeting with the General (with witnesses because she felt her views would be misrepresented). After a long but fruitless discussion she presented Bramwell with a petition known as "The Fifteen Points," the two major of which were that Bramwell should not exercise his right to designate his successor and that he should initiate a method for *electing* future generals. "You know," she wrote, "that I have held these convictions for a long time, and have both spoken and written to you regarding them. They grow with time and conditions. I again repeat them, only with increased emphasis, and can assure you that they represent the views of a large number of commissioners and leading officers. A change is inevitable, and the only question is whether you will bring it about during your lifetime, which is the most desirable, or risk the Army splitting upon this issue."[3]

On all issues Bramwell Booth proved intransigent. He had no inclination, even if it could legally be done, to alter the 1878 Deed. "It would serve no useful purpose to cancel the General's power of appointing his successor," he replied. Circulating Bramwell's response and her next rebuttal to all high-ranking officers, Evangeline Booth renewed her assault with unassailable arguments, drawing most of those officers to her side. "The implication so pervading your Memorandum that the Foundation Deed of 1878 is complete, final and unalterable, and that it must remain untouched as the Alpha and Omega of our Constitution, forever defiant of every amendment that development, progress, or future generations may demand, fails to accord with our experience as an Organization, and is utterly repugnant to the responsibilities that attach themselves inalienably to God-guided and Christ-following men and women."

Casting her net yet farther than she had done, Evangeline took issue with many of the other causes for complaint within the ranks, the most serious being that of autocracy and nepotism, leading to growing unrest: "Since you cite the possibility of 'personal seekings and rivalries' being associated with this 'theoretical' (?) reform, may I not reasonably ask whether the possibility of that very thing is not the greatest blight that attaches to the present system? You are a father with sons and daughters whose rapid advancement both in rank and position has been and is the subject of world-wide unfavourable criticism. Should one of the children be appointed as your successor it would be strongly resented, especially by those very officers whose hearty co-operation is so essential, if your successor is to have the strong confidence of Salvationists in all lands." A council composed of fifty Commissioners, she suggested, would be less liable to corruption than one man, and "far less exposed to the temptation of personal seeking or personal favouritism."

Warning Bramwell of the serious consequences of his intractability, knowing that her voice, and the voices of others, "are but whimpering sounds scarcely to be heeded," Evangeline ended her missive with a warning: "I cannot help but say that it would indeed be an unjustifiable and most flagrant action on the part of the Chief Executive to our international peoples to answer the prayer for fuller liberty with a course of further repression and deprivation. It is unthinkable. We must not shipwreck our glorious Army."

Though support for Evangeline Booth came primarily from America —it being easiest to do so from a distance— it is necessary to point out that there were a few high-ranking officers at the centre (in London) who took the risk of making known that they too were appalled by the 'new' autocracy. In March of 1928, in fact, they were forced to intervene when it became known that the General was consulting the Army's solicitors with a view to altering the 1904 Deed Poll so that the High Council would not have the power to remove him or his successors. In a letter to Bramwell Booth, seven commissioners —Samuel Hurren, David Lamb, Charles Jeffries, Henry Mapp, Robert Hoggard, Richard Wilson and Arthur Blowers— along with Colonels John Carleton and Frederick Booth-Tucker, made known their sympathy with Eva Booth's position and suggested it would be wise to consider change before the matter became a public controversy. "We regard the deed of 1904 as the complement of the original Deed, but more particularly of the method of the appointment of future Generals, and as a sacred trust and responsibility bequeathed to and imposed upon not only yourself but all the Commissioners of the Salvation Army. We therefore most seriously and respectfully beg you to reconsider your intention to proceed with amendment of this Deed for which we can see no reason useful to the Organization, and we think it only proper to inform you with the greatest and most respectful submission that we can in no manner be parties to the action proposed and that should the matter most unfortunately be proceeded with, we would to our infinite sorrow and regret feel compelled to jointly advise our comrades to also withhold the consent required under the provisions of the deed in question."

How matters might have proceeded, had General Bramwell Booth remained healthy, is open to conjecture. But fate intervened in the whole affair, and by May of 1928 the 72-year old General was physically incapacitated, stricken with neurasthenia. He was, by the terms of the 1904 Deed, practically 'unfit to hold office.' Out of respect, the reformers waited as long as they could; until, that is, they felt that the General's death might cheat them of their opportunity and deal them another hereditary successor. On November 28, therefore, seven Commissioners —Hurren, Lamb, Hoggard, Mapp, Jeffries, Wilson and Wilfred Simpson— requisitioned the Chief of Staff, Edward Higgins, to convene the High Council. Taking legal advice, Commissioner Higgins immediately complied and within days the High Council's sixty-three members had been informed that they were to meet at Sunbury Court, London, on January 8, 1929.

For the first three days High Council members established protocol, debated procedure, and then studied how best to deal with the issue of the succession without unduly grieving Bramwell Booth and alienating the public. The issues were complicated, the arguments painful and the decisions sometimes heart-breaking. On the third day, for example, High Council members considered a suggestion made by Bramwell Booth himself, to the effect that he would appoint a five-person committee to carry out his duties until he fully recovered. As with most submissions by the General, this one was not without some small attempt at intimidation. Rather than making it a private matter, as The High Council would have liked, Bramwell Booth released his letter to the *Daily Mail*, thus making it a public appeal. It was, according to the New York *Times* a thwarting manoeuvre carried out with "the skill of a Machiavelli." Further complicating the issue was his (or his family's) attempt to have the letter published in the *War Cry*. Again the New York *Times*:

> There was a sensation when the high council was considering the General's letter yesterday. A councillor who has long been associated with the General and is familiar with his writing questioned the authenticity of the document. Then followed an uproar caused by the appearance of a breathless junior officer who burst into the chamber. At the same moment the lights in the room went out, adding to the excitement.
>
> The newcomer groped his way through the darkness to the presidential dais and handed a note to Commissioner James Hay. By the aid of a flashlight, the president found the note contained the information that an officer of the army had been to the army's printing works and stopped an edition of the 'War Cry' then on the presses and ordered an insertion of the General's letter. This was done, apparently, on his own authority and without consulting those in charge of the army's publicity department.
>
> This announcement created another uproar, but the council soon came to a decision in the matter. It was quickly resolved that it would be undesirable to make the General's letter public, and an order immediately was telephoned to the printing works that every copy containing it should be destroyed. This was done, although it involved more than 20,000 copies (Jan. 11).[4]

Following this excitement, and a full discussion of Bramwell Booth's proposal, the High Council issued a statement (on January 10) indicating that they had passed a resolution asking General Booth to retire from active leadership. After placing on record the members' "high appreciation of the life and labours of the General," the resolution continued as follows:

> The Council being, however, unable to see the practicability of the suggestion made by the General, and realizing that it is most unlikely that at the General's advanced age he can ever recover sufficiently again to take up the burden under which he collapsed, takes the opportunity of requesting him to co-operate with the Council in securing the future welfare of the Army, and to that end it resolves that the General being, as his doctors assure us, capable of considering important questions and giving decisions thereon, the president, vice-president, and five members of the High council be deputed to see the general and suggest that he now retire from office, retaining his title of General and continuing to enjoy the honours and dignities attaching thereto.

In what was called "an impressive silent ceremony," all members of the Council signed the letter and empowered a deputation to take it to the General's residence at Southwold the following day.

The High Council deputation to see Bramwell Booth on Friday, January 11, consisted of Commissioners Samuel Brengle, John Cunningham, William Haines, James Hay, George Mitchell, Gunpei Yamamuro and Colonel Mrs. Trounce. The visit was graphically described by almost every major newspaper in England, that of the *Manchester Guardian* being typical of most:

> The red-brick villa in the quiet Suffolk resort presented a particularly isolated appearance today, the rain beating wildly against its windows. A number of Southwold people waited in the driving rain, in the mud and puddle of the unmade roadway outside, to watch the arrival of the deputation. . . .
>
> The members of the deputation were at once taken upstairs to the sick-room, the curtains of which were drawn. In single file they advanced to the bedside, bent over the General to express greetings and wishes for his recovery, and clasped his hand. A little more than an hour passed and then the deputation left the house. None of them would make a statement.
>
> A Press Association reporter was admitted to the house, and was given the authorised statement on General Booth's behalf by his chief nurse,

Brigadier Smith, who had been in the bedroom during the interview between the general and the deputation.

The authorised statement —the first issued on behalf of the General since the calling of the High Council— ran: 'The General has seen the deputation, and has received through them the long letter from the High Council. After listening carefully to all that was said he announced that he would give his answer on Monday. It will probably be conveyed to the High Council either by Mrs. Booth or by his daughter, Commissioner Catherine Booth.

'The General received the deputation very calmly and wonderfully like the saint of God he is. He has stood this business from the beginning all through very well indeed. He has never uttered a word of complaint even from the moment that he heard the High Council were being called together from all parts of the world. He then only said, "I think this is a bit rough on me." He heard the decision of the High Council yesterday evening from his wife. He took it beautifully; and with the utmost calm. The only remark he made was, "I wonder who is in this?"'

As expected, and as newspapers predicted, Bramwell Booth's response to the deputation's proposal was an unequivocal "no." To the High Council he stated (in part): "Were I to yield to a request for retirement presented under these conditions, I should not be acting in the strong and consistent manner which the Founder would have desired." For the general public, he went into considerable more detail, making a full case for his position:

In view of the widespread interest which is being shown by all classes of the people in the important question of the future of the Salvation Army, I feel it my duty to issue a plain statement concerning my present position. For 54 years I have spent all my time and energy and toiled incessantly amidst burdens of anxious care such as few men are called upon to bear, in extending and leading the Salvation Army. I have never before had a prolonged rest, but some months ago I was ordered away by the doctors so that I might have a complete cessation from work. I, of course, made arrangements for the carrying on of the responsibilities which rested upon me. The Chief of the Staff, Commissioner Higgins, is the Second-in-Command, and he has had full powers to act for me during my absence. I have yet to hear where he has failed. . . .

It has been said that had the seven Commissioners who requested that the council be called, believed that I should recover, this step would not have been taken. This has, however, been done, and the High Council has met to adjudicate upon my fitness for my position, and with a desire to discuss proposals for radical changes in the constitution of the Salvation Army. Legally the High Council has absolutely no power even to propose, let alone to make, any changes in the constitution; but I wrote the Council stating that I should be prepared to consider any feasible scheme for broadening the constitution, and suggested appointing a special commission to consider what changes were desired and how far they were practicable. I also asked for a little time in order to regain my normal health, which my doctors advised me I have every hope of doing.

I am informed that my letter to the Council was scarcely considered, and I was asked in reply to retire from office under what amounts to nothing less than a threat of expulsion. The only ground for this request, so far as I can ascertain, is that I am ill. There is not even the excuse that I am a burden upon the Army's funds, as my personal needs have been provided from a trust fund supplied by a personal friend for this express purpose. Why should I retire? My leadership at the moment may not be what it was; but what guarantee or assurance have I that I should be replaced by one who would seek first and foremost to maintain the principles of the Salvation Army? I am responsible before God for the well-being of this great organization, to which I have devoted my life, and which in less than 70 years has achieved a success unique in the history of the world.

I have carefully and prayerfully considered the entire question in all its bearings, and much as, in some respects, I should welcome complete rest and relief from responsibility, I feel I should be less than a man, let alone the leader of a great religious organization, if I agreed to the request to retire at a time when, as I understand, there is agitation to change the foundation upon which it rests. Therefore, I am compelled to refuse to do so (*Times*, Jan. 16).

On Thursday, January 17, just after the midnight of a very stormy English day, the High Council decided, by a vote of 55 to 8, that General Bramwell Booth was physically unfit to continue his command of The Salvation Army. An 'official statement' declared that the result of the vote was "a complete vindication of the seven Commissioners who requested the calling of the High Council. Their action was unprecedented, but under the circumstances with which they were confronted they felt there was no alternative."

There was, then, but one matter to be attended to: the election of a successor to Bramwell Booth. But, if most High Council members believed that the affair would be so quickly settled, they were soon visited with a vast disappointment. There had, of course, always been a possibility that Bramwell Booth would challenge the High Council's decision (even its right to make a decision) in the courts, but most Salvationists believed (or hoped) that the General would not resort to legal action. Not only had he been a party to the 1904 deed poll, but Army regulations expressly forbade Salvationists to "go to the law in the ordinary way" because it was "prohibited by the Holy Spirit." Nonetheless, on Friday, January 18, Bramwell Booth's lawyer's applied for an injunction, prohibiting the High Council from proceeding any further until rulings could be made on two issues: that the deed poll of 1904 was *ultra vires* (beyond one's legal power) on the grounds that the constitution of a charitable trust could not be altered by a trustee of his own will; and that the High Council violated natural justice by not permitting Bramwell Booth (or his solicitor) to put his cause before them. Mr. Justice Eve granted the injunction until Monday when the case could be heard.

That the future existence of The Salvation Army depended on the outcome of the legal hearing no one could deny. For now Bramwell Booth had hardened almost everyone against him. The rank and file in great numbers were sending their protests to London. The few High Council members who had sided with the Booth family —notably Commissioners Cunningham, Theodore Kitching and John Laurie— publicly withdrew their support. And those who had laboured to find other solutions to the problems —who had tried to give the General's position a fair hearing— felt that, by his action, Bramwell Booth had "struck a blow right at the heart of the Army." One of these was Commissioner Edward Higgins who, upset by the turn of events, expressed his determination to resist Boothism to "his last drop of blood." To his fellow officers he wrote:

I could never have believed that General Booth could have dealt such a ghastly blow at the Trust passed on to him by his predecessor. The 1904 Deed was the work of our Founder, assisted by his son Bramwell, heralded by both as an additional safeguard for the Army's protection. General Bramwell Booth accepted office upon and subject to the terms not only of the said deed poll of the 7th August 1878, but also of the said deed poll of 28th July 1904. (I quote this from his acceptance of office document.) Now, he has appealed to the Court to declare this deed 'ultra vires' and should he be successful —which I do not think he will— the Army will be left without this part of our foundation, upon which we have built for nearly twenty-five years, and God alone knows what legal complications may ensue.

It seems unthinkable that General Booth could have adopted this course of action, and the only charitable construction I can place upon it is that he is in too enfeebled a condition to fully appreciate the seriousness of his action.

And to Bramwell Booth, Edward Higgins wrote the following:

> Your action in securing an injunction has entirely changed my view upon one of the main grounds of my confidence. I held on in spite of many things which I have been bewildered about to the belief that you had no self-interests in endeavouring to continue in office in spite of your enfeebled condition of health.
>
> That is shattered, and I can only see in your attitude a determination to try and keep the power and position which has been yours in the Salvation Army, even if in the trying to do so you bring ruin to the Salvation Army.
>
> That you could be guilty of going to the courts and securing an injunction upon the plea that the 1904 deed is ultra vires has so stirred me and produced such indignation that, in the interests of the Army, which to my surprise in your letter you say you are seeking to secure, I have consecrated myself to resist to the last drop of blood I have this attack upon a trust which you have received from the Founder, and which both he and you have said over and over again was made in the highest interests of the Salvation Army.
>
> General, you have alienated the sympathy which was felt for you. You have isolated yourself from the comrades who have served you all these years, and even the men who have stood by your cause in this difficulty, have had now to step aside, so that plea you are making is purely a family one, and in the light of all that will be revealed that will be apparent to the world.
>
> I am grieved beyond words. My heart is stricken, but I brace myself for whatever demands this may make upon me.

Clearly, given this kind of commitment on the part of most Commissioners, if the eventual court ruling had gone against the High Council The Salvation Army would probably have been irreparably ruined.

Perhaps through Divine intervention, though acting on legal advice, Bramwell Booth did not proceed with the first of his claims (it was left open to future action). Instead, Mr. Greene, acting for the General, pleaded for an extension of the injunction until Bramwell Booth could defend himself, holding that if he had had the opportunity to refute the charges against him he might have been able to persuade the High Council that there were no grounds for his removal from office. "The General must be given a fair opportunity of meeting the charges against him, and if the result were to confirm the resolution which has passed, he must and would accept it." Mr. Justice Eve, while appreciating the respect shown Bramwell Booth by the High Council and without entering into the substance of the case, agreed that, as a technicality, Bramwell Booth should have been given the opportunity "of stating the grounds on which he was seeking to continue in office for the present." He therefore granted an injunction "to restrain the defendants from acting on the resolution passed on January 17th until after the holding of a meeting of the council and after the plaintiff had had that opportunity" (*Times*, Jan. 31).

Anxious to return to their various appointments, and confident of their position, the High Council resolved to have the matter concluded as soon as possible. General Booth was asked to have his counsel set a date for his (or his representative's) appearance, and on February 13, 1929, their final meeting took place at Sunbury —almost five weeks after they had first met. No arguments were heard in support of the motion; only those for Bramwell Booth, presented by his solicitor, Mr. Jowitt, in an eloquent two-hour oration. Shortly thereafter the final vote was taken. Of the sixty-one members present (one had died; two were ill), fifty-two voted in favour of deposing General Booth, five voted against, and four abstained. The resolution read as follows:

> That this meeting of the High Council doth hereby, in exercise and performance of its duties conferred upon the High Council by the provisions of the deed poll of July 26, 1904, under the hand and seal of William Booth, founder of the Salvation Army, adjudicate William Bramwell Booth unfit for service as General of the Salvation Army, and remove him therefrom, and doth hereby declare, by way of record, that this resolution is based upon the state of health of the said William Bramwell Booth.

The High Council then proceeded, for the first time in the history of The Salvation Army, to *elect* a General. Edward J. Higgins was their democratic choice.

The affair was, to all intents and purposes, concluded in November, 1930 at a Commissioner's conference. The two lasting decisions were as follows: (1) the General would no longer designate his successor; instead future Generals would be elected by the High Council; (2) the General would no longer be sole trustee of Salvation Army property; boards would be created in England and Northern Ireland (as they already had been in many other countries). It was too much for the Bramwell Booth family, and too little for Evangeline; but The Salvation Army, from that time on, was run along more democratic lines, free of the threat of nepotic tyranny. And once again it had weathered a storm of controversy —the most concentrated in its history— to emerge a better, more spiritually-alive organization.

"All the world loves a religious fight, and this one has been more than usually spectacular." That quote from the New York *Nation* typifies the public curiosity which greeted the 'Bramwell Booth Affair.' Though public interest was of a short duration —coinciding exactly with the High Council meetings— it was intense, thorough, pervasive, and compelling.

Bramwell Booth's deposition came, in fact, as a shock to the general public and to ordinary Salvationists as well. Of the unrest within the Army's upper echelon and of the various attempts at reform they had heard very little, the 'manifestoes,' private meetings between Evangeline and Bramwell, and the many letters being known to only a very few senior officers. Now, in January and February of 1929, they were suddenly being told that Bramwell Booth was likely to be deposed —and as suddenly confronted (often in glaring headlines) by accounts of family quarrels, officer intrigues, and abuse of power; of the convening for the first time of a High Council to judge the fitness of their leader; and of legal wranglings in the Court of Chancery. Though obviously dramatic (not to say worrisome) to Salvationists, it was all quite confusing: sorting through the various opinions, the speculations, the allegations and the sudden turns of events was a difficult task. About the only certainty was that this was the "most serious crisis in the history of The Salvation Army" and its resolution

General Bramwell and Florence Booth who 'ruled' the Army from 1912 to 1929.

Cartoon in the London *Evening Standard* depicting the 'Bramwell Booth affair' as a 'family act'.

would, if it did not destroy the organization, alter it forever. Every newspaper in the world stated that conviction without hesitation.

Public proof of their certainty lay in the fact that the story was given great coverage, as universal as that which reported the death of William Booth in 1912. Most non-English papers paid 'special correspondents' to cable them news of the latest developments which they printed on their front pages. In England, where news about royalty nearly always took precedence over any other event, the 'Booth Family Affair' (as some newspapers termed it) actually received priority (in prominence and length) over reports of King George's grave illness. As the correspondent for the Montreal *Standard* put it, "With evidence that King George's illness has definitely taken a favorable turn, public interest has shifted from the royal patient to the bedside of General Bramwell Booth, who has become the centre of a drama in which the whole future of the Salvation Army is involved. The core of that drama is whether the Salvation Army is to remain a despotism or become a democracy." In the United States, where the public felt they had a stake in the outcome (the possible election of Eva Booth), newspapers were ablaze with speculation, the New York *Times* making it front-page news for five days in a row. It was, for them, the culmination of 'eight years' effort by a 'reform' movement within the Army, headed by Commander Booth, to persuade her brother to give up the autocratic and dynastic powers now vested in him by the constitution." The 'Bramwell Booth Affair' was, then, treated very seriously. And yet, as is usual in such cases, most newspapers were pre-occupied with (and some only interested in) the drama of the event; what got most coverage were the spectacular or unusual or bizarre aspects, some newspapers creating spectacle where sometimes it could not be found.

In fairness to the journalists, it must be admitted that the affair lent itself to journalistic extravagance. There were, to begin with, present in London more than sixty of the Army's highest-ranking officers, from all corners of the globe, from the well-known Dr. Samuel Brengle to the mysterious Gunpei Yamamuro and the flamboyant Evangeline Booth (now closeted in her hotel room with other Commissioners, now dashing off to Southwold to try and see her brother). One pictures them ever valiantly trying to evade the hordes of reporters waiting as they entered or left the gates at Sunbury Court

—those gates, stoutly manned by four 'burly Salvationists' who demanded to see the official passes of each visitor, even that of the morning milkman. "Elaborate precautions have been taken to ensure absolute secrecy today. All the indoor and outdoor staffs of the court will not be allowed to leave until the council meeting is over. A special force of police will be on duty inside and outside the grounds, and no one without one of the special permits provided for those immediately concerned will be admitted. No pressmen will be admitted even to the grounds" (*Manchester Guardian*, Jan. 28, 1929).

Quite naturally, in such a highly-charged and secretive atmosphere, so tantalizing to reporters, peripheral events often gained unwarranted prominence and speculative journalism —in which innuendo played a leading part— dominated the newspapers. Journalists reported everything from the frivolous to the very sad. In one story, for example, under the headline "Stranger Within the Gates," the public was treated to a humorous account of how the population of Sunbury Court was added to, in spite of the diligence of the guards, by the unauthorized birth of a baby to the wife of one of the Army's chauffeurs. Another told of an automobile accident involving Commissioner Higgins, who then had to 'beg a ride' with a passing labourer, who, on later learning the identity of his passenger, expressed great delight and surprise.

More substantial than these, however, was what the *Manchester Guardian* called "A Clumsy Plot," an attempt to undermine the legitimate business of the Council. On January 14, the High Council was deluged with telegrams from officers all over the world, responding to what they thought was a directive from Commissioner Higgins, asking them to petition the Council to "stop further action." The telegram read as follows:

> Do you realize that the doctors say the General will recover within six months? The General has asked the High Council to give him time, and the reply to this is a demand for his retirement. Is this fair after the General's lifelong work? The Chief of Staff is well able to carry on during the general's continued absence. There is a growing indignation among the British public at the Council's action. Do you desire the General to be given time? If so, telegraph immediately to Chief of Staff, Sunbury-on-Thames.

Disavowing any involvement, Commissioner Higgins branded the telegram as a "clumsy plot to frustrate the Council in their work."

Such attempted interferences were not uncommon throughout the affair. F.A. McKenzie, a noted journalist and long-time friend of the Army, suggested that he had intervened in a positive way to ensure that one essential strategy was not overlooked. It was at his suggestion made in the *Daily News*, he claimed, that the High Council decided to send a delegation to the General to try and persuade him to voluntarily retire. This was indeed done, but the request made to no avail. In a less-constructive way, some ex-officers also tried to influence public opinion. One of these was Mr. A.G. Pollard, a former Commissioner in the Army who had resigned because of ill health, had become a wealthy businessman, and was now appalled by what he thought to be the unjust treatment of his former leader. "He swept down to Southwold," says one account, "saw his old chief and took over the direction of the defence. Lawyers were immediately instructed to proceed with the application for an injunction against the High Council." Making no secret of his views and involvement, Mr. Pollard sent the following letter to every member of the High Council:

> When I learned a few weeks ago that the general was lying ill at Southwold with no one at hand to help or advise him at the most critical period of his wonderful life, I went down to see him, and I found him anything but helpless so far as his mental powers were concerned.
>
> The spectacle of a body of men, every one of whom owes his existence as an Army leader to the general, refusing such an eminently reasonable request as time in which to regain health is repulsive. Such a request in similar circumstances would be readily granted by any third-class business house, leaving religion out of the question altogether.
>
> The general public take this view and regard the action of the High Council as a determined effort by hook or by crook to get power and property into their own hands. The influence and work of the Army are already damaged for all time, whatever happens.
>
> I regard the whole action and attitude of the High Council towards the general as ungrateful, harsh, unchristianlike and unjust, and in forcing an issue as they are doing at the present time, instead of calmly taking time to arrive at the broader constitution they desire, they are alienating the sympathy of thousands of friends and the loyalty of tens of thousands of the rank and file, and inflicting irreparable damage to the Army's best interests.[5]

And just as commentators tried to link such outside influence to Bramwell Booth's decision to "take the matter to court," so they also attempted to make the court's granting of an injunction for a stay of proceedings a direct cause of the death of one of the High Council members. Whether it was so or not is impossible to determine, but the fact that Commissioner William Haines died almost immediately after receiving news of Bramwell Booth's counter-move made the unfortunate episode much more sensational than it might otherwise have been:

> Commissioner Haines had been making an impassioned speech denouncing one-man rule in the Army, which rule every one thought had been ended when Bramwell Booth had been declared unfit by the council this week.
>
> Towards the end of Commissioner Haines's speech a telephone bell rang in an adjoining room and Commissioner James Hay, presiding officer, went to answer it. It was a call from the Salvation Army's solicitors in London. The look of dismay on Commissioner Hay's face as he resumed his place was only a hint to the delegates of the bad news to come.
>
> After a few more sentences Commissioner Haines sat down and those near him could see that he was exhausted by his effort. Then, speaking slowly and with the utmost seriousness, Commissioner Hay announced that the Chancery Division of High Court at London had issued an injunction in favour of the ousted General. The court order, he said, forbade the council to act on its resolution on the General's unfitness and restrained it from electing a successor until Monday at the earliest, when the court hearing would be held.
>
> Silence fell over the council room. Not another word was uttered until Commissioner Hay from the platform said 'Let us pray.' The sixty-three delegates, in their blue uniforms, then stood with bowed heads and prayed for God's guidance.
>
> The meeting decided to adjourn at once and Commissioner Haines was seen to walk into the anteroom with his friend, Commissioner Henry W. Mapp. He complained of feeling ill and lay down on a sofa. Scarcely had he done when he had a severe attack of acute indigestion. A doctor was rushed in and gave emergency heart treatment, but it was of no avail.
>
> 'How did they hear it?' were Commissioner Haines's last words, spoken to Commissioner Mapp, who stood anxiously at his side. He wanted to know how the delegates had received the news of the court

injunction, but death came before he could be told. Commissioner Mapp went out to give the tragic tidings to the council members, who were still dismayed by the news from London (NY *Times*, Jan. 20).

All of these seemingly peripheral happenings illustrated, in journalists' eyes, the essentially dramatic nature of the whole affair —an affair marked by secrecy, intrigue and suspense. For it was, they felt with some justification, a contest between 'two camps' —the Booth family (and a few supporters) and the reformers. In some quarters, this was presented to the public very crudely, especially by papers not friendly to the Army. The New York *Nation*, for example, talked of Bramwell Booth as having 'absolute powers' of which "the Pope or Mussolini might well be envious." It therefore felt that Evangeline Booth, "the vigorous commander of the American army," was quite justified "in organizing the reformers and taking away the control of the organization from a decrepit old man whose relatives were misusing his dictatorial powers" (Jan. 30: 124).

It was this kind of depiction that resulted in letters and articles defending one side or the other (chiefly in an emotional manner), suggesting that a small group of malcontents were taking advantage of an old man's illness, perhaps aggravating that illness through a "knowledge that a movement was on foot directed not against his own personality but against his possible successor."

> Propped up in bed reclines an old man, his features wasted with sickness, his enfeebled frame covered by a black dressing gown. To one side is a window, on which patters a gloomy rain that all but obscures the North sea pounding on England's east coast shore at Southwold. Into the room file six men clad in dark blue uniforms, and one woman. Each is greeted by the old man.
>
> 'Let us pray,' he says after a moment's silence.
>
> When he has prayed for them and their families, one of the men steps forward. Slowly he reads a document thanking the old man for his life of devoted service, but informing him that he has been deposed from command of the world-wide organization he has ruled, for nearly two decades, as a general rules an army.[6]

It was also this kind of 'two-camp' reporting which brought into the debate such former supporters as A.G. Pollard and Frank Smith who, remembering fondly the Founder's benevolent regime, launched into a public defence of Bramwell Booth and placed their money at his disposal for his legal costs. On the other hand, it was the same kind of reporting which caused the public to withdraw its support from Bramwell Booth when they saw that, by going to court, he was acting more out of self-interest than for the good of the organization. And, finally, it was the 'family' versus the High Council aspect which made reporters (and thus the public) see intrigue in every action that took place at Sunbury and Southwold, causing them to write (and the public to read) such melodramatic accounts as this:

THE RED CAR

A closed red car making journey after journey between Sunbury Court, where the High Council of the Salvation Army is sitting, and a little villa which is being rented by the Booth family was an object of mystery at Sunbury-on-Thames today.

The Booth family, with the exception of Commander Evangeline Booth, the leader of the Army in America, have come to the Council meetings to defend the 72-year-old General, the supreme head of the organization, against the charge of unfitness. They have established a headquarters under the shadow of the Georgian river-side mansion. Here it is known that they are constantly in telephone communication with the General, who is recovering from a long illness at Southwold. It was to this secluded villa that Commissioner Catherine Booth and Colonel Mary Booth, daughters of the General, hurried after the Council had adjourned for luncheon. Commissioner Catherine was hatless, and there was a grave expression on her face. The two women were joined by Commissioners Kitching, Laurie, and Cunningham, and these, the chief supporters of the General, remained in close consultation for nearly an hour with their representatives.

Long before the Council meeting was resumed the mysterious red car was seen making its way at a fast speed between the court and the villa. Always in it was a uniformed secretary and Miss Catherine Booth. They had with them piles of legal documents. Seven journeys were made in under an hour, and the telephone bell within the villa could be heard ringing at frequent intervals (*Manchester Guardian*, Jan. 10, 1929).

It seems to be true, then, as some historians assert, that when some members of the public and of the Salvation Army became acquainted with the 'Bramwell Booth Affair' they saw it primarily as a struggle between two power-hungry factions. It was, they thought, an opportunistic bid for control. In this rather simplistic, and sensational, view there was little cognizance of the real issues, nor of the soul-searching struggles over "affection and duty" endured by all major participants. It is little wonder that those (not very many, I think) who accepted such a view should have severed their connection with or discontinued their support of The Salvation Army.

But, it is quite clear, on reading a sampling of the world's leading newspapers, that this was not the prevailing view of the affair. Only a very few newspapers —and then only through private commentary— saw the High Council's actions as "a determined effort by hook or by crook to get power and property into their own hands" and still fewer felt that the Army's influence and reputation would be significantly damaged by a decision to depose Bramwell Booth. In fact, recurring throughout the editorials is the clear recognition that the first duty of the seven requisitioning Commissioners was to the Army and that every decision in favour of duty was tempered by expressions of devotion to the General. As the *Review of Reviews* put it, "No personal animosities moved the reformers to revolt. All felt a deep and real affection for the sick man they came to depose. But stronger than this was their desire to see the Army shake off control of what they call the Booth dynasty" (Mr 1929: 135). And, as the Toronto *Globe* asserted, "[High Council members] are Christian men and women who have devoted their whole life to the things for which the Salvation Army stands. In a matter of this kind it is not likely that they would act hastily or wittingly follow a divisive course that must eventuate in disruption unless they were convinced that no other way was open to them (Jan. 18)." One could not, the London *Times* argued, believe that the Commissioners, by convening the High Council during the General's illness, were acting mercilessly, but that this was merely "an opportunity which could not otherwise have occurred without doing harm to the army." Indeed, it reminded its readers, all impartial observers had been struck by the dignity of the proceedings and the courtesy extended to Bramwell Booth. "Here again, however, there should be nothing in the least surprising. Distressing as the circumstances have been, the gathering at Sunbury has been all along one of General Bramwell Booth's personal friends and devoted followers; and the deputation who were under the trying necessity of having to wait upon his sick bed, if they were driven there by the force of hard facts, took with them one of the most Christian of virtues —courtesy. That all these qualities in the negotiators, this careful procedure, and the obvious crisis lying behind it, should have issued in the conclusion announced yesterday is a matter for sincere regret" (Jan. 18).

Most world newspapers agreed with that position —a position summed up by the Montreal *Star*: "Although unstinted tribute is paid to General Booth's character and leadership of the Salvation Army by the British press today, the whole tendency of comment on the crisis in the Army's affairs is towards supporting the decision reached yesterday by the High Council to ask General Booth to voluntarily retire from active duty" (Jan. 11). The Toronto *Globe* echoed this affirmation, stating that "the attitude of the Council, so far as it has been made public, has commended general support. It seems inevitable that some changes in the internal administration of the Army will have to be made if it is to cope with modern conditions and keep pace with the times" (Jan. 11). Similarly, most newspaper commentators felt that, justice being on the reformers' side and that side being represented by a vast majority of High Council members, The Salvation Army would not suffer a diminution of morale or support, but "unity and fresh zeal" would eventuate. For as the Norfolk *Virginian-Pilot* observed, "When men and women have given that much of their lives to an organization, they may be expected to use every effort to preserve its spirit and to promote its welfare." That proved to be the case. A slight decrease in public giving in 1930 was overcome in 1931 and continued in subsequent years until it mushroomed during the war years.

As Frederick Coutts points out in *The Better Fight*, "There were those who genuinely feared that the introduction of the principle of freedom of election as a permanent means of appointing future Generals must bring the decay of a General's independence of action, unhealthy rivalry and intrigue, and the eventual disruption of the Army as an international body. But time has proved these fears unfounded. The international unity and solidarity of the Army is now [in 1973] as strong, if not stronger, than ever. Wisdom was justified of her children" (p. 101). As far as the public is concerned, though there was a kind of voyeuristic fascination with the drama and personal dynamics of the affair, it is clear that, on the whole, the public interest was primarily a result of a genuine concern that the 'good work' of the organization would not be interrupted. "The world knows of its good works," stated the editor of the Toronto *Globe*, "not through the hearing of the ear, but through practical service to the human race among many nations. . . . It is for this reason that friends of the Army everywhere hope and pray that the difficulties confronting it will be cleared away and that it will embark on a new era of service to mankind" (Jan. 16, 1929).

NOTES

Introduction

[1] *Orders and Regulations for Staff Officers* (1895), Part X.1.

Essay One

[1] Quoted in Robert Sandall's *History of The Salvation Army*, Vol. I, p. 1.

[2] *Review of Reviews*, 4 (1891): 571.

[3] One of the surprising aspects of these defections is not just how many early Salvationists left the ranks (disgruntled or disappointed), but just how many were educated enough to write about their experiences. When one is led to believe that most of the Army's recruits were drawn from the lower classes, such widespread articulateness (combined with the knowledge that many early officers were drawn from the 'artisan' classes) helps to dispel the myth.

[4] Investigator, *Behind the Scenes With the Salvation Army* (London, [1881]).

[5] "The Last Revival," *Contemporary Review* 42 (1882): 186-87.

[6] "The Lay of the Loud Salvationist," *Punch* (July 12, 1890): 14-15.

[7] "The Last Revival," 185.

[8] Investigator, op cit.

[9] "The Salvation Army," *Contemporary Review* 42 (1882): 342.

[10] *Catholic Review*, 51 (Sept. 1890): 745.

[11] See Roger J. Green, *Catherine Booth: A Biography of the Co-Founder of The Salvation Army*, chapter 5.

[12] p. 17.

[13] *The Month*, 44 (1882): 482.

[14] The Salvation Army," *Harper's Magazine* 82 (1891): 903.

[15] "Some Aspects of the Salvation Army," *National Review* 5 (1885): 71.

[16] "The Salvation Army: A Note of Warning," *Contemporary Review* 74 (1898): 441.

[17] Cunningham Geikie, "Introduction" to *An Ex-Captain's Experience* (London, 1888): ix-x.

[18] *The New Papacy: Behind the Scenes in the Salvation Army* (Toronto, 1889): 7.

[19] "The Methods of the Salvation Army," *Contemporary Review* 42 (1882): 195.
[20] *Harper's Magazine* 82 (1891): 903.
[21] *Eclectic Magazine* (1885): 855.
[22] *Contemporary Review* 42 (1882): 191.
[23] p. 743.
[24] *Harper's Magazine*, 82 (1891): 906.

Essay Two

[1] *The Life of General William Booth*, Vol. II, p.4.
[2] For an of account of the existence of Skeleton Armies, see Glenn Horridge, *The Salvation Army: Origins and Early Days*, pp. 101-02, 198-203, 205-06.
[3] The Super-Weston-Mare riots occurred as follows: for many months prior to March 23, 1882, Salvationists had marched unmolested through the streets of that quiet seaside town at the mouth of the Severn River. On that day, however, for reasons known only to their opponents, they were "attacked by a band of roughs. . . who maltreated some of their members and seized and destroyed some of their musical instruments, the police failing to apprehend any of the disturbers." As a consequence of the disturbance, the local magistrates issued a proclamation requiring all citizens to "abstain from assembling to the disturbance of the public peace in the public streets within the said parish of Weston-super-Mare." On Monday, the 26th, the Army, with Captain William Beatty in charge, marched out in defiance of the order (but without any music). When Beatty declined to desist at the request of the police he, along with his two assistants, Bowden and Mullins, was arrested and eventually convicted by the town's magistrates of having "unlawfully and tumultuously assembled with divers other persons to the number of 100 or more to the disturbance of the public peace." All were fined and bound over to keep the peace for twelve months; but, on failing to pay the fines, they were sent to Shepton Mallet jail for three months. Though a segment of public opinion, taking the form of a petition for release signed by thirty-two leading citizens, felt the Army had been unjustly dealt with, an even larger segment, making itself known through a counter-petition signed by a hundred others, supported the magistrates. When, in June of 1882, the Army appealed the magistrate's decisions, two judges of the Queen's Bench —Justice Field and Justice Cave— concurred in finding for the Army and against the magistrates.

[4] *Saturday Review* (Oct. 18, 1884).

[5] Ibid (Nov. 5, 1884).

[6] It should not be forgotten that, though time may have proved Mr. Morrison and other opponents wrong, his belief that the Army was a form of 'religion gone wrong,' was sincerely held. In 1910, writing in his *Eastbourne Memories*, C.F. Chambers still believed strongly in the stand he had taken: "My deliberate conviction that the desecration of Sunday which has now reached such alarming proportions in the shape of Sunday concerts, Sunday travelling, Sunday trading, Sunday newspapers, etc.— lies in no insignificant degree at the door of 'General Booth' with his Sunday Bands, Sunday journeyings and Sunday hawking of newspapers [i.e. *War Crys*]."

[7] To be fair, it must be pointed out that, while many Salvationists were prosecuted for breaking the law, quite a number of Eastbournians were also fined or jailed for assaulting Salvationists.

[8] It should be pointed out that determining support by virtue of votes is somewhat dubious. It was not a 'one-man-one-vote' system: many property-owners, those entitled to vote, had two votes, one for the person and one for the property. It is, indeed, quite provable that quite a number of Eastbourne citizens supported the Army's cause and deplored the treatment they received. In fact, some fishermen —such as Tom and Henry Boniface (who later became Salvationists)— marched with the Salvationists to protect them.

[9] Quoted in Wiggins, *The History of The Salvation Army*, Vol 4, p. 279.

Essay Three

[1] Raymond L. Schults, *Crusader in Babylon: W.T. Stead and the Pall Mall Gazette,* p. 129.

[2] Quoted in Robert Sandall, *The History of the Salvation Army*, Vol. 2, p. 9.

[3] *Echoes and Memories,* p. 127.

[4] Ibid, 129.

[5] Charles Terrot, *The Maiden Tribute: A Study of the White Slave Traffic of the Nineteenth Century,* p. 157.

[6] See "The Maiden Tribute of Modern Babylon," *Pall Mall Gazette,* July 7, 1885.

[7] Schults, 140.

[8] *Echoes and Memories*, 137.

[9] Ibid, p. 139.

Essay Four

[1] Carolyn Scott, *The Heavenly Witch: The Story of The Maréchale*, p. 24.
[2] Ibid, 79.
[3] *Twenty-One Years Salvation Army* (1886), 121.
[4] Ibid, 78.

Essay Five

[1] "Canada and Imperial Federation," *Fortnightly Review* 49 (1891): 466. For an in-depth discussion of these views and Canada's attitude towards imperialism, see R.G. Moyles and Douglas Owram, *Imperial Dreams and Colonial Realities.*
[2] From statistics cited in a private statement regarding the "Philpott difficulty" written by Rev. George A. MacKenzie, formerly Chief Secretary under Commissioner Herbert Booth in SA Archives, Toronto.
[3] Ibid.

Essay Six

[1] W.D. Bowman, The Story of 'The Times' (1931): 1.
[2] It was Bramwell Booth's opinion that Huxley's 'attack' on The Salvation Army stemmed from a personal grievance. It seems that, at some early time, William Booth had ridiculed the evolutionists in a sermon. He stated, facetiously, "that evolution began in the mud, and that after a long time —ages, and ages, and ages (one needed to hear him drawl it out to get the true humour of the telling)— out of the mud there came a fishy creature, something like a shrimp, and then, after more ages, and ages, and ages, the shrimp turned into a monkey, which, after yet more ages, and ages, and ages, turned into —an *infidel*!" The 'Darkest England' debates was Huxley's chance to get back at William Booth (*These Fifty Years,* chapter 21).
[3] William Irvine, *Apes, Angels & Victorians,* p. 254.
[4] Ibid, 254-55.
[5] Frank Smith, a brilliant young man, well-versed in socialism, was, most historians now believe, the 'brains' behind Booth's venture into large-scale social work. He headed up the Social Wing but, in what seems a power play, fell out with Booth over the direction that

wing should take and resigned as a consequence. The Smith resignation was widely reported and commented on. Smith returned to the Army's ranks in 1902; but resigned again a few years later to become a Member of Parliament and one of the founders of the Labour Party.

6 *Those Fifty Years,* p. 206.

Essay Seven

1 See Herbert A. Wisbey, *Soldiers Without Swords: A History of the Salvation Army in the United States,* p. 112.
2 This letter of resignation, as were most letters between the General and Ballington, were made public and are now to be found in various archives.
3 This, of course, raises this question: to what extent was the New York *Times* initiating the debate and/or was being fed information by someone in the ranks who knew the Army well and wanted an autonomous American organization. Given the intimate knowledge of the Army displayed in some *Times'* reports, the latter does not seem unlikely.
4 Quoted in the *Literary Digest* (March 14, 1896): 577.
5 Wisbey, p. 110.

Essay Eight

1 Denton Prout, *Henry Lawson, p. 109.*
2 *Poetical Works,* p. 236.
3 *Complete Poetical Works,* p. 357.
4 G.B. Shaw, 'Preface' to *Major Barbara.*
5 Ruff, *Edward Sheldon,* p. 62.
6 Ibid.

Essay Nine

1 Begbie, *The Life of General William Booth,* p. 432.

Essay Ten

1 *A Talk With Mr. Gladstone* [1897].
2 Herbert Wisbey, *Soldiers Without Swords: A History of the Salvation Army in the United States,* p. 182.

[3] Most of the quotations from private manifestoes and letters are to be found in the appendices of F.A. Mackenzie's *The Clash of the Cymbals*. They have been verified in the Army's London archives.

[4] This was a mistake on the part of the High Council since it had no legal right to control *The War Cry*, the trusteeship still being the general's. Fortunately, it did not proceed to 'court martial' Commissioner Kitching, the editor, as some suggsted it should do. That would have been a damaging tactical error.

[5] Mackenzie, 114.

[6] *Review of Reviews* (March 1929): 134.

WORKS CONSULTED AND CITED

Begbie, Harold. *The Life of General William Booth*. 2 vols. New York: Macmillan, 1920.

Bengough, John Wilson. "The War Cry," in *Motley: Verses Grave and Gay* (Toronto: Briggs, 1895): 19-22.

Bevington, M.M. *The Saturday Review 1855-1868*. New York: AMS Press, 1966.

Booth, Bramwell. *Echoes and Memories*. 1925. Rpt. London: Hodder & Stoughton, 1977.

Booth, Bramwell. *These Fifty Years*. London: Cassell, [1929].

Booth, William. *In Darkest England and the Way Out*. London: Salvation Army, [1890]. Rpt. 1970.

Buchan, John. "A Captain of Salvation," *Yellow Book*, 8 (Jan. 1896): 143-58.

Buchanan, Robert Williams. "The Last Christians," in *The Complete Poetical Works of Robert Buchanan* (New York: AMS Press, 1976): Vol. 2, pp. 356-60.

Charlesworth, S.B. *Sensational Religion*. Ipswich: p.p., [1885].

Chesham, Sallie. *Born to Battle: The Salvation Army in America*. New York: Rand McNally, 1965.

Chichester, C. Raleigh. "The Salvation Army," *The Month*, 44 (1882): 467-83.

Cobbe, Frances Power. "The Last Revival," *Contemporary Review*, 42 (1882): 182-89.

Cudmore, J.T. *The Doctrines of the Salvation Army and the Bible Compared*. Charlottetown, PEI: Cudmore Press, 1889.

Dicey, A.V. "The 'Salvation Army' as an Index to Public Opinion," *The Nation*, 36 (1883): 77-78.

Duncan, Sara Jeannette. *The Path of a Star*. Toronto: Gage, 1899.

Earle, Elliven. "A Salvation Lass," *Belgravia*, 83 (1894): 274-90.

Farrar, Archdeacon F.W. "The Salvation Army," *Harper's Magazine*, 82 (1890-91): 897-906.

Farrar, F.W., et al. *Essays and Sketches*. London: Salvation Army, 1906.

Green, Peter. *Beyond the Wild Wood: The World of Kenneth Grahame*. Exeter: Web & Bower, 1982.

Green, Roger. *Catherine Booth: A Biography of the Co-Founder of The Salvation Army*. Grand Rapids, Mich.: Baker Books, 1996.

Heathcote, Rev. Wyndham S. *My Salvation Experience*. London: Marshall, [1892].

Hodges, Samuel H. *'General Booth', 'The Family', and the Salvation Army.* Manchester: n.p., 1890.

Hollins, John. "The Salvation Army: A Note of Warning," *Contemporary Review*, 74 (1898): 436-45.

Horridge, Glenn K. *The Salvation Army: Origins and Early Days 1865-1900.* Godalming: Ammonite Books, 1993.

Huxley, T.H. *Social Diseases and Worse Remedies: Letters to the 'Times' on Mr. Booth's Schemes.* London: Macmillan, 1891.

Investigator. *Behind the Scenes with the Salvation Army.* London: Civil Service Printing Co., [1882].

Irvine, William. *Apes, Angels and Victorians.* London: Weidenfield & Nicholson, 1956.

Katscher, Leopold. "Some Aspects of the Salvation Army," *National Review*, 5 (1885): 71-93.

Lawson, Henry. *Poetical Works.* Sydney: Angus and Robertson, 1964.

Lewis, Mary A. "The Salvation Army," *Macmillan's Magazine*, 46 (1882): 403-16.

Lindsay, Vachell. "William Booth Enters Into Heaven," *Poetry: A Magazine of Verse*, 1 (1913): 101-03.

Machar, Agnes Maule. *"Red Cross Knights —A Nineteenth-Century Crusade,"* Andover Review, 2 (1884): 193-210. Rpt. as *Red Cross Knights of the Salvation Army.* Toronto: n.p., 1884.

Mackenzie, F.A. *The Clash of the Cymbals.* London: n.p., 1929.

McKinley, Edward H. *Marching to Glory: The History of the Salvation Army in the United States.* San Francisco: Harper & Row, 1980.

Manning, Cardinal Henry Edward. "The Salvation Army," *Contemporary Review*, 42 (1882): 335-42.

Marshall, A.F. "The Salvation Army," *Catholic World*, 51 (1890): 738-46.

[Mearns, Andrew]. *The Bitter Cry of Outcast London.* London: n.p., 1883.

Moyles, R.G. *A Bibliography of Salvation Army Literature in English.* New York: Edwin Mellen, 1988.

Moyles, R.G. and Doug Owram. *Imperial Dreams and Colonial Realities.* Toronto: University of Toronto Press, 1988

Moyles, R.G. *The Blood and Fire in Canada.* Toronto: Peter Martin Associates, 1977.

Murdoch, Norman H. *Origins of The Salvation Army.* Knoxville: University of Tennessee Press, 1994.

Peek, Francis. "The Salvationists," *Contemporary Review*, 49 (1886): 55-62.

Philpott, Peter and A.W. Rolfe. *New Light: Containing a Full Account of the Recent Salvation Army Troubles in Canada*. Toronto: n.p., 1892.

Prout, Denton. *Henry Lawson: The Grey Dreamer*. Sydney: Angus and Robertson, 1963.

[Railton, George Scott.] *Twenty-One Years Salvation Army*. London: Salvation Army, [1886].

Redstone, J.J.R. *An Ex-Captain's Experience of the Salvation Army*. London: Christian Commonwealth Pub. Co., [1888]

Ruff, Loren K. *Edward Sheldon*. Boston: Twayne, 1982.

Sandall, Robert, et al. *History of The Salvation Army*. 6 vols. London: Nelson and Hodder & Stoughton, 1947-73.

Schults, Raymond L. *Crusader in Babylon: W.T. Stead and the Pall Mall Gazette*. Lincoln, Neb.: University of Nebraska Press, 1972.

Scott, Carolyn. *The Heavenly Witch: The Story of The Maréchale*. London: Hamish Hamilton, 1981.

Shannon, Richard. *The Crisis of Imperialism 1865-1915*. St. Albans: Paladin, 1976.

Shaw, George Bernard. *Major Barbara*. London: Constable, 1912.

Sheldon, Edgar. *Salvation Nell: A Play in Three Acts*. New York: A. Kauser, 1908.

Stafford, Ann. *The Age of Consent: The Law and Eliza Armstrong*. London: Hodder & Stoughton, 1964.

Stead, Estelle W. *My Father: Personal and Spiritual Reminiscences*. London: William Heinnemann, 1913.

[Stead, W.T.] "The Maiden Tribute of Modern Babylon," *Pall Mall Gazette*, 42 (July 6, 1885): 1-6; (July 7): 1-6; (July 8): 1-5; (July 10): 1-6.

Sumner, Arthur. *The New Papacy: Behind the Scenes in the Salvation Army*. Toronto: Britnell, 1899.

Terrot, Charles. *The Maiden Tribute: A Study of the White Slave Traffic of the Nineteenth Century*. London: Frederick Muller, 1959.

White, Arnold. "Truth About the Salvation Army," *Fortnightly Review*, 58 (1892): 111-24.

Wilson, Andrew. *The Salvation Army, Its Government, Principles, and Practices*. Toronto: James Bain, 1884.

Wisbey, Herbert A. *Soldiers Without Swords: A History of The Salvation Army in the United States*. New York: Macmillan, 1955.